Also available at all good book stores

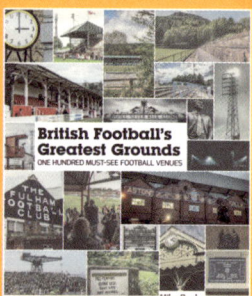

9781785316470

9781785313929

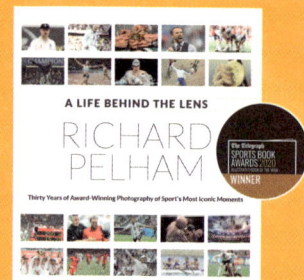

9781785315466

9781785316531

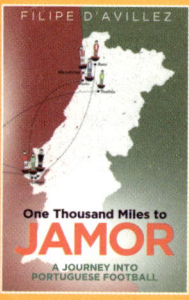

9781785316258

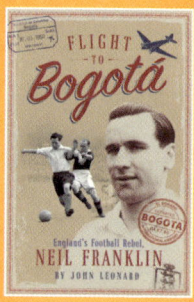

9781785316548

9781785317262

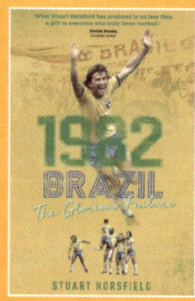

9781785316869

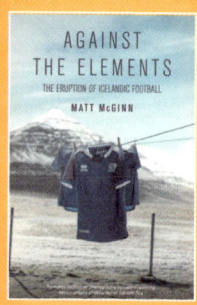

9781785317200

TEARS AT LA BOMBONERA

TEARS AT LA BOMBONERA

FOOTBALL • TRAVEL • CULTURE • HISTORY • GROUNDHOPPING

STORIES FROM A SIX-YEAR SOJOURN IN SOUTH AMERICA

CHRISTOPHER HYLLAND

First published by Pitch Publishing, 2021

Pitch Publishing
A2 Yeoman Gate
Yeoman Way
Worthing
Sussex
BN13 3QZ
www.pitchpublishing.co.uk
info@pitchpublishing.co.uk

A CIP catalogue record is available for this book
from the British Library.

ISBN 978 1 78531 759 0

Typesetting and origination by Pitch Publishing
Printed and bound in Great Britain by TJ Books Limited

Contents

Dedication

To Rafael, Siri, Nicolas and Fride

Foreword

Football is just there – at the bus stop, the water cooler, the internet chat room. We take it for granted. We take the size of football crowds for granted – numbers that equal the population of a reasonable-sized town crammed into a single building. We take the importance of the game for granted, the way that it is so central to the identity of millions and that its development serves as an alternative history of the last century and a half.

But let's go back, say, to 1880. No one could possibly have predicted that the game would take on such status – and even less that, in just 50 years, South America would have become its centre.

As late as 1922 one of Brazil's greatest writers couldn't see it. Graciliano Ramos wrote a piece arguing that this football lark would never catch on, that it would be nothing more than a short-lived craze and that his country had no need for such foreign cultural imports.

How could he have got it so extraordinarily wrong? Ramos was undoubtedly brilliant, and, with communist leanings was at least theoretically equipped with an internationalist perspective. But he was writing from a small town far from the big urban centres further south, where the dynamism of change was bewilderingly fast. Cities like Buenos Aires, Montevideo, Rio de Janeiro and Sao Paulo had gone through a remarkable expansion, swollen by waves of immigrants. A new urban population was ready for fresh traditions – and football was the new phenomenon they found.

The game was simple to learn and with few barriers to entry. It arrived full of First World prestige, introduced by the British. As it went down the social scale – with remarkable speed – it was re-interpreted by the locals, transformed into a graceful, balletic activity ideal for those with a low centre of gravity. And this re-interpretation led to international triumphs and recognition for a region that otherwise felt peripheral, far away from the rest of the world.

The First World War is clearly vital. It may well have spread the popularity of the game in Europe – playing football was a vital rest activity for troops behind the lines. But Europeans were primarily concerned with killing each other in a grotesque industrial slaughter. South America, meanwhile, forged ahead with a much healthier form of pseudo-conflict. The first Copa America was played in 1916, with Uruguay, Argentina, Brazil and Chile competing. In the early years it was held annually, and it brought about a rapid rise of standards, the consolidation of a distinctive South American style and the idea that national prestige was at stake.

For Uruguay and Argentina, and soon afterwards Brazil, football was a chance to shout to the rest of the world the powerful message that 'we are winners'. Later, the game spread north, often carried by Argentines and Uruguayans. The diaries of the future 'Che' Guevara, when he wanders on a motorbike up through South America in the early 50s, show that the mere fact of being from Argentina gave him and his friend credibility and status as football experts. The countries of the north of the continent have little pretension of shouting 'we are winners'. For them, reaching the World Cup and hearing their national anthem played in front of the planet is a way of shouting out a message that 'we exist!'

This is the broad sweep of the process, seen from on high. But football takes place close to the ground, on the bus to the stadium and in the bar after the game, among the dreams and frustrations of daily life.

Christopher Hylland has ridden the bus, has drunk at the bar, has got close enough to the coal face to see whether those tears in La Bombonera are shed in triumph or sadness, in joy or in despair. Welcome to a land of a thousand stories.

Tim Vickery

An Introde to Eduardo Galeano

EIGHT HOURS. The double-decker coach left the Retiro bus terminal and drove out of the sprawling city of fury, *la ciudad de la furia*, Buenos Aires. The tall buildings of the city centre were soon replaced by two- or three-storey apartments, before an open, vast nothingness dominated the scenery out of the window. The lights of the bus were switched off and it quickly became pitch-black outside. I fell asleep.

The journey took us up the River Paraná to the carnival town of Gualeguaychú. Across the river, Fray Bentos was peering over from Uruguay and it was here we had to alight at 2am to pass through the small immigration office. Back on the bus and back to sleep, the next stop was Montevideo. I was finally making a pilgrimage to Eduardo Galeano's home city. Apart from a handful of footballers, no Uruguayan is more famous than the writer and intellect Galeano. I had pored over his books *The Open Veins of Latin America* and *Football In Sun and Shadow* upon arriving on the South American continent in 2013. Galeano died aged 74 in 2015 and the whole continent mourned his death.

I had hoped to make the trip earlier. In 2014 a friend and I had bought tickets for the ferry crossing the River Plate in the hope of catching the *superclásico del fútbol uruguayo*: Club Atlético Peñarol versus Club Nacional de Football. However, due to Paul McCartney playing at Estadio Centenario the same weekend as the scheduled *clásico*, something had to give and the match was postponed by a week. The ferry tickets were inflexible and non-refundable – not that my Spanish was up to demanding my money back.

After the McCartney-postponement, it took me another four years to get over to Estadio Centenario. A friend from Buenos Aires had a Nacional-supporting cousin living in Montevideo who could sort out tickets. All I had to do was get on the right bus and find a hostel. The first part went smoothly enough. The second part, less so. At 7am I got off the bus at Terminal de Buses and walked towards the town centre. I had chosen a hostel across the road from Café Brasilero, a place where almost every day Galeano sat down to write. And around the corner was a bookshop, Linardi y Risso, where a young Galeano attended deep, intellectual debates which formed his political ideations.

None of these places would be open. The hostel door was locked and nobody answered, despite furiously ringing the bell for 15 minutes. I was more disappointed that the café and bookshop were closed. Montevideo was a sleepy town compared to Buenos Aires across the river, which was strange because Uruguayans drank more of the stimulating and insomnia-inducing yerba mate than even their Argentinian cousins. Every third person on the street was carrying a mate and a thermos. The bus drivers were the worst: they would drive with one hand on the wheel, the other holding a mate gourd with the thermos tucked under the same arm, every other minute leaning forward to pour a little bit more water into the green leaves.

I had set aside Sunday for the continuation of the Galeano tour but, at a loss with what to do with myself, I bought a different green-leafed product. Marijuana had been legalised by Pepe Mujica's government in 2012 and edibles were available in a handful of shops. I would have to keep the visits to the café and the bookshop on the list for another visit. The first stop on the Galeano tour, however, would be a success.

Galeano was a big Club Nacional de Football fan. I woke up early on Saturday and walked back to the bus station to meet my friend from Argentina. Elián had me worried: he was over an hour late. He had my ticket and I was forced to wait. He wasn't answering his phone and the majority of fans who had been gathering at the terminal had already left to walk the one mile through Parque Batlle to the ground. Getting to the stadium, there was a long queue to get in but we didn't miss any of the game. We made it into the historic Estadio Centenario and took our seats for the 1-1 draw between Nacional and Peñarol.

Galeano's men took the lead but a late equaliser from Peñarol would see the spoils shared. More importantly, the equaliser denied Nacional the chance to close the gap at the top of the league. With only two rounds to go and a four-point lead, Peñarol as good as secured the 2018 Clausura title with the draw. Nacional had won the Apertura by two points in May and Peñarol's Clausura win would ensure that the two heavyweights would meet in the championship play-off final three weeks after the 1-1 draw. It was a game Peñarol would win after extra time, triumphing 2-1 in the same stadium.

Peñarol and Nacional were by far the two biggest teams in Uruguay. The others didn't come close. The Uruguayan *superclásico* is the oldest rivalry outside of the British Isles, the first encounter having been played on 15 July 1900. Peñarol – then known as Central Uruguay Railway Cricket Club, CURCC – won 2-0. The long rivalry has its anecdotes, myths, legends and tragedies. And one of the earliest and most dramatic fragments of Nacional's history was staring me in the face as I sat on the concrete steps enjoying the draw.

We were sat under the stadium's 100-metre-tall watchtower on Tribuna Olímpica (so called for Uruguay's Olympic football gold medals in 1924 and 1928). To my left, the Tribuna Colombes was adorned with the yellow and black of Peñarol, their hinchas forming five vertical stripes across the stand. In the Tribuna Amsterdam to my right sat the Nacional *hinchada*, resplendent in their blue, white and red. Directly in front of me was the face of former Nacional captain Abdón *El Indio* Porte.

Porte had died 100 years earlier. Nacional's 2018 away shirt commemorated his passing with a circular badge – just under the collar on the back of the kit – showing Porte's portrait.

In 1918, Abdón Porte committed suicide in the centre circle of Nacional's stadium, Estadio Gran Parque Central. The defender had been a mainstay of the Nacional team, playing over 200 games, and had been part of the Uruguayan team that won the 1917 Copa América on home soil. But El Indio's form waned and he fell out of favour. The club bought in a centre-half called Alfredo Zibechi from Montevideo Wanderers to replace Porte. The writing was on the wall.

After playing 90 minutes in a 3-1 home win, Porte left his team's post-match dinner and returned to the stadium.

At midnight on 5 March 1918, he pulled the trigger to end his life before his time as a Nacional player could be ended for him. The 25-year-old's body was found the next day by the groundsman's dog. A stand at Nacional's ground was subsequently named after Abdón Porte.

I had first learned about Porte's fate in Galeano's book, *El Fútbol: A Sol Y Sombra* (*Football in Sun and Shadow*). The book taught me Spanish. Not many people could claim to have Eduardo Galeano as a Spanish teacher. I sat with the book hour after hour, studying the wonderful football stories and the Spanish words and grammar within them. Being a page or two long, I could read a story, look up the words, re-read the story before recording it in an audio message in Spanish to send to friends. It was invaluable speaking practice whether or not the audio was listened to. Does a falling tree make a sound if no one is there to hear it? My Spanish certainly did, regardless of a lack of audience, and eventually I became fluent.

I had been able to speak about football in Spanish before I could speak the language. Galeano helped me talk about other topics in his own tongue. Football was my social lubricant in South America. And combined with beer, the potent mix allowed me to engage with new friends and other football enthusiasts even when a common language was absent. In Argentina and Uruguay there was always someone willing to talk about the sport.

And talk we did. And play and drink and groundhop we did. The following 20 chapters are an account of what living abroad taught me about myself, about my new countrymen and about the beautiful – and, at times, ugly – game.

List of important phrases

CONMEBOL = the *Confederación Sudamericana de Fútbol*, the governing body of football in South America (South America's equivalent of UEFA).

Copa América (the Campeonato Sudamericano until 1975) = South American equivalent of the UEFA European Championship, the Euros.

Copa Libertadores = South America's equivalent of the Champions League (formerly European Cup). Nicknamed *La Gloria Eterna* (eternal glory).

Copa Sudamericana = South American equivalent of the Europa League (formerly UEFA Cup and European Cup Winners' Cup). Nicknamed *La Otra Mitad de la Gloria* (the other half of the glory).

Primera División/'La Primera' = Argentina's top tier (equivalent of the English Premier League or Italian Serie A).

Primera B Nacional/'La B' = Argentina's second flight.

The Big Five (Argentina) = Boca Juniors, River Plate, San Lorenzo, Independiente and Racing Club.

La Albiceleste = the white and light blues, the Argentina national team's nickname.

La selección = the Spanish translation of *national team*, e.g. the English national team in Spanish would be *la selección inglesa*.

Latin America = South America and Central America form Latin America, from Mexico to Argentina.

Gringo = traditionally a national from the United States of America, the term can be used to offend or simply as a label for either 1) a Yank, or 2) anyone speaking English. (Latin Americans often can't distinguish between the English spoken by Americans, Brits or any other visitor – the foreign tongue used between any backpacker is, of course, English, hence why we are all now gringos!).

Argento = the Spanish spoken in Argentina, incorporating their slang (*lunfardo*) with the unique dialect.

Boring, boring Arsenal de Sarandí

AS THE Uruguayan author and fellow football enthusiast Eduardo Galeano wrote in his book, *Football: In Sun and Shadow*: 'The goal is football's orgasm. And like orgasms, goals have become an ever less frequent occurrence in modern life. Half a century ago, it was a rare thing for a match to end scoreless: 0-0, two open mouths, two yawns. Now the eleven players spend the entire match hanging from the crossbar, trying to stop goals, and they have no time to score them.' The two 0-0s I saw at Arsenal de Sarandí resulted in many an open mouth, but not from spectators stunned by any brilliance witnessed at the Estadio Julio H. Grondona.

Boring, boring Arsenal, indeed – a 1990s British football chant that could easily be applied to The Arsenal's namesake 7,000 miles diagonally across the Atlantic. The London club I inherited from my English grandparents played a brand of football in the 1990s that wasn't pleasant on the eye. Very little football in Argentina was pleasant on the eye, but fans of the Arsenal in Avellaneda might resent the modern incarnation of their club being labelled *boring*. In their 60-year existence, Arsenal de Sarandí may have contributed very little to Argentinian *fútbol*, but the last two decades have seen them promoted to the top tier and lift, amongst other things, the 2011 Copa Sudamericana and the 2012 Clausura league title.

From The Arsenal to their Arsenal. I left London on Wednesday, 23 October 2013 to fly to Buenos Aires. A connecting flight in Madrid gave me four hours to wander around the empty airport. But it was being refurbished. There was nothing to do there: no bars, no restaurants, no shops to browse. I had hoped to find a bar to watch the Champions League in whilst waiting for my onward flight to Argentina. In the end I had to make do with buying four cans of San Miguel from the tiny cafeteria and paying an extortionate price for 24-hour wi-fi to watch a 90-minute football match on my laptop. Arsenal lost 2-1 at home to Borussia Dortmund, but the four beers served as an effective nightcap ahead of the 12-hour flight.

From Ezeiza Airport I took a *remís* taxi into town. *De dónde sos?* the taxi driver asked me. *Where are you from?* I had been studying Spanish for a couple of years, yet fell at the first hurdle. He changed the question: *De dónde ERES?* We tried to chat the rest of the journey but didn't get very far. He dropped me off at the door of the house where I was staying. It was 9am. Once I had been given the tour and was settled, I went online to have a look at the football fixtures.

I had already visited several grounds around the world without really even being conscious of what groundhopping was. I was a *groundhopper* before *groundhopping* as a concept had presented itself to me. Nearly a decade earlier, when I was in Berlin for a meeting, visiting the Olympiastadion was high on my list of sights to see. Had I been a fully fledged member of the football subculture groundhopping back then, I could have gone to see Union Berlin before they became admired around the globe. I could have even visited the Poststadion, which I have learned was where Adolf Hitler watched his only-ever game of football (when Norway beat Germany in the 1936 Olympics football quarter-finals). Hitler was apparently so disgusted by the result that he never returned to a football stadium.

But I hadn't thought to visit other grounds, only the biggest and most famous one – the only one I was aware of at the time. I wouldn't make the same mistake in Buenos Aires. Argentina's capital is home to an astonishing number of teams, making it one of the best cities for football in global football – if not *the* best. More than half the clubs in the top two tiers have a stadium in the capital or within an hour of the city's limits. And naturally each has its own unique history entangled with glorious stories of victories, defeats and everything in between.

First on my list, however, were Arsenal de Sarandí. That initial search of fixtures showed that Arsenal de Sarandí were playing at home only 48 hours later. A Friday night. Adopting *El Arse* as my Argentinian team and going regularly to the ground was the plan, a plan cooked up long before I had learned anything about the club. I didn't even know how far the ground was from the barrio of Colegiales where I was staying. I soon learned that this was an overly ambitious plan.

I went online to find out more. I contacted a couple of people on social media, asking about Arsenal de Sarandí on a Friday night. The response was an unequivocal *DO NOT GO*. Why would you be so stupid as to visit such a dodgy neighbourhood, an hour and a half from home, having just landed and not knowing your way around, let alone speaking the language? All that aside, who in their right mind would want to watch this team? And this was coming from one of their own fans.

Santiago was an Arsenal fan. He had lived in New Zealand for a year and, luckily for me, spoke perfect English. He put me off the idea of going to the ground and invited me instead to watch the game at his flat. It just so happened that he lived a short walk down Avenida Lacroze from my rented digs. A mate of mine came along and we found the 25-storey modern block of flats where Santi lived. The building looked very out of place amongst the mostly three- or four-storey buildings in the residential neighbourhoods of Colegiales and Chacarita in the north of the city.

My first cultural shock was awaiting me behind the door as I arrived on the 14th floor at Santi's flat. I knocked on the door. A few seconds passed before an Argentine man launched himself forward to kiss me. I'm slow at the best of times. I closed my eyes and accepted my fate. Without any pretence whatsoever, Argentines – men and women alike – embrace each other with the right cheek touching. To call it a kiss would be inaccurate; it's a brief hug in which the cheeks are the main protagonists.

Whilst this first experience of the Argentinian *beso* felt a little more homoerotic than I was used to, it was something I would grow to love. As a way of greeting a friend, or even meeting a friend of a friend for the first time, it broke down an invisible barrier whose existence I hadn't been aware of. (Later, when I was travelling through Bolivia and living in Perú and Colombia, I would miss the *beso*). But there were also times when it was a pain in *el arse*. Leaving a pub after getting together with Arsenal Argentina Supporters Club to watch an Arsenal game in the Premier League, I would feel obliged to go around the 15 Argentines, kissing my

22

farewells. A few times, after a few beers and a disappointing result, I would just sneak out.

Saying hello would be easier in these situations. Thirsty and excited about the game ahead, I was often the first to arrive at the pub. One by one others would arrive, and I could spread the kissing out over half an hour. Those who arrived last would have to do a lap around the table. One young Argentine would always arrive late. Sebastian also spoke perfect English, having lived in the US. I always hoped he would come so that I had someone to talk to. Sometimes he would arrive at half-time, other times not at all. If he did come, he wouldn't be in much state to hold a conversation: he had come straight from one of those Buenos Aires nights out that start at midnight and last until lunchtime.

The *beso* greeting could be something for my mates back home, I thought. But England and Norway are a lot *colder* than I had ever realised. Argentines would say to me that 'in colder countries the people are *colder*'. Were they trying to say we are unfriendly and maybe even hostile? At first, I felt this was unfair. We might not be as warm as people in South America, I countered, but I didn't feel we were cold. The problem lay in the comparison. It's like saying Argentina is not a footballing power just because Brazil have won more World Cups, I would say.

After a few years, however, I had to concede that, yes, people in my countries are generally quite cold. When I told my Peruvian girlfriend that Norwegian couples often sleep with separate duvets, she was dumbstruck. It was difficult to deny we were cold, having admitted that.

Before any talk of watching the English Arsenal with Argentines, I wanted to watch the Argentinian Arsenal with an Argentine. We walked into Santiago's flat and settled down for a male bonding session talking about football over a few beers. I don't remember much from the 1-1 draw between Arsenal de Sarandí and Gimnasia, just that watching it on telly was probably a better option than trekking down to the Estadio Julio Humberto Grondona in Sarandí.

It would take a few months before I made the trip to Arsenal de Sarandí's ground. Julio Grondona was an interesting, if not infamously outspoken and controversial, character who had risen to the top of the world game as president of the Argentine FA, as well as being the vice-president of FIFA. In the 1950s Julio and his brother Héctor founded the current Arsenal de Sarandí. There had been an amateur club called Arsenal in the neighbourhood for a decade up until that point. Naturally I was interested in the name, but no one could tell me definitively. Most suggested that *it probably came from the English Arsenal*. With the first Arsenal in Sarandí starting out in the 1940s, and the English Arsenal FC having had an iconic and successful team in the 1930s under the tutelage of Herbert Chapman, this may well tally.

So the name probably *did* come from London. But they hadn't adopted the red and white of the London club. The idea for their kit came from combining the colours of the two big clubs in Avellaneda, a town just outside the city limits of Buenos Aires. Racing Club and Independiente are the more traditional clubs of Avellaneda, two of Argentinian football's *big five*. Like any area with two big powers, the two clubs split many families, much like Arsenal and Tottenham or Liverpool and Everton do back home. But no concern was given to the revolting result of such a mix: Racing Club wear light blue shirts, Independiente red. Imagine a Manchester

City shirt slashed diagonally from one shoulder to the hip in a red sash representing Manchester United. Half-and-half scarves are unpopular enought amongst many football fans; I think this combo would cause a riot in the UK.

The club had languished in the lower divisions throughout the first couple of decades of their existence, reaching the Primera División in 2002 (with 1986 World Cup hero Jorge Burruchaga as coach). Their rise through the leagues – promotions in 1986 and 1992, before that last push in 2002 – coincided with Grondona's rise to power at the Argentine FA and at FIFA, which also included a stint as president of Independiente.

In fact, it turned out that I was living with a member of Grondona's family. Of sorts. I was staying in a gorgeous old house in Colegiales, renting a room from a teacher who worked where I was going to be taking an English teaching course, and where I would later be offered my first teaching job. My landlady's eldest daughter was married into the Grondona family. I began thinking about interviewing him. I wasn't a journalist, but I thought that Arsenal fans in the UK and beyond would be interested to know more about another Arsenal. And that if I had a link to the founder of the club, why not try my hand at writing about a topic close to my heart? Nothing came of it. Grondona died in 2014 aged 82. I had to be careful of what I said about the man around the house. I had heard a lot about nefarious things that implicated the man and I didn't want to offend my host. This was just another – allegedly – highly corrupt man in a country struggling with crippling corruption. Why could Argentina never get its act together? The C word.

When I did finally make it to Estadio Julio H. Grondona, it was with another new friend I had met in my first few weeks in Buenos Aires. Juance was what I never became: a double Arsenal fan. He was a Gooner and *hincha* of *El Arse*. More than a fan, Juance worked closely with Arsenal de Sarandí as a journalist with *Hablemos de Arsenal*.

We met in the pub watching the English Arsenal. Juance promised to take me to Sarandí. I had been putting off going on my own after what I had been told about the area. But Arsenal were due to play a Copa Libertadores quarter-final. It was as good a game as any to tick off a new ground, one I had been anticipating for a while. It was an evening kick-off and getting down to Avellaneda in rush hour was problematic. Juance lived in Belgrano, a neighbourhood close to where I was staying, and we met at Olleros tube station in Colegiales to go into the centre. From there we were supposed to get a bus from near the city's iconic Obelisco, but by the time three full buses had passed without stopping we decided to jump in a taxi.

Pre-match rituals are important in Argentina. Juance would always stop off at a pizza restaurant near the ground. The place was grubby, but the pizza was decent, the beer was served by the litre, and football shirts adorned the walls. Fans would either nip in for a slice to take away or they were propping up the counter, eating and talking. We wanted to sit and enjoy more than one litre of beer. We grabbed an empty table and marvelled at the shirts hanging around us. Naturally, there were a number of Arsenal shirts and of the rivals Racing and Independiente, as well as several smaller local teams that I had never heard of and would never hear of in the following years living in Buenos Aires.

It was just the kind of place I adored. Along with our pizza and beer, we had time for Juance to explain the ever-changing Argentinian league format. The following year it would change, but in 2014 the Primera División consisted of 20 teams with the season being split in two. It followed a European schedule with the *Apertura* or *Inicial* ('opening') starting in August and a *Clausura* or *Final* ('closing') played from February until June. Both Apertura and Clausura halves were played over 19 games and two champions would be crowned. (Sometimes there would be an outright winner after a final between the two winners, but not always.) It's a common setup throughout South America. That's not to say it's a permanent setup.

The 2011/12 season saw Boca Juniors lift the Apertura – their 30th league title – and Arsenal de Sarandí win the Clausura, their first. Arsenal winning the league wasn't the fairytale story of Leicester City winning the Premier League in 2016. It wasn't uncommon for smaller teams to win either the Apertura or Clausura, or at least challenge for them. Sustaining a title challenge over 19 games was easier than over a 38-game season.

Many changes have been made to how Argentinian football is played, particularly over the last ten years. In one way it's admirable that changes are readily made to the format in an attempt to improve the general footballing landscape. I have always wished that European football would be equally dynamic. Cynical observers of South American football would suggest that the seemingly constant tinkering of the structures makes Argentinian football chaotic and too random. It's certainly difficult for foreigners to understand until they really get to know the league and the teams. And after a lot of online study or football chat over beers. More cynical still, maybe the whimsical reformatting isn't always with the game's best interests in mind. In a corrupt country on a corrupt continent, there are probably other motives.

In 2015 the Primera División was expanded to 30 teams and named in honour of the late Grondona. But with 30 teams, playing each team home and away wouldn't have been possible. Fifty-eight league games would certainly make for a lot of football in Buenos Aires, but it wasn't viable. The solution was to play every team once, either home *or* away. That would mean a 29-game season. A second game against your closest rivals would give the 30-team league a 30-game season. El Campeonato de Primera División 'Julio H. Grondona' 2015 would be played from February to November – it was the first and only time since 1966 that a full season would be played in a calendar year.

With the new 30-team format, Boca Juniors and River Plate would play each other twice a season, home *and* away. Against the other three big clubs, however, Boca would be drawn to play either at La Bombonera or away. Boca having to play two of these three teams away would be a clear disadvantage (assuming that these three clubs were all at full strength, something which was never guaranteed as Argentinian clubs are also always in a state of flux). But a seeding system was devised to make it as fair as possible.

Baked into this pie was a derby match planned for every weekend. Clubs were paired up with a rival with whom they would spend a weekend with the eyes of Argentinian and South American football solely on them. One weekend Boca Juniors would face River Plate, another Newell's Old Boys versus Rosario Central. In the middle of the season a weekend was marked for *all* derby matches to be played. Boca versus River *and* Newell's versus Central *and* San Lorenzo versus Huracán. The setup meant that four teams would play their two derby matches on back-to-back weekends. Two rivals meeting the weekend before the big derby weekend, only to do it all again a week later. Another two teams would meet the weekend after the derby bonanza.

Of course, not everyone had a natural rival in the league. Once all the traditional derbies had been drawn up, the odd ones out – or *bichos raros* ('strange bugs' in Argentinian Spanish) – would simply be assigned a partner. Where maybe there was no rivalry before, for the coming season they became your most hated, despised rival. In theory, at least.

In English football, Arsenal-Spurs, Liverpool-Everton, United-City would be the first derbies to be scheduled, should such a season be adopted in England. But what about Norwich City? Norwich would wait until the end, picked last much like when playing football in the school playground. Is Norwich versus Newcastle an anticlimax of a rivalry?

Arsenal de Sarandí was a *bicho raro*. All of Arsenal's neighbours had a hated rival with whom they could spend two weekends during 2015. Arsenal's assigned *clásico* for this newfangled 30-team season was Defensa y Justicia. DyJ were another small team punching above their weight, but were certainly no direct rival for Arsenal and there was little head-to-head history to talk of. Arsenal fans will tell you that they have no particular disdain for Defensa. Porvenir, a team I only came across in the last few months of living in Buenos Aires, would be a more fitting fixture, had they not been separated by three tiers of Argentinian football. Arsenal toiled for decades in these lower divisions, after all. Quilmes, another southern Buenos Aires team, would have been a more viable rivalry, but Quilmes had been assigned neighbours Temperley as their derby partner for the season.

The 2015 campaign would be a one-off. In the first half of 2016, two 15-team leagues were contested between

February and May. Rivals were in different halves of the two zones but would play each twice in two interzonal games. Boca Juniors played 14 games, either home or away against the teams in Zona 2, but home and away against River Plate (both games ended 0-0). After the 2016 Copa América in June, another 30-team season was embarked upon between late August 2016 and late June 2017.

All this had been difficult to follow ahead of my first visit to Estadio Julio H. Grondona. The beer was flowing and the pizza was tasty, but the league formats were difficult to swallow. I resolved to read up on it the next day. First up was a Copa Libertadores quarter-final first leg between Arsenal and Club Nacional of Paraguay.

There are a lot of Paraguayans living in Argentina and, whilst away fans had recently been banned from domestic games, visiting fans were allowed for continental competition. It was one of few occasions when the ground would be full. Despite the decent atmosphere, the hosts couldn't break down the visiting defence and the game ended 0-0. Arsenal had lost the first leg in Asunción a week before and Club Nacional went through to the semi-final.

My second trip to watch *El Arsenal* also ended 0-0, this time in their so-called *clásico* versus Defensa y Justicia on the weekend of derby matches. Juance said he would take me, getting me into the *platea* section for free. It was on the condition that I didn't mind hanging around in the players' car park after the game while he interviewed players for *Hablemos de Arsenal*.

I didn't recognise any of the players. That wasn't really my thing. I might have tried getting a picture had it been Carlitos Tevez or Fabricio Coloccini or any other easily recognisable returnee to Argentinian football. I could probably only name a total of seven or eight players when Boca Juniors and River Plate played one another. When it came to Arsenal de Sarandí I struggled to name even one player. But I had nowhere else to be other than hanging around amongst the wives, girlfriends and young children of these top-division footballers, even if it lacked a lot of the glamour I would have expected.

Only 900 other spectators bothered, and it wasn't quite what one would expect of a Latin American – let alone an Argentinian – *clásico*. The fact that it wasn't really a derby, but just a regular game between two teams who were on borrowed time in the top division, might have explained the lack of enthusiasm. We did get an early red card for the home fans to shout about, but if anything this encouraged the away team to be even more defensively minded. The 0-0 seemed inevitable and the atmosphere never got going. Dotted across the little, blue-painted concrete terracing were groups of fans. And a street dog sat at the feet of an elderly man to my left. Behind one goal, there was a bigger cluster of fans and *barra brava* trying their best to support the team, but to no avail. People around us seemed resigned to a dull game early on. Oh well, there were much bigger games on that weekend anyway.

It was always disappointing to leave a stadium without having seen the home team score. The roar of the home crowd, that release of energy, was an essential part of visiting a new ground. In the coming months and years it was something I experienced several times across the continent, but particularly in Argentina. The result wasn't important to me: I was impartial but for wanting the home team to score at least once. 1-0, 1-1, 1-5.

My spreadsheet with data of games attended and grounds visited has a slew of yawning mouths, with half of the games

I went to in my first year in South America ending 0-0. There was nothing worse than returning home from a goalless draw to watch the goals in the other games on TV. An Argentinian goals show consists solely of the screaming of GOOOL a couple of dozen times over a 45-minute period. Commentators never deviate from the classic goal commentary and a review of Primera goals would feel like the television taunting the fan who attended the 0-0 draw.

Another three games ended without the home team scoring. A game which didn't end 0-0 was All Boys versus Olimpo at the Estadio Islas Malvinas. The only goal of the game was scored in the fifth minute. We arrived in the sixth and enjoyed 84 minutes of goalless action.

Situated in the south-west of Buenos Aires, All Boys play at Estadio Islas Malvinas. An uncomfortable name for Brits: *Las Islas Malvinas* is the Spanish name for the Falkland Islands. Most prominently, Godoy Cruz in the city of Mendoza and All Boys play in a stadium named after the islands. Apart from these, any stadium you visit in Argentina will have graffiti of the scraggy islands inside or outside the stadium, on items of clothing or even on the kits themselves. Upon seeing bucket hats sold outside River Plate's El Monumental stadium, with Las Malvinas and their famous red sash going through the middle, I had to buy a couple for my collection.

The issue of Las Malvinas was ever-present in Argentina and always seemed to be topical when it came to politicised events, which was essentially everything. The Argentine writer Jorge Luis Borges had suggested that the Falklands War was 'two bald men fighting over a comb', but the issue of whose islands they really were was still topical over 30 years later. Gatherings, celebrations, protests, elections, football matches: the islands were mentioned in many contexts that defined daily life in Argentina. Grondona had called the English 'pirates and liars' whilst he was on the board at FIFA, something he later had to apologise for. The resentment towards the UK (more specifically, England) on the topic was very real.

Argentines say that there are two things that are best not spoken about, namely football and politics. Touching on either subject is guaranteed to lead to disagreements, arguments and possibly fist-fights. Best to keep the peace and talk about the weather, maybe. However, football and/ or politics is generally *all* the locals talk about. And with Las Malvinas, every Argentine going to a football game will agree that *Las Malvinas Fueron, Son y Serán Argentinas* (' … were, are and will be Argentine'), so rather than causing disagreements, these two topics go together like red meat and red wine, bringing the locals together.

But being English or British in Argentina, one could expect a degree of animosity. I didn't experience any, possibly because I mostly came across a younger generation of Argentine who were more likely to ask about music or football than the Falklands. But I did have English students of mine ask me, either through curiosity or friendly teasing. A 12-year-old student, a smart and funny kid who later became an (English) Arsenal convert, stood up in our kids' class one day, put his hand on his heart and started singing the 'Las Malvinas' song they are taught in school, apropos of nothing. I didn't mind. Despite being half-English, I had no strong opinions about the Falkland Islands; it was before I was born. What's more, having read Naomi Klein's book, *The Shock Doctrine,* at university as part of my degree, I had been exposed to a slightly more sinister angle on Margaret

Thatcher and her motivation for fighting for the islands. But, as the Argies say, politics are best left out of it.

Teaching English in South America is a popular, almost clichéd, profession for expats. Considering that the vast majority, like myself, arrive without speaking much (if any) Spanish, this isn't so surprising. What other local job could you do without speaking the local tongue? Being British carried a lot more weight when working as an English teacher, more so than other nationalities. Argentine teachers of the English language suffered the most discrimination in this sense, even if they had come from Anglo-Argentine families. It was unfair considering the local teachers I worked with had studied English, in some cases for decades. They understood and could explain the grammar better than most native speakers, especially me at the outset of my teaching career. But being native had gravitas; not all native English speakers, however. I lived briefly with a South African who struggled to get work and moved home within a year in Argentina. Some Irish teachers had the same problem.

It served me well to say I was from the UK when working as an English teacher. Otherwise I would say I was Norwegian. I had been born in Oslo after all and had moved from Norway to Argentina; I felt I could say I was Norwegian without it seeming disingenuous. Norway was quite exotic to an Argentine. England was less so, as they already knew a lot about the country. Anyway, there were many British expats, long- and short-term, living in Argentina.

When backpacking in southern Patagonia towards the end of my sojourn in Argentina, I hitched a lift with an Argentine from the town of El Calafate to the Pan-American

Highway *Ruta 40*. We started chatting and I said I was an English teacher. I had said I was Norwegian, but I always felt it necessary to qualify myself as an English teacher by saying my mum was from the UK. (It didn't really matter, most people in South America – more so in Perú and Colombia than in Argentina – would ask if English was the main language in Norway, so either I confused them with my mixed heritage or maybe they were just confused generally.) The driver, an Argentine man in his mid-40s, had never bothered to learn English. I asked whether it had had anything to do with Las Malvinas, to which he said yes. He had never wanted to learn the language of the coloniser, whether that be the UK or the US (the latter were very active in many other parts of Latin America, from Mexico's northern border to the southern tip of Chile and Argentina, some 7,000 miles). The driver, however, felt that he needed to learn it now. The rancour of the war had diminished, and it was inconvenient not speaking the language when travelling, he said.

I had never had to talk about Las Malvinas because I said I was Norwegian. A mate of mine had said that he was Scottish when sitting on a barber's stool, a tactic that worked as they didn't associate Scotland with Britain, luckily for him. He was from Cambridge, but his grandad was from north of the border. Worse was my mate Ilan's story of when he was visiting London. With his light-blue-and-white Racing Club scarf on, he knocked on the window of a white van to ask for directions. The driver asked what his scarf was, to which Ilan answered Racing from Argentina. Without helping him out, the driver just wound the window up again. I'm sure there are Argentines who could be equally petty, but luckily I didn't come across them.

Racing Club's *mufa*

AFTER ARSENAL'S 0-0 against Defensa y Justicia, I was hoping to catch a better *clásico* the following day. I was making what by now was my third trip to *El Cilindro*, also known as the Estadio Presidente Juan Domingo Perón, Racing Club's ground. Argentinian grounds always have two names – an official name, often of an earlier club president, and a more informal nickname. It's the informal one that's used by the fans and media alike.

The first two trips to *El Cilindro* had been very different affairs. I had first seen Racing at the end of the 2013/14 season (the first half, the *Torneo Inicial*) and, with nothing to play for, the stadium was more than half empty for their routine 2-0 win at home to Godoy Cruz. The second game was a sell-out against Independiente, a 1-0 win that I watched with *La Guardia Imperial* from behind the goal.

On the third occasion I was taking a Norwegian girl I had got to know over the past few months. Synne wasn't a big football fan, but I had been telling her and anyone else that would listen that no one can live in Buenos Aires without going to watch a game. And not any game, it had to be a *clásico*. But I was probably the wrong host. With all the 0-0s I had attended, I had already become *mufa*.

Mufa is the opposite of *cábala*: two terms that are specific to Argentina. Argentines are very superstitious and the concepts of *cábala* and *mufa* are essential to their *fútbol* as well as daily life. Arguably, daily life for Argentines *is* football. *Cábala* could translate as a good omen, or a good-luck charm, whereas *mufa* is bad luck or a curse. I had been to enough games that had ended goalless to suggest that I was *mufa* for anyone wanting to attend a high-scoring game. Or even a game that featured just one, solitary, single goal, (preferably for the home team).

Shouting *goooal* before the ball had hit the back of the net was *mufa*. Whether watching on TV, in the stadium or playing football with friends, a dirty stare could be expected if you dared to pre-empt a goal by vocalising anything before the net rippled. Outside of football, Argentines don't wish anyone a happy birthday before midnight. The party itself will often start at 9–10pm the day before the birthday. At midnight the birthday song is sung, at which point anyone can congratulate the host. Before midnight, it's a regular party without any mention of the occasion.

A former student and now good friend of mine, Matías, is a huge River Plate fan. When River Plate were due to play Boca in the much-maligned 2018 Copa Libertadores Final, Matí turned down a ticket to his team's home leg for fear of being *mufa*. River Plate's home leg was the second leg of the last-ever two-legged Copa Libertadores Final. The decider of deciders for the *superclásico* of all *superclásicos*. He hadn't been able to attend any of his team's games in the Copa Libertadores all season as his university classes were in the afternoon and early evening. To suddenly turn up for the final would be a bad omen. So as not to risk River Plate losing against their rivals in the final of the biggest tournament in South America, he sacrificed himself for his team.

Another good friend, Roberto, told me the legend of an Argentine journalist who was considered *mufa*. The journalist had travelled to the World Cup 1986 in Mexico with many other Argentine colleagues. With the reputation of bringing bad luck to the *selección argentina*, the journalist only attended and reported on other games at the tournament.

Even when Argentina reached the World Cup Final, he stayed away. Sacrificing himself for the happiness and glory of his nation, he watched the game in a bar close to the Estadio Azteca in Mexico City. Diego Maradona's Argentina took a commanding lead in the final: goals from José Luis Brown and Jorge Valdano gave the 1978 winners a 2-0 lead before the hour mark. The journalist was now itching to join the action. His Argentina team were going to win the World Cup! He made the short walk to the stadium and, using his media pass, joined his colleagues. But he received a cold reception. Everyone knew that this man was *la mufa*.

And sure enough, Germany scored shortly after. Everyone in the Argentinian delegation of journalists threw an aggressive stare over at *la mufa*. Nine minutes later, in the 83rd minute of the 1986 World Cup Final, Germany equalised. If the journalist wanted to live, he would have to leave the stadium. He had watched 20 minutes and seen his team surrender a 2-0 lead and lose the all-important momentum going into the last five minutes.

But leaving the stands and looking for the exit, he found the gates closed. He couldn't get out of the Azteca. Still in the stadium, he knew his presence was sure to see Germany score again. The metal bars denying free entrance to the ground were too tall to climb over and too narrow to squeeze through, but putting his feet through so that they were touching the ground outside the stadium, surely that would be enough?

With the journalist halfway in and halfway out of the stadium, he hears the roar of the Argentinian crowd celebrating Jorge Luis Burruchaga's winning goal. The three minutes it had taken the journalist to leave the stadium were all Argentina needed to regain the lead and win the World Cup. Superstition in Argentinian football is a serious matter.

As *mufa* and as expected, the Racing-Independiente derby finished 0-0. Luckily, so did six of the 15 *clásicos* I could have gone to that weekend, including *all* of the games played on the Sunday. How many mouths yawning? I had seen a 0-0 on the Saturday in Avellaneda, and made the hour-long journey back to Avellaneda for another 0-0 on Sunday.

Game week 12 of 16 of the 2016 Argentine Primera División:

Saturday, 23 April 2016

Atlético Rafaela	3-1 Patronato
Olimpo	2-1 Aldosivi
Vélez Sarsfield	1-0 Argentinos Juniors
Unión	1-0 Colón
Arsenal de Sarandí	**0-0** Defensa y Justicia
San Lorenzo	1-0 Huracán
Godoy Cruz	1-0 San Martín
Lanús	2-0 Banfield

Sunday, 24 April 2016

Gimnasia La Plata	**0-0** Estudiantes
Newell's Old Boys	**0-0** Rosario Central
Boca Juniors	**0-0** River Plate
Racing Club	**0-0** Independiente

Monday, 25 April 2016
Belgrano   **0-0** Atlético Tucumán
Tuesday, 26 April 2016
Tigre   2-0 Sarmiento
Quilmes   2-0 Temperley

The highlight of our trip to *El Cilindro* this Sunday was *el recibimiento*, the reception of the Racing players coming out of the tunnel and on to the pitch. Flags unveiled, ticker tape and the whole stadium singing in unison to welcome the home team's players on to the pitch. It's always something to behold. Unfortunately, not much else happened. Teams are generally much happier to avoid losing than trying to win these games and the inevitable result is that more often than not they end scoreless, as was seen that weekend. There is said to be a lot of pressure on players coming from various quarters, none more so than the *barra brava* who demand a positive result from such an encounter. A negative result could be met with threats of violence and grave consequences.

My first *clásico de Avellaneda* had been better. Since arriving in the country I had been playing football with a group of expats, through whom I had met a Frenchman named Sylvain. He was a quiet bloke, but a very good footballer, and he had adopted Racing as his team. Sylvain sorted tickets out and eight of us – several Dutch, two French, a Brazilian and I – caught the bus down to Avellaneda. A mother and her daughter found this big group of foreigners intriguing and chatted to us during the long journey from Palermo to the stadium. The daughter was an avid Boca Juniors fan but regularly attended Racing games on a mother-daughter day out. Once we had arrived, we were asked to line up to have a picture taken with the two Argentines and from there our paths took different directions.

Our tickets took us on to the terraces behind the goal where the group known as *La Guardia Imperial* stand. We got in relatively early and found our spot. As it filled up, however, it got tighter and tighter for space. Moving around freely became difficult. The hardcore fans made their entrance and headed for the reserved space in the middle of the terrace. A makeshift brass band with drums and trumpets led the way, followed by people twirling umbrellas, marching in file, singing. As they filled their self-assigned turf there was much less space.

As the game kicked off the lack of space became a big problem. Racing Club started the game well and were creating chances. The block of people surged forward with every shot or attack. We were helpless to stand against it. I was perched on the edge of a concrete step. There wasn't enough room to firmly plant my foot on the ground beneath me. I had a Dutch friend directly behind me and the rest of our group were by now spread out on the terraced steps around us. I glanced back at Joop, and the look on his face confirmed my unease at the situation. When Racing went close with another shot, the surge was so strong that I saw a man in his fifties fall in the *avalancha*. I feared for him. I was sure he had been trampled on. It was difficult to imagine that it could have possibly ended well for the fan. There were *paravalancha* barriers, but very few of them, and those prime spots had been taken early, probably a good two hours before kick-off.

Once it had settled again, I saw the Racing *hincha* being dragged to his feet by his son and his daughter, a hand each under his arms. His face was pale white with fright, but he seemed unhurt. He had been lucky. Falling on these concrete steps with an unstoppable herd of people behind and then over you wasn't something I was keen on experiencing.

Morbidly, the situation made me think of Hillsborough. Nick Hornby told of similar experiences at Highbury in *Fever Pitch*. Here we were, more than 25 years after 96 people had died at an FA Cup semi-final in Sheffield, and the danger of something similar happening here in Buenos Aires in the here and now felt real.

Clearly, the circumstances surrounding Hillsborough were very different. The context of this game at *El Cilindro* wasn't comparable and there was enough space in other parts of the stand. As people began to realise the danger, they started to move. Whether they moved to a different part of the stand or a different part of the ground, I'm not sure. Maybe they left the ground altogether. By the time Racing had taken the lead in the 23rd minute, the crush had thankfully subdued.

The referee awarded Racing a penalty in front of *La Guardia Imperial* and, for 60 seconds of anticipation of a goal, the noise became deafening. *Vamos Vamos Vamos Acade*. There were ten rows left clear at the bottom of our terracing to allow for the avalanche of fans rushing towards the pitch (but not on to the pitch: there is a moat separating the pitch from the terraces). Diego Milito, who had won everything there was to win in Italy, scoring both goals in the 2009/10 Champions League Final against Bayern Munich in Madrid, scored the penalty against Racing's biggest rivals. It was the only goal of the game. But at least we had seen the home team score and run out worthy winners. More importantly, we were now safe on the terraces.

In the intervening 18 months between my first and second visit to Racing, the club had won only their second league title since 1966. One of the big five clubs, the lack of a title had haunted them and led to much ridicule from other fans, none more so than from fans of their neighbours, Independiente. Their two grounds are 1300 metres from one another – two behemoths in an otherwise flat part of Avellaneda staring each other down.

In 1967, Racing won the prestigious Intercontinental Cup, the precursor to the modern-day Club World Cup. Then, as is now, South American club football was much overlooked, but this tie gave the winners of the Copa Libertadores the chance to match themselves against Europe's best team. Glasgow Celtic were the European Cup holders and faced Racing Club for the title of the best club side in the world.

Having won the 1967 Copa Libertadores, Racing beat Jock Stein's Lisbon Lions over three games. Although initially a two-legged affair, a third game was needed to settle the tie after a 1-0 home win in Glasgow and a 2-1 home victory in Avellaneda in front of 120,000 spectators (an Argentinian record). The away goals rule had only been introduced by UEFA in 1965 but wouldn't be used in the Intercontinental Cup until 1969. A tie-breaker was needed and the Estadio Centenario in the Uruguayan capital, Montevideo, just across the Rio de la Plata, was chosen. The third game was so infamously violent that it's dubbed The Battle of Montevideo. Six red cards were brandished, although several players got away with infractions worthy of a ten-game ban in modern football. Celtic had four players sent off but finished the game with eight men after Bertie Auld refused to leave the pitch.

The Intercontinental Cup of 1967 was settled by a 30-yard left-footed screamer from Juan Carlos *El Chango* Cárdenas. Shoot, kid! his team-mate Mashcio had screamed. The Celtic net rippled 55 minutes into this third game and after over 235 minutes across two continents and three countries. It was a goal of the highest order that won the 'world cup' for Racing Club de Avellaneda. Returning from the airport, the players headed for *El Cilindro* and were met by fans of all Argentinian teams waving their clubs' flags in support of Racing, who had been representing Argentina when playing in the Intercontinental Cup.

However, Racing wouldn't maintain their position at the top. On 22 December 1983 they suffered relegation at the hands of neighbours and rivals Independiente, losing 2-0 on the last day of the season. Racing went down, Independiente won the league and huge riots broke out among Racing fans and the police.

Racing were cursed. The same night that Racing became world champions in 1967, a group of Independiente fans broke into *El Cilindro* and buried seven black cats. The *mufa* was planted and years of mediocrity followed. The players were aware of it and spoke about it openly. One evening in 1992, Racing were hosting Independiente. A fierce wind was blowing, and the advertising hoardings were close to flying off into the night. Racing's Claudio *El Turco* García predicted that the wind would lift the curse and that night Racing did have luck on their side. *El Turco* himself opened the scoring by punching the ball into the back of Independiente's net in their 2-1 win. 'I thought the goal had been like Diego's against the English, but it had been more like Daniel Castellani in the volleyball World Cup.' But the *mufa* hadn't gone.

Independiente fans continued to tease and taunt and Racing eventually tried to lift the curse by digging up the pitch. The remains of six dead cats were found, but the seventh remained elusive. In 1998, an exorcism was staged with white-hooded men carrying flaming torches. It looked more like a Ku Klux Klan event. It's said that the chaplain assisting the exorcism was a Boca Juniors fan. Needless to say, it didn't work. In the next game they lost 2-0 to Colón.

However, in 2001, whilst redeveloping *El Cilindro*, the seventh and final cat was found. The same year Racing won the 2001/02 Apertura. It was their first title in 35 years. It wasn't without its drama, though. Racing were top of the league with only one round to play, but the country was burning after the 2001 economic crash. Violent riots took place on the streets of the capital and 39 people lost their lives. The final round of fixtures was suspended. But finally, on 27 December 2001, Racing beat Vélez Sarsfield to win the title.

Another 13 years would pass until they won another league title, this time in 2014. This half-season title, however, was neither the Apertura nor the Clausura. It was a one-off, transitional half-season title, *Torneo de Transición*. None of the 20 teams competing in this league campaign was relegated, and ten teams were subsequently promoted from Nacional B.

Racing's relegation in 1983 was a humiliation, made worse by the fact that it came at the hands of their fiercest rivals as they were winning the title. Arguably worse still was the relegation of River Plate in 2011. Despite the biggest teams in Argentina having been for many years effectively protected from relegation, two of the big five – River Plate and Independiente – have both suffered this fate (in

2011 and 2013, respectively). In Argentina and across the continent, an average point system over three seasons is used to determine who goes down to the second tier. The biggest teams can therefore afford to have one bad season, but they normally wouldn't get relegated off the back of one below-par campaign. The timescale – three full seasons, six halves where applicable – gives the biggest teams, who have more money to spend, time to improve a squad whilst at the same time often weakening others in the process. Smaller teams' *promedio*, or average, is calculated over fewer games than those who are permanent fixtures in the league (or who *should* be permanent fixtures, anyway).

For example, in a traditional 20-team league, each team would play 38 games. Multiplied by three seasons: 114 games. However, a newly promoted team who has only spent one season in the top division will have their average calculated over only 38 games. With this system, it's not unthinkable to have a team near the top of the league based on the current season's efforts at the same time as they are languishing near the bottom of the three-year averaged relegation table. It hasn't yet happened, but in a magical football world where Eric Morecambe's dream East Fife 4 Forfar 5 scoreline can happen (albeit after a penalty shoot-out), an Argentinian team could theoretically win the Primera División and get relegated at the same time.

Cursed or not, Racing Club's stadium is another iconic ground in Buenos Aires. The ground's official name is Estadio Presidente Juan Domingo Perón, after the Racing-supporting president of the time of its inauguration. (Officially Perón supported all Argentinian teams equally.) It sits between the streets Diego A. Milito and Corbatta Oreste Omar, two legendary players of the club. Oreste

Osmar Corbatta's story is a tragic one: born into poverty and illiterate to Argentina's greatest-ever winger to destitute drunk living under one of the stadium's stands. 'Do you know why they couldn't take the ball off me? Because she didn't want to leave my side. Other things, yes, were taken from me, but never the ball,' he once exclaimed. Corbatta died aged 55 in 1991. The street adjoining *El Cilindro* was named after him two years later.

The stadium is perfectly circular – hence the nickname – with a 75-metre tower and another 15 metres of flagpole above it. The tower has a curious significance, which was only discovered in 2016, 66 years after its construction. When the blueprints of the stadium were handed over to the club by head engineer Eduardo E. Baumeister's family, the tower's position revealed a secret. On 28 September of every year at exactly 3pm, the tower casts a shadow that aligns perfectly with the stadium's halfway line. Baumeister was born at 3pm on 28 September.

But for the first four years after the 2016 discovery of the fact, it hadn't been possible to determine whether or not this was the case. Every 28 September was cloudy, until 2020. When 3pm came around, the shadow didn't land where it was supposed to. But then 2020 was a leap year. Those Racing fans who want to believe, will believe regardless.

Martyred Markitos at *Defe*

ARSENAL DE Sarandí fan Santiago – who planted that first Argentinian kiss on me – wasn't from Avellaneda, but from Núñez. The posher northern neighbourhood of Núñez was more famous for River Plate and Argentina's El Monumental than for the other teams who also called this part of Buenos Aires home. The area had four teams a short distance from one another: Platense, Defensores de Belgrano, Excursionistas and River Plate. *Defe* – of the third tier – was his other team, and a month after Arsenal-Gimnasia, he took me to a game there.

I had been in Buenos Aires a month and just completed a four-week, intensive English-teaching course. Intensive in terms of the amount of time spent on the course, but also the pressure of preparing and delivering classes. On the second day of the course, wannabe teachers are expected to stand in front of a class to teach English for the first time. The idea of standing in front of a class of eager students was made worse by my severe lack of knowledge of English grammar. I could barely explain what a noun was. We simply didn't learn much grammar at my 'less than comprehensive' comprehensive school. What made it more terrifying still was that the other people on the course –

11 Brits and one Argentine girl – would be in the room watching, encouraged to make notes on your performance over the 45-minute class.

I spent several hours the first evening of the course preparing a lesson for the next day and was nervous waking up on the Tuesday knowing I had to perform. It would be the first of about ten classes I would have to teach to complete the course; by the tenth class I actually started enjoying teaching, which was a good sign, as teaching English was the only prospect of income for me, having just moved. The students made it easier as they wanted their trial teacher to do well. The class was mainly made up of older ladies who were either retired or who simply didn't work (this was the rich part of Buenos Aires) and therefore were able to attend a free, two-hour English class every day, Monday to Friday. They were our guinea pigs, but their maternal instincts helped, and they guided us through it.

On the course I was reunited with a Barnet fan I had met a few years before. Barnet in north London is where my English family come from, and Barnet FC has always been my second team. I had been to Underhill several times, and when they were drawn away at Charlton Athletic in the Johnstone's Paint Trophy, I fancied the trip up from Brighton. Going on my own to my first Barnet away game, I got chatting to two fans at Clapham Junction. They followed Barnet up and down the country. They took me under their wings: we found the away pub for some beers and stood together on the terraces. Barnet lost 4-1 and we parted ways without exchanging phone numbers.

Four years later, as our group of 12 trainee English teachers was enjoying its first tea break from the intensive course, I overheard Marco telling one of the tutors that he was a Barnet fan. Then it dawned on me: this was the same Marco I had stood next to on the terrace at The Valley. Meeting again at Barnet FC's old ground Underhill would have been plausible, but meeting in a small language institute, doing an English-teaching course in Buenos Aires – what are the chances? Neither of us had recognised the other; it was only when I put his name and his club together that I realised that there can't be many Barnet fans named Marco whose parents run an Italian restaurant in Whetstone, over the road from where my mum grew up. We became good friends at the second time of asking.

Four weeks later, with a new mate and the course out of the way, I could relax. I wanted to go to a game. Santiago said that *Defe* were playing at home and off we went. The club provided an interesting juxtaposition in the posh neighbourhoods of Belgrano and Núñez. These are predominantly upper-class neighbourhoods. The Avenida Libertador cuts through the whole northern part of the city – from the centre near the postcard-famous Obelisco and the Avenida 9 de Julio, past Recoleta and Palermo before reaching Belgrano and Núñez. It's here, before the city limits, that Avenida Libertador becomes home to tennis courts, golf courses, gyms and private, member-only country clubs (some of which, even today, don't allow female membership).

Estadio Juan Pasquale seems to hide in amongst all of this. On the corner, backing on to the stadium, is a Starbucks. On matchday, heavy-set *barra brava*-looking football fans can be seen hanging around drinking beer and Fernet y Cola while young students with the latest fashion wander out of the air-conditioned coffee shop chain.

Who looked most out of place here? Interestingly, neither. Whilst neither group had much in common with the other, both seemed to respect the other's existence. In fact, the men and women, girls and boys coming out of the Starbucks were probably football fans themselves and people who are not in awe of or intimidated by football crowds.

Defe were a proud club, but that hadn't been in the top division for over 90 years. Ariel *El Burrito* Ortega – *el burrito* meaning 'the little donkey', an intriguing nickname – finished his career at the club on loan from River Plate, having gone back to *Los Millonarios* after spells in Spain, Italy and Turkey. Unfortunately, 'the little donkey' retired the year before my visit to the ground. Their attendances ranged from 1,500 to 7,000 on big occasions; the game we attended was probably nearer the lower end of this scale.

Santi explained that supporting a small club in Argentina wasn't for the faint-hearted. 'The lows are constant and the highs few and far between.' Similar to many lower-league teams in England, I thought. If football were all about winning, why would anyone support these teams when supporting River Plate/Boca Juniors or Liverpool/ Manchester United was easier? But the smaller clubs – in Argentina like in the UK – have more of a community feel about them, 'a family vibe' as Santi described it. Added to that, the stadiums were much smaller, and you were close to the action. 'You can stand right next to the corner-taker and distract him.'

'I also love how, even though it's a small team, we have our derbies, our rivalries, our legends and fables of things that happened in the past – like any other team. Our biggest derby is against Excursionistas – another small barrio team whose stadium is maybe two miles away from ours. My favourite bit of history happened on 27 May 1995. Excursionistas were having a shit time in the old Primera B and were about to get relegated if they lost – we played the derby against them, beat them 2-0 and that was it. They stayed in the fourth division for almost 25 years! The man who scored those two goals, Almanza, is a massive local hero – he comes to the club once in a while and re-enacts the second goal he scored that day. It's remembered as one of the most important wins in our 100-plus-year history. Sending your rival down is maybe the best thing that can happen to you in Argentinian football culture, even more than being crowned champion. I don't exaggerate if I say that it has been sung about in various football chants in every single *Defe* match since then.'

We finished our cans of beer and went to find the ground's entrance. We walked past a mural of a young man wearing a red-and-black-striped kit. It was Markitos Zucker and we were entering the roofed stand that bore his name behind the goal.

Markitos was the son of a famous Argentine actor – Marcos Zucker. As a political activist he would become one of an estimated 30,000 'disappeared' Argentines, victims of the brutal military dictatorship of 1976 to 1983.

Argentina – much like the rest of Latin America – has had a turbulent existence with several military coups and dictatorships plotted over the past 100 years. By the 1970s Argentina had already had six military coups in the 20th century and the majority of Latin American countries were under military rule. The early to mid-1970s saw such civil unrest that it bordered on a civil war, with bombings in the streets of Buenos Aires and the kidnapping of people on both sides of the political spectrum. Having himself been ousted by a military coup in 1955, Juan Domingo Perón returned from exile to Argentina in 1972. However, two years later he was dead. Perón's third wife, Isabelita, became president but her unsuitability to the job formed a huge power vacuum. This led to civil unrest bordering on civil war, with a political assassination every five hours and a bomb exploding every three hours at the height of the disorder.

Unable to stabilise the situation, Isabelita was ousted on 24 March 1976 and replaced by General Jorge Rafaél Videla, Argentina's newest military dictator. Many Argentines were in fact happy to see an end to the conflict being fought on the streets of Buenos Aires and other cities, but what followed – the so-called 'dirty war' – was beyond all reasonable force.

A campaign of state terror saw anyone considered 'subversive' or to be politically opposed to the military junta picked up off the street by one of the secret police's Ford Falcons. Invariably, suspects would be tortured upon arriving at secret concentration camps and, with few exceptions, killed or 'disappeared'. Captives taken from the streets of Buenos Aires were taken to ESMA – Escuela de Mecánica de la Armada, or the Naval School of Mechanics – in the same neighbourhood as *Defe*, Platense and River Plate. Club Atlético River Plate got their name from the river a stone's throw from El Monumental, the same river into which captives were thrown from planes to their death. It was when bodies began washing up on Uruguayan beaches that news of the extrajudicial killings made headlines around the world.

I had picked up Horacio Verbitsky's *The Flight: Confessions of An Argentine Dirty Warrior* before moving to Argentina. A member of the armed forces, who had taken part in two such 'death flights', had approached the well-known left-wing journalist on the metro in Buenos Aires in the early 1990s. Seemingly without remorse, Adolfo Scilingo told Verbitsky all about his participation in the state's National Reorganisation Process. Scilingo told how prisoners were given injections on the premise that they were vaccinations ahead of being transferred to a prison in another part of the country. But instead they were being sedated, left pliable, but not fully conscious, ahead of their 'transfer'. He admitted that some prisoners woke up as they were about to be thrown out of the military aeroplane's door.

I consumed this book in a matter of days and it would haunt me to think of the horrors this city had seen. The Ford Falcons became symbolic of the terror, and seeing one driving down the road would send shivers down the spine of many an Argentine. After reading the book I often saw old Ford Falcons parked innocently in my neighbourhood and it would make me think about what I had read, almost transferring me back to that decade. But I could never understand what people had gone through.

Some Argentines were sensitive to the number of deaths touted. Twice I experienced someone taking exception to talk of 30,000 disappeared *argentinos*. 'It was only 8,000!' I felt it was an odd way of denying the brutality and horrors of a dictatorship: 8,000 dead and disappeared is still an awful lot of victims.

ESMA was the largest and most notorious of all such clandestine detention centres in Argentina and is located directly opposite Defensores de Belgrano's ground. The mural of Markitos Zucker faces the former naval site, where his life was most probably taken. When the mural was commissioned, *Defe*'s then-president said that Markitos's portrait would protect the entrance to the stadium and the fans watching his club.

Markitos's two passions were football and politics. For his politics he was picked up off a Buenos Aires street in 1977 and detained for nearly 50 days until he was eventually released. He was one of the lucky ones and subsequently fled the country, moving to Brazil and then later to Spain. But in 1979 he returned to Argentina. The dictatorship didn't give him a second opportunity. Markitos was never seen again.

There were 25 million people living in Argentina in 1975, compared to 45 million in 2020. Some 30,000 people disappearing out of 25 million inhabitants is the equivalent of more than one in every thousand people. River Plate and Argentina's El Monumental holds over 70,000 people. In an attempt to provide a context to the extent of the horror, imagine 1,000 football fans being escorted from an Argentina game, taken from their seats to a detention centre. Nobody knows where they have been taken. They have disappeared. The now-empty block serves a warning to the rest that illegal and secret detention, torture and death are the consequences of living in a society ruled by the junta. You don't even have to be guilty of a crime, let alone suspected of any crime, to be victim of this punishment.

I visited ESMA a few times. The former military base has been transformed into a memorial site and museum. It's a respectfully classy place but the visit is nonetheless chilling. The horror lives in the walls. The videos, the photographs, the belongings of the victims and their stories leave a profound sadness for people who you didn't know and who you will never meet. I had students who told of family members who had been disappeared as teenagers. I taught 17- and 18-year-old students who would never meet the uncles and aunts they were already older than. It affected me profoundly to hear the next generation of Argentines talking about a dirty war that took place before they were born yet impacted their lives 35 years after the fact.

A friend of mine came to the *Defe* game and later went on a tour of ESMA. During his guided visit of the site a lady broke down as they were walking through the cold, narrow corridors of one of the buildings. She was sobbing uncontrollably. She blurted out that she had been detained at ESMA in the late 1970s and that this was the first time she had been back. Whilst I had been impacted, my mate Rob left the museum with a greater sorrow, having met one of the few victims to survive the dirty war. Hopefully the visit served as closure for her and helped her at least partially come to terms with what she had been through there.

The 1978 World Cup was held in Argentina amidst the backdrop of this severe violence. The junta – the army, navy and air force coming together – were only two years into the dictatorship. There was pressure from international human rights groups to boycott the tournament and it's said that 1974 finalists the Netherlands considered withdrawing from the World Cup. The *Oranje* ended up travelling, albeit without Johan Cruyff. Many thought that this was a political statement by Cruyff, but he wrote in his autobiography that he had stayed at home for reasons concerning threats to his family in Barcelona, nothing related to the situation in Argentina. Even without their talisman, the Dutch were the favourites and they progressed through the two group stages to the final. Argentina made it through their half of the draw, albeit with allegations of match-fixing.

As with any tournament held in the context of a dictatorship, there were questions around the legitimacy of

Argentina's first World Cup victory. The format of World Cups up until 1978 had been ever-changing, with both knockout and mini-league formats. In 1978 the top two teams qualified from four groups into two new groups of four, with the winners of these two second-phase groups meeting in the final. There were no quarter or semi-finals as is common in the knockout tournaments of today.

In their final and decisive second-phase group game, Argentina needed to beat a decent Perú side by four goals. Brazil topped the group and would be heading to the final, unless Argentina could pull off a miracle. The game was played in the city of Rosario, at Rosario Central's ground, El Gigante de Arroyito. Argentina won 6-0. It was an eyebrow-raising result. *Los Incas* had won their first group by finishing ahead of Argentina's opponents in the final, the Netherlands, and had only conceded four goals. But against Argentina, Perú had nothing to play for other than pride. Or maybe self-preservation.

General Jorge Rafael Videla was the junta's leader and the de facto President of Argentina during the World Cup. Videla didn't like football but he understood the game's power to deflect attention from the atrocities of his dictatorship to a potential national joy of winning the country's first World Cup. Before the Perú game, Videla – accompanied by former US Secretary of State Henry Kissinger on behalf of Operation Condor – paid a visit to the Peruvian dressing room. Naturally, no one knows what was said in that dressing room, but of course suspicions were raised by the result.

Other conspiracies have been discussed. One suggests that Argentina's military dictatorship entered into deals with Perú's then-military dictatorship for corn (supposedly one million tonnes). Another talked about the return of Argentinian dissidents imprisoned in Perú.

Rumours that bribes had been taken were also commonplace and were given credence when a Peruvian player – Rodulfo Manzo – claimed that his national team had been bought and told to throw the game. Manzo was playing in Buenos Aires at the time of his comments. He realised that he wouldn't be popular with the ruling junta and left Vélez Sarsfield after only 15 days, escaping the country on a motorbike and ending up at Ecuadorian Emelec. It's rumoured that he drove the whole 3,000-mile distance between Buenos Aires and Guayaquil, leaving his wife and children behind.

Whatever the circumstances of their win, Argentina would contest the 1978 World Cup Final with the Netherlands at El Monumental. The stadium is only one mile from ESMA. Very few of those held at the detention centre would survive their internment, but the handful that did would reference hearing the crowd celebrating Argentina's three goals in the World Cup Final against the Dutch and the cheers when the trophy was lifted. From the small cages under the low ceilings of the loft or from the basement where the torture sessions were carried out, detainees managed to follow the final before many of them were disappeared. Some prisoners were even taken out into the streets to see the crowds celebrating before being driven back to the grounds of a place that nobody knew was being used as a torture centre.

An information board at the modern-day ESMA tells the story of the guards during the tournament. Inmates experienced more cruelty after an Argentina win, the euphoria of the triumph seemingly giving the guards more justification to carry out *El Proceso*, the 'National Reorganisation Process'. The prisoners soon learned that a victory for Argentina would increase the thuggish violence.

Pregnant women were amongst the detainees fearing *la victoria argentina*. Upon giving birth, the mother would be tortured and disappeared. The newborn would often be given away to a family on the right side of the political sphere – 'right' in both senses of the word, according to the military personnel involved, at least. The fiercest – and only – lobby group the dictatorship had was *Las Madres de la Plaza de Mayo*. *Las Madres* were the mothers of the disappeared who demanded to know what had happened to their children. Some of these mothers were themselves disappeared for their protesting. The remains of two of the founders of *Las Madres* washed up on a beach 200 miles south of Buenos Aires in 1977. Another founder was disappeared in the same year, her body dumped in a mass grave; only 28 years later did her family learn of Azucena Villaflor's fate.

During the World Cup, (West) German goalkeeper Sepp Maier tried to meet with mothers from the *Las Madres* group to find out more about their campaign and the political situation in the country hosting the tournament. FIFA, however, warned that any such visit would lead to Germany's expulsion from the World Cup. Sepp Maier might have been scared off, but *Las Madres* weren't; they continued to protest outside La Casa Rosada every Thursday, without fail. And whilst *Las Madres* were asking questions about their children, *Las Abuelas* – the grandmothers – were specifically asking about the children of the pregnant women disappeared.

Now, 35 years after these terrible events, I was taking my seat on the concrete steps in the Markitos Zucker stand facing ESMA. I still had an awful lot to learn about my new home and its recent history. But on this hot Saturday at the start of the Argentinian summer, with the smell of weed wafting throughout the terrace, we were solely thinking and talking about football.

Defe were facing Club Deportivo Morón, a club a short train ride west of the city limits. Moronic of me, maybe, to be so fascinated by the name, but it was a fascination that led to me buying several bucket hats and other souvenirs when I finally made it to their ground a few years later.

The novelty of the name momentarily subsided once the game had started. Within a minute of the Primera B Metro clash, the Argentinian third tier, Morón took the lead. But I was looking the other way. Not only did I miss the goal, but it also took me several minutes to find out that *Defe* were behind. Without away fans, there had been no roar of emotion at the opening goal. Any noise coming from Morón's bench was drowned out by the brass band and the singing in the Markitos Zucker stand. Morón's second goal I did catch, but it was irrelevant. The away side could have scored ten for all I cared. I was happy for them to win as long as I could see one home goal and experience the home roar. But it wasn't to be, and the curse continued.

Not having away fans would be something I would miss. But Argentinian football had been struggling with violence for several years, with on average one death every month between 2009 and 2011. One solution was to ban away fans altogether. With over 30 grounds in Buenos Aires, the authorities and police were unsurprisingly overwhelmed by the management of a dozen or more games on a weekend.

The police have enough on their hands controlling just the home supporters. Football violence in Argentina isn't necessarily between fans of rival teams but rather rival factions within a supporter group.

The *barra brava* are organised gangs akin to mafia. They look to curry favour within a club, not necessarily the club they support. Friends and students talked about the *barra brava* as football hooligans, but that's not the case. Hooliganism is much less nuanced. British football 'firms' of the 1970s and 1980s may have been organised to an extent, but they didn't have access to the club like the *barra brava* do. At some clubs, the leader of a *barra* can let themselves into the stadium when they want. With this access and all that comes with it, lots of groups are constantly vying for control of the fanbase. There is a lot of money to be made from football in a country like Argentina, from petty cash to million-dollar deals a club negotiates.

The genesis of the *barra brava* was a lot more honest than what it would become. Originally, in the 1950s, groups of fans were paid by their club to travel to away games. Whilst modern-day players at Europe's top level rarely, if ever, experience discomfort travelling to away games, the reality is different in South America, even today. But more so in the past. Fierce and violent home fans, often backed up by local police, applied pressure to visiting teams and, unsurprisingly, many teams buckled, underperforming. In an attempt to come away with a positive result from trips to other grounds, club directors in Argentina paid fans to travel to support their team – the team's 12th man. Not *any* fans, of course, but rather the *barra* – a hardy set of young men who could look after themselves. Travelling *barras* were a lightning rod for the aggression meted out by the locals, allowing the team to focus on the job at hand.

Once in the door, the *barras* made more demands and levied more power. The result of this is that today they control large aspects of Argentinian clubs. It starts on the street: *barras* charge for parking in the streets around the ground, their territory, Monday through Sunday. *El trapito* (the cloth man, a symbolic cloth suggesting the car will be cleaned while the owner is away) promises to look after the vehicle upon receiving a small sum of money. There are no parking meters, there is no app on your phone. Just *los trapitos*.

From the street to the boardroom, *barras* demand money from the club's hierarchy. Free tickets are handed over, which are resold on the streets, bringing in 100 per cent profit. More lucrative still are the cuts taken from players' wages or big transfer deals taking players to Europe (or elsewhere). Protection money and extortion are commonplace, as if from a Hollywood gangster film; money is made both from selling drugs to players and the potential blackmailing further down the line should the player decide to go against the club's or the *barra's* demands. The *barra brava* can force a player to sign a new contract.

The *barras* work as freelancers. Politicians use them as bodyguards or henchmen. A friend told me of his experience. Martín had gone along to a protest in a southern suburb of Buenos Aires. The ecological reserve was being used to dump rubbish and Martín and his friends went to the town hall with a big group of local residents in support of a professor presenting to the municipality. There to greet the protestors was a group of 50 thugs linked to Club Atlético Los Andes. Holding sticks and throwing stones, the Los Andes *barra* first intimidated Martín and others present before attacking and hospitalising the professor after he had given his scientific findings. The politician behind the violence went on to become president of a big team in the Primera División.

During the 2014 World Cup, stories circulated that certain *barras* had been flown out to Brazil. These types of trips were even given either as a present to reward certain groups or as payment for jobs done. The well-connected politicians and club presidents could guarantee tickets upon their arrival.

Santí had another story for me like any good story, it involved Ronaldinho. At the beginning of 2013, Ronaldinho's Atlético Mineiro side were visiting Arsenal de Sarandí in the group stages of the Copa Libertadores. People flocked to the Estadio Julio H. Grondona in Avellaneda to see the former Barcelona and Brazil legend. The Arsenal de Sarandí *barra*, however, noticed that the crowd for this game had swelled beyond normal proportions, so they closed the turnstiles. Getting out black bin liners, they reopened the turnstiles on the condition that everyone queuing paid an extra 20 pesos (about £2 in 2013). Supporters threw their cash into the black bags as they passed through the gate. Call it demand and supply – the more demand for something, the higher the price becomes. These were basic economic principles that a capitalist football club would be naïve to ignore, but Argentinian clubs as not-for-profit members' clubs? The gap between the reality and the potential is filled by the *barra*.

But the *barras* have far too much control, and in an already corrupt country, they are a cancer that will be difficult for Argentinian football to rid itself of. The violence had been brewing for decades until it reached boiling point. That's when away fans were banned. And without them, there was something missing. In the biggest games, it felt unfair that 50,000 people's hatred would be focused on those 11 souls on the pitch. Even a small section of away fans to act as a lightning rod to absorb the pressure on behalf of the players would have helped.

Very occasionally, Argentinian football would be treated to visiting fans. Continental club competition allowed away fans from foreign teams (but not when Argentinian sides met one another). For Arsenal de Sarandí's quarter-final against Club Nacional the away end was full, but the significance of their being there hadn't yet dawned on me. After a few years of having been starved of away fans – and therefore the full, matchday experience – seeing and hearing away fans was a strange and wonderful thing. I would never take them for granted again.

The theft of the
Argentinian Wembley

ALL OF the other big five teams in Argentina had won the Copa Libertadores, but not Club Atlético San Lorenzo de Almagro. Rival fans would mock *los cuervos* (the crows). Vélez Sarsfield, not considered one of the big teams in Argentina, would remind their visitors of their 1994 Copa Libertadores trophy every time San Lorenzo made the short trip to the Estadio José Amalfitani.

The club's acronym, CASLA, was reworded by rival fans to spell out *Club Atlético SIN Libertadores de América* (*sin* meaning without). Finally winning the trophy in 2014, San Lorenzo got a huge monkey off their back. But was it all of their own doing, or did they get divine help?

For years the club had been exposed by the lack of the Libertadores, the most prestigious on the continent. Argentinian clubs are the most successful in the competition and Independiente have won the tournament seven times, followed by Boca Juniors with six (having competed in 11 Copa Libertadores Finals since 1960). River Plate now have four titles (at the time only two) and Racing Club one (1967). Outside of the big five, Estudiantes de La Plata won three in a row between 1968 and 1970, with Juan Ramón Verón scoring in all three final games in 1968 (two legs and a tiebreaking third match). His son, Juan Sebastián, captained the same team to victory in 2009. Argentinos Juniors and Vélez also have one title each. For San Lorenzo, it was an embarrassment not to appear on this list. But that was about to change.

In March 2013 a new Pope was elected. Jorge Mario Bergoglio was born in the Buenos Aires neighbourhood of Flores. The biggest club in his neighbourhood was San Lorenzo. Upon his succession to the Vatican, Pope Francis's San Lorenzo began winning again after having been threatened with relegation the year before. They picked up the 19-game Torneo Inicial title, which qualified them for the Copa Libertadores the following year, which they finally won for the first time in their history.

Since his election as Pope, San Lorenzo have won several trophies. On each occasion they send a delegation of players and management with the latest trophy to the Vatican to show Pope Francisco. At the time of winning the Copa Libertadores, their kit sported a halo above the CASLA badge. I had assumed the halo was a symbol of pride for the Pope being one of their own, but San Lorenzo fans set me straight. I had only just arrived to their country; my ignorance was partially excused.

Club Atlético San Lorenzo de Almagro were founded by a priest called Lorenzo, who was later canonised to be a saint (Saint Lawrence in English, San Lorenzo in Spanish). Lorenzo Massa was a priest born in Morón, just outside the border of the city of Buenos Aires. Working in Boedo, a neighbourhood within the city limits, he saw children playing football in the street. A group of friends in their early teens had formed a team called Los Forzosos de Almagro and played under the streetlights at the intersection of the streets México and Treinta y Tres Orientales.

One day, one of the Forzosos fell in front of a tram. Juancito Abondanza was kicking the ball on the tracks when he tripped. The streetcar managed to stop just in time, bumping into Juancito, who jumped up shouting and swearing at the driver. The priest summoned the Forzosos' 15-year-old captain, Federico Monti, and told him that his team could use the church grounds to play in. *Los Forzosos* could use the grass as their football pitch on the condition that they attended mass every Sunday. Eventually, the team took their name from the priest who had opened his church's doors to them, whilst also taking the *azulgrana* colours of the Salesian Order to which Massa belonged. The nickname *cuervo* also comes from the priest Lorenzo: priests dress in black, as do crows.

From humble beginnings to the big five and eventually to winning the greatest tournament in the Americas. I had only been in the country for a matter of weeks when I was invited to see San Lorenzo win the league at home to Juan Sebastián Verón's Estudiantes. It was 1 December 2013, and three points at the Estadio Pedro Bidegaín, more popularly known as El Nuevo Gasómetro, would see them over the line. It was scorching hot, with the mercury hitting 35°C, and there was only a roof on the main stand opposite us. We had to get there early to get a good seat, so rather than for two hours, we sat in the baking sun for four hours.

The fans in the terraced end behind the goal were given relief from the heat. Not by a roof, but by the fire department who took pity on the multitude assembled behind the fencing in the south curve, *Los de la Sur*. Before the match and during half-time, the firefighters sprayed their water cannons into the crowd. It was a preventative exercise: at any moment the crowd could burst into flames in the searing heat. Oh how I wished I had been standing amongst them for those refreshing droplets.

And oh how I wished San Lorenzo had scored, but the game ended 0-0. Of course it did. The prospect of seeing the crowning of the league champions had been tempting, but San Lorenzo had bottled it. They would have to go to rivals Vélez in the final round where, for the last time, they would be taunted about not having won the Copa Libertadores. A 0-0 draw (and a 2-2 draw between Newell's and title rivals Lanús) saw San Lorenzo crowned champions.

Four months later the Copa Libertadores was on television. In the group stage of the successful 2014 campaign, San Lorenzo went to Ecuador to play Independiente del Valle, a small team who had never won their domestic league and had only gained promotion four years earlier (they would reach the 2016 Libertadores Final, beating both Boca Juniors and River Plate along the way, and win the 2019 Sudamericana). San Lorenzo were leading 1-0 in the final minute of their penultimate group match. It was a result that would have seen *los cuervos* through to the knockout stages.

But with four minutes added on and 93:30 minutes on the clock, a clumsy challenge gave the referee a chance to award a penalty to the home side. The penalty hit the back of the net and the official immediately blew for full time. At the final whistle, San Lorenzo players surrounded the Paraguayan referee to remonstrate. As the Ecuadorian riot police stepped in to protect the match officials, both players and police got carried away. A brawl began with emotional

San Lorenzo players attacking the baton-wielding police, who retaliated. The drama was over in a flash but it's an image that stuck with me.

As a result of the melee, two San Lorenzo players received four-match bans from CONMEBOL. They would re-join the matchday squad only in the quarter-final second leg. After Ecuador, San Lorenzo had a nervous two-week wait before the final group match at home to Botafogo. They won 3-0, taking them above Independiente del Valle on goal difference in a very tight group: two points separated first from fourth and only one goal separated San Lorenzo and Independiente del Valle.

The third goal was decisive. Independiente del Valle had won a crazy game in Chile, beating group winners Unión Española 5-4. From 1-0 down to 3-1 up to 4-3 down, the game finished with an Ecuadorian win. So 2-0 wouldn't have been enough for San Lorenzo, and they pushed for a third goal, which they duly got when Ignacio Piatti struck in the 89th minute.

One of four Argentinian teams in the last 16, San Lorenzo were seeded 15th. Being ranked below Lanús and Arsenal de Sarandí was bad enough, but to see Vélez Sarsfield ranked first was a bitter pill to swallow. Having beaten one Brazilian team in Botafogo, *El Ciclón* were drawn to play 40-year-old Zé Roberto's Grêmio. But it was the 19-year-old Ángel Correa who would dictate the first leg, starring and scoring the goal that gave San Lorenzo a slender first-leg victory. It was a performance that would earn Correa a move to Atlético Madrid a few months later. A 1-0 defeat in Porto Alegre took the game to penalties. The penalty shoot-out victory in southern Brazil took San Lorenzo into the quarter-finals where they would meet yet more Brazilians, their friends Cruzeiro.

Their *amistad* stems from 1998 when the two clubs met four times in the Copa Mercosur, a precursor to the modern Copa Sudamericana. Cruzeiro played twice in Buenos Aires, first in the group stages and then in the semi-final second leg. The leader of Cruzeiro's *barra brava* (*torcidas* in Portuguese) visited the Estadio Pedro Bidegaín and fell in love with the passion of the home fans. From that day on he would support San Lorenzo as well as his beloved Cruzeiro.

In May 2014, Cruzeiro once again visited the Bajo Flores neighbourhood of Buenos Aires. San Lorenzo's *barras* received the Brazilian *torcidas* and enjoyed an *asado* together before watching *El Ciclón*'s 1-0 home win. In the crowd, San Lorenzo fans were wearing the blue of Cruzeiro in honour of their visiting amigos from Belo Horizonte. In Brazil a week later, the second leg finished 1-1 and San Lorenzo had reluctantly knocked out the last remaining Brazilian side.

While San Lorenzo fans were being wined and dined in Belo Horizonte, I was off to watch the other quarter-final involving an Argentinian club: Arsenal de Sarandí's 0-0 home draw with Club Nacional of Paraguay. The team seeded 16th of the last 16 in the knockouts would find their way to the final, beating Uruguayans Defensor Sporting 2-1 on aggregate in the semis.

San Lorenzo's semi-finals were easier. A 5-0 home win against Bolivians Bolivar all but sealed a place in the final. The Bolivians had hoped to play out a scoreless draw to take back to the altitude of La Paz. San Lorenzo themselves were forced to attack to ensure they avoided having to travel to the Estadio Hernando Siles at 3,600m altitude needing a result. An aggressive performance made the second leg a formality. The game ended 1-0 to the hosts in La Paz, the consolation goal coming in the 90th minute.

In the first leg of the 2014 Copa Libertadores Final, San Lorenzo travelled to Paraguay. A draw in Asunción was a decent result to take back to Bajo Flores, but a last-minute equaliser was inconvenient. The second leg was won with a 36th-minute penalty in Buenos Aires. The rotund central midfielder Néstor Ortigoza, Argentinian-born but a nationalised Paraguayan, put away the spot kick and ended 54 years of hurt in the Libertadores for *El Ciclón*. Two weeks later, 77-year-old Pope Francisco received Edgardo Bauza's team in the Vatican, inspecting the immense, iconic trophy.

Pope Francis remembers having been to see San Lorenzo play with his father. Bergoglio senior had been a successful basketball player for San Lorenzo *basquet*. In 1946 father and son went to see the title-winning San Lorenzo *fútbol* team. Aged 12, Jorge Mario would have been spellbound by a team who played with such intensity and aggression entwined with skill and attacking verve that they romped to the top of the table, grabbing this young boy on the way. After 30 games they had scored 90 goals. The moniker of *El Ciclón* given to them in the 1930s had reappeared to pull up trees once again. (*The Cyclone*'s rivals, Huracán – *hurricane* – were blown away when they heard of this new nickname.)

Nearly two decades later came the 1968 version of *El Ciclón*. A new nickname was added: *Los Matadores* (the killers). This team became the first in Argentinian football to go the season unbeaten. They played 22 league games, plus two subsequent play-off games to win the title. (Without taking anything away from this great team, going unbeaten in Argentinian football is somewhat easier than in other countries as they play fewer games. Boca Juniors,

Racing Club and San Lorenzo have gone unbeaten ten times between them since 1968. Either way, San Lorenzo can forever boast to have been the first to achieve the feat.)

The next six years would harvest another three league titles, again going unbeaten in their successful 1972 campaign (only 13 league games, plus a play-off final). But with the start of the military dictatorship the following year began the downfall of the great San Lorenzo. With a global economic crisis on top of what was happening locally, many institutions were feeling the pinch, and San Lorenzo were no different. Debts were growing, bankruptcy was looming.

As with any polarising event in Argentina, there are two diametrically opposed versions of the same story. The fact is that San Lorenzo played their last game at their stadium *El Gasómetro – el Wembley porteño* – in 1979; a 0-0 draw with Boca Juniors. Little did the players or fans know that it would be the last time they would ever play there. It would be the last time San Lorenzo would play in a stadium they could call their own for the next 15 years.

The stadium represented the neighbourhood. The first game had been played there in 1916, and in 1928 it had been expanded to accommodate a rapidly growing club. By the 1940s, San Lorenzo had more than 40,000 *socios* (paid-up, card-holding members) using the various sporting facilities and attending social events. The stadium was a cultural centre, housing one of the city's biggest libraries and organising dances and carnivals. Children would grow up playing football in the belly of the stadium, flanked by the concrete pillars that supported the wooden terracing above. They would meet friends there that would last a lifetime. Romances were made and families were started amongst the club's membership.

The stadium represented so much more than a place where professional footballers plied their trade. It was called *Tierra Santa* (the holy land) and selling up and moving out wouldn't have been an easy, let alone popular, decision. The club might have been broke, the stadium might have needed repair, but surely the club's heart belonged in Boedo and at *El Gasómetro*?

Around the same time as San Lorenzo's financial strife, Osvaldo Cacciatore was installed as the new Governor of Buenos Aires by the de facto military government. Insisting that the plot of land where San Lorenzo's stadium sat was needed for the development of an intercity motorway and housing, the junta began applying pressure on the club to sell. Other clubs had received financial support from previous governments, as well as the dictatorship, yet San Lorenzo were being ostracised. A famous San Lorenzo song aimed specifically at River Plate outlines this. The song, a whole verse, is sung on the terraces whenever the two clubs meet. In Spanish it rhymes, but even in English the *azulgrana* message is clear:

> 'River, you are chickens, you attend games [only] when you're winning or playing at home, Today San Lorenzo will tell you about the sensations that football can give you. Happiness and sadness is what living a passion is all about, Something that fans of River don't bear in their hearts.
>
> For this reason, I want to explain to you, the importance of football is the passion.
>
> If it was just about winning, it would be the same as watching it at home.

Whilst you put armchairs on your terraces,

The San Lorenzo party is something you'll never emulate.

We are so different; you're sat in the stands, we're stood on the terraces,

It's not the same way of thinking.

Our fanbase built our ground, and it will never be forgotten,

Yours was built by the military government!'

San Lorenzo fans felt aggrieved, even to the point of conspiracy about how the junta attempted to destroy their club (not just football club, but social and sporting club). The more sinister version suggests that San Lorenzo's administration were powerless against a dictatorship intent on depriving them of the social fabric that made them who they were (and still *are*). San Lorenzo and its fans had an activist temperament, rebellious in nature, and regularly protested against right-wing political policies. Something that the junta would have wanted to crack down on was the club's link to *Las Madres de la Plaza de Mayo*. Having been founded in April 1977, *Las Madres* protested against the disappearance of their children for the first time at San Lorenzo's stadium on 20 June 1977, an act in and of itself enough to unleash the wrath of the dictatorship.

A couple of years after this defiant act, San Lorenzo de Almagro's president, Vicente Bonina, received a visit from governor Cacciatore to talk about the plot of land owned by the club. With a vast number of university students already dead, it's reported that Bonina was asked whether he had children attending university, to which the answer was *sí*. 'I suggest, then, you pay attention to what I am asking of you,' responded Cacciatore. With this pressure, the club sold the majority of the land for a paltry US$900,000. The buyers were two so-called phantom companies, or dummy corporations which had only been registered two days' earlier in Montevideo. Whilst initially the contract forbade the building of supermarkets on the site, in 1985 the site was sold for US$8,000,000 to the French multinational Carrefour. Nothing came of the promised redevelopment of the area, such as housing developments and primary schools.

The same year that *El Gasómetro* was demolished – 1981 – was the same season San Lorenzo were relegated. They became the first of the big five clubs to suffer this humiliation. Needing a draw at home to survive (*home* being Ferro Carril Oeste's ground in Caballito), they lost 1-0 to Argentinos Juniors. If the goal of the junta had been to cripple the club, it had momentarily worked. It could have gone either way for a club in dire straits financially and now playing in *La B*.

The following year would, however, be a record-breaking season for *El Ciclón*. In 1982 they won the second division with a greater average crowd than all other teams in the country, including all of the first division. And that despite not having their own ground. San Lorenzo played the majority of their games at Vélez Sarsfield's ground in Liniers, with two home games played at Ferro and another two played at River Plate.

San Lorenzo's first game of the 1982 season was played at Ferro, where they had suffered their relegation only a few months earlier. A strange twist of fate – before the invention of 'the fixture computer' – had them playing Ferro away only a week after losing to Argentinos Juniors as hosts at the same ground. It saw an immediate return to the stadium at which they had just been relegated at. For 90 minutes the San Lorenzo fans sang: 'Wherever *El Ciclón* choose to go, we will follow.' So impressed were Ferro's players that they applauded the away fans before leaving the pitch.

Despite this, the club's administration underestimated how many fans would attend their first game in the second division back at the rented Estadio Arquitecto Ricardo Etcheverri, also known as *El Templo de Madera* (the wooden temple, a ground I was lucky to visit before the old wooden terraces were demolished in 2014). Ferro's stadium wasn't big enough and a larger stadium was needed for the large crowds that would attend their 21 home games that season. Upon San Lorenzo's return to the first division, the military dictatorship were on their way out, and within a decade the club had built El Nuevo Gasómetro in the neighbourhood of Bajo Flores, two miles from their spiritual home in Boedo. Officially named Estadio Pedro Bidegain after one of the first *socios* and former club president, construction was finished in December 1993, and by June 1995 they had been crowned Primera División champions, winning the Torneo Clausura with a win at Rosario Central on the final day of the season to leapfrog Gimnasia. Things were looking up for *El Ciclón*.

El Nuevo Gasómetro within a few years would host continental football, receiving teams from all over the continent and making new friends. But, while San Lorenzo have friends in Brazil, another Argentinian club have enemies.

Two months after having visited San Lorenzo's ground for their 0-0 draw with Estudiantes de La Plata, I went to Club Atlético Tigre's Estadio José Dellagiovanna for another 0-0 draw. With two friends, we got the train from Belgrano north towards the river delta formed at the town of Tigre. Getting off a few stops before Tigre at Victoria, we wandered a few blocks to find tickets for Tigre versus Argentinos Juniors.

The streets were full of Tigre fans enjoying the summer warmth. Sleeveless blue-and-red training tops with shorts was the dress code. People were mingling, drinking litre bottles of beer and/or Fernet and Coca-Cola as we made our way to the ticket office. An old school bus parked on a side street was where we were encouraged to buy our *entradas*. We stood in the queue and were eventually served out of the back window of the bus.

Only 14 months earlier, Tigre had contested the Copa Sudamericana Final against Brazilians São Paulo FC. It was only the second time the club had qualified for the continent's second most prestigious tournament and had done so by finishing second to Arsenal in the 2012 Torneo Clausura. It had been a historic league campaign.

Tigre finished second for only the third time in their history, having done so for the first time only five years earlier in 2007, and then again in 2008. But 2009 had started badly. In the 19-game Torneo Apertura, Tigre amassed only eight points, losing 15 games. Having done well in the two seasons prior, their three-year average was good enough to avoid relegation. But by 2012 they were struggling to keep their heads above water.

With two games left of the Clausura, Tigre needed a win to stay in the race for the title and, more importantly, to stave off relegation. A 1-0 win in Vélez's Estadio José Amalfitani ensured that Tigre wouldn't be relegated directly, although a relegation play-off game against a second division team was still on the cards. With Vélez also in the chase for the title, it was a big game, a championship six-pointer. With the three points in the bag and going into their last game, Tigre were joint top with Arsenal.

Tigre drew 2-2 at home with Independiente on the last day of the season, while Arsenal beat Belgrano 1-0 in Sarandí. Tigre lost out on the title but maintained their Primera División status. A bittersweet end to the season for Tigre, but the drama wasn't over yet.

With their second-placed finish, the small club from the northern suburbs had qualified for the Copa Sudamericana for only the second time. With the Copa Libertadores played between January and June, the Sudamericana started in July and finished in December. Tigre met Argentinos Juniors in the second round, winning 6-2 on aggregate, saving the 0-0 for my visit.

Ecuadorians Deportivo Quito (4-2 on agg.), Paraguayans Cerro Porteño (4-3 on agg.) and Colombians Millonarios (1-1, away goals) were beaten on the way to the final, where Tigre would meet São Paulo.

The first leg of the final was played at Boca Juniors' La Bombonera, the Estadio José Dellagiovanna deemed inadequate for hosting such an occasion, despite its nickname *El Coliseo de Victoria*. The game finished 0-0. To win their first-ever major honour, Tigre would have to win in a real coliseum, the Estádio Morumbi.

The Argentinian club have many complaints from their brief time in Brazil. It started when they landed at Guarulhos airport. The coach they had booked was nowhere to be found. The Tigre squad waited for two hours before getting another bus to drive into the huge, sprawling city. But they travelled without a police convoy from the airport and the following day without an escort to take them to the ground. The dressing room they were given was a mess and they weren't allowed to go on to the pitch to warm up. A warm-up would have to take place inside the concrete underbelly of the stadium.

These complaints pale into insignificance when compared to the treatment they received at half-time. With the Brazilians leading 2-0 in the first half and cruising to another continental title, their players started showboating, with the *paulista* crowd egging them on with cheers of *olé, olé* for every successful pass. It wasn't even half-time, and the score was *only* 2-0, but the home team's players in their white shirts, shorts and socks were walking lazily with the ball, stopping to put hands on hips in a provocatively arrogant manner. The Argentines understandably took exception.

When the Chilean referee blew for half-time, Tigre players went after Lucas Moura. Moura had been on the receiving end of a tough challenge, leaving him with a bloody nose. Taking out the bloodstained cotton from his right nostril and showing the Tigre defender as the teams were walking off the pitch was enough to start a 50-man brawl involving both benches and, of course, armed riot police.

Arriving at their away changing room, Tigre's players and staff were confronted by *torcidas* of São Paulo. Tigre's manager Néstor Gorosito and his goalkeeper Damián Albil revealed that a Brazilian security guard had used a gun to hit Tigre players, at one point pointing the gun at Albil. In the dressing room, the military police came and, rather than diffusing the situation, made matters worse. Using batons, the police began hitting players. There were images of blood on the walls of the changing room.

Gorosito, talking to the media at Buenos Aires' Ezeiza Airport, said that the referee had seen the blood and had been aware of the hostility at half-time. Tigre didn't go out for the second half. They stayed in that changing room for another three hours until a coach came to transport them to the airport. The referee awarded the game to São Paulo, who promptly celebrated and lifted the cup in front of their raucous home fans.

Fourteen months later I was standing under a summer deluge on the terraces at Tigre's ground. The 0-0 draw had been uninspiring – two more mouths yawning. Despite the result, it had been another good outing and a new neighbourhood explored. I was now turning my attention to getting tickets for Boca Juniors against River Plate, the first *superclásico* scheduled since my arrival in Argentina. That wouldn't be quite as straightforward as buying out of the back window of an old school bus.

Tears at La Bombonera

BOCA-RIVER. RIVER-BOCA. *El superclásico* evokes an image of a different species of football match, closely related to what many of us are used to. But at some point in its evolution, it and Argentinian football as a whole took a unique direction. Maybe we think we know what to expect when the two biggest clubs on the continent go mano a mano.

Whilst for many a visitor to Argentina it may be a once-in-a-lifetime match, I was lucky to experience three *superclásicos* during the four years I lived in Buenos Aires. I almost feel guilty as if I'm boasting of the feat. I became a Boca-River junkie, chasing the dragon looking for a hit to rival that first high, the derby game at La Bombonera on 30 March 2014.

Upon landing in the country, I had immediately noted down the date of Argentina's and arguably Latin America's biggest fixture. I had plenty of time to find tickets. I would have to pester people, butter people up, brown-nose. I asked around. I hadn't lived in Buenos Aires very long but had started working as an English teacher with a handful of private students who I spoke to about football; men, women, young and old alike, they were all keen to talk about football. I had started regular private classes with two students, both called Pablo, and later a pair of 50-something female doctors who wanted classes together at the hospital where I would go every Tuesday for a few months.

Young Pablo, an 18-year-old aspiring pilot – who had taken up English only two years earlier and by the time I met him spoke better English than me – wasn't especially interested in football. Like most Argentines, he knew a lot about football and had a team, but 'I'm not a *fanático*'. This was an Argentine's way of saying that they didn't watch or go regularly to the stadium, but they knew where their allegiances would be should they choose to take it up more 'fanatically'. The second Pablo was a 40-year-old former journalist. He, *sí*, was a *fanático* and was proud to tell me that he had interviewed Diego Armando Maradona in the 1980s. Ferro Carril Oeste of Caballito was his team.

Ferro-Pablo lived and breathed football. Our Friday morning lessons would invariably fly by with nothing other than football chat. I ended up giving Pablo a copy of Nick Hornby's *Fever Pitch*, and a couple of years later I received a message from him saying he was penning his own version, a story of his life as a Ferro Carril Oeste fan. Outside of the big five teams of Argentinian football there are lots of teams with charm and history. Pablo would be the first to highlight Ferro's greatest era, winning the Primera División title twice in the early 1980s, not an insignificant time in Argentinian football considering the fact that the national team won the World Cup in both 1978 and 1986.

Pablo was a good person to ask. He might not have been a Boca fan, but I could start by interrogating him about how I might come across a ticket. By having the conversation in English I could also justify my AR$100-a-class wage (about

£6). I would get on the Subte, the Buenos Aires metro, in rush hour and a ridiculously humid 35°C heat, arriving sweaty and slightly traumatised at his flash, downtown office in Corrientes street. His secretary would bring me a buttery *medialuna* and cup of coffee and I would sink into one of the chairs, enjoying the air conditioning and a moment's peace.

But my pleas for help were met with deaf ears. Pablo wasn't a *bostero*. I hadn't heard this word before. Pablo explained.

Various theories exist for both the origins and meaning of Boca fans' nickname. Some claim that it means *shit collector*, from the word *bosta*, meaning animal faeces. Rival fans say the neighbourhood stinks, due to the sewage that spews out into the river Riachuelo. Others say the nickname comes from *botero*, or boatmen, with La Boca serving as the old port of Buenos Aires (*boca* meaning mouth in Spanish). Argentines swallow the letter *s*, so *bostero* from *botero* is almost indistinguishable, especially for a foreigner.

Bostero or *botero*, it wasn't meant as a compliment from opposing fans. It never is. As for River Plate, *gallina* means chicken. The nickname derives from a Copa Libertadores Final loss to Peñarol in 1966. River Plate were leading 2-0 only to lose 4-2. River Plate and the Uruguayan giants Peñarol had met home and away, both teams winning one game each: 2-0 to Peñarol in Montevideo and 3-2 to River Plate in Buenos Aires. Without aggregate scores, the final went to a third and deciding game played in Chile's capital, Santiago. At half-time, River Plate were leading by two goals, but Peñarol scored twice in the second half, forcing extra time. Two more Uruguayan goals sent a third Copa Libertadores title back to the Peñarol trophy cabinet. River

Plate would have to wait another 20 years for their first Copa Libertadores trophy.

The bottling of the final was only the first part of the humiliation. The nickname *gallina* was hammered home when River Plate travelled to Banfield in the next round of league fixtures. Banfield fans threw dead chickens on to the pitch to taunt the River fans and players. From that day forth, the moniker was fixed. As with all football fans, however, self-deprecation is essential, and they have accepted the story as part of their history. Boca fans proudly call themselves *los bosteros* and River Plate *las gallinas*.

I had met a handful of people in my first six months living in Buenos Aires and I was hopeful that this network would allow me to get a ticket for the *superclásico*. The lady running the English institute where I had some classes told me that her husband was a Boca fan and could maybe get me a ticket. That would be handy. But I wasn't resting on my laurels and kept asking around, making a nuisance of myself. Everybody wanted a ticket to these games, so why should I jump the queue?

Alas, when the weekend finally arrived, I had nothing. I had resigned myself to the fact that I would miss the game. I could watch it on TV, but I wouldn't be there in the flesh to experience it. Not yet. It would have to remain on the list of unfulfilled fixtures. It wasn't the end of the world; I had already been to La Bombonera back in 2009 and there were another 35 grounds to visit in greater Buenos Aires alone. Eight grounds had already been ticked off in those first few months; 11 in total, having visited the trio of Newell's, Boca and River in 2009. Hardly prolific but I had time.

I woke up on the Sunday morning of the big game and began planning my day. The sun was shining as it so often is in Buenos Aires. The Argentinian flag pays homage to the blue skies with the celestial bands top and bottom and the sun on the silver band in the middle. Paula, a *porteña* I had met on a month-long exchange trip to China back in 2007, had told me that they would be selling any returned tickets at a place called La Casa Amarilla in La Boca before the game. I had nothing to lose.

Maybe I did. La Boca isn't known to be the safest neighbourhood in a city and country that at the time was experiencing increasing levels of poverty and subsequently violence. I left my ageing smartphone at home, took my SUBE smartcard for the bus, 900 pesos in cash (about £65 at the time) and my donor card. I was only going down there to experience the build-up to a *superclásico*, and if I managed to find a ticket then I had what I was willing to pay on me.

Apprehensively, I got on the bus and made the 45-minute journey from Colegiales in the somewhat *cheto*, well-to-do north of Buenos Aires to La Boca in the industrial south. There were still about four hours to go until kick-off, and as I got off the *colectivo*, I started looking for La Casa Amarilla, the so-called 'yellow house'. Initially, I stuck to the main *avenida* Admirante Brown, looking into pubs and restaurants and getting a few odd looks. Maybe it was more my paranoia telling me that I was out of place rather than any special attention I might have interpreted as receiving.

The locals are very welcoming. During my four years in the city I never felt any animosity. Whilst not quite on the level of the modern-day Premier League in terms of attracting tourists, La Bombonera is a place where football fans and football ignoramuses flock alike, more so than any other football ground in South America. Estádio Maracaná in Rio de Janeiro might be on par or a close second.

I hadn't found what I was looking for in the main *avenida* and I couldn't really ask anyone as my Spanish was still very poor. I ventured down one of the streets leading to the stadium itself. From the main road, between two blocks of flats, a preview of the yellow concrete stadium can be seen. But after about 50 metres down I got cold feet. On subsequent visits to La Bombonera I would learn that this area is where the *barra brava* park up and hang out, drinking their *trago locos*, smoking weed and building up to the game.

The *barra brava*'s mode of transport is another iconic element of Argentinian football. They deploy old school buses – either retired or still in use – that are either hired or commandeered for the day. Or they pile on to the city buses, either in service or not, driving in convoy, sometimes with a police car or two in front leading the way. The *hinchas* hang out of open doors and open windows, extending both arms as if fanning themselves in the heat. This is the typical expression of supporting your team. It belongs to the large family of hand gestures deployed by Argentinian football fans and Argentines in general. Reaching out with one or both arms, flicking your wrists forward as if swatting two flies with the outside of both hands, extend your fingers out before bending your elbows and bringing your hands towards your face in a fanning motion. And repeat. The more fanatic the arm-flailers, the more it looks like the person is having an aggressive convulsion, but only from the shoulder down. An intense religious experience where they might as well have been speaking in tongues, as I didn't understand the songs being sung.

Before I could experience the *aguante* and almost religious fanaticism inside the ground, I would have to find a ticket. On this particular day, alone and unfamiliar with the area, I was being extra cautious. I wasn't expecting to get a ticket. The *barras'* buses were parked up further down the side street and I decided to turn around and head back to the main road. Turning those 180 degrees was the best thing I could have done as I immediately bumped into two Boca fans walking towards the ground. One of them asked me if I was looking for a ticket – in perfect English. I didn't know what to say. Obviously, I was, but I had to play it cool. *How could I know if the tickets were real?*

Bruno explained that his father – whose ticket he was carrying – was under the weather and had decided at the last minute to stay at home. Bruno was tall and good-looking. He spoke calmly but with authority. He said that he wasn't desperate to recoup any money; as *socios* (members), they had paid a standard price for that ticket, the same as a ticket to any other league fixture. His *bostero* pal had his seat in a different section and would be heading off to the other side of the ground. A quick *beso* to say goodbye and good luck, and his friend left.

Bostero Bruno seemed like a decent bloke. He had light brown hair like me, and green eyes like me. He could have been from any European country. I told him I had AR$700 on me and he was happy to accept that. We set off towards the ground. The encounter was the stroke of luck I felt I deserved for having made the trip down there.

AR$700 was above the face value of the ticket, but he could have got a lot more for it had he offered it around elsewhere a few days in advance. I played football with two English lads who had paid AR$3,000 each (around £225), albeit in the executive balconies opposite the corner where I ended up sitting. Paying £65 for my ticket wasn't too bad.

The Argentinian peso was still a foreign currency and I hadn't quite learned instinctively whether it was a lot or not at the time of handing over the cash to Bruno. But it was a price I was more than happy to pay.

'Keep your head down and don't speak English,' was Bruno's advice as we walked past the *barras*' buses. There were more than two hours to go until kick-off, and without too much hassle we were in the concourses of La Bombonera. Coming from the north, we walked through an open plot of land. There was a train track, which came from the La Boca port and up along Puerto Madero, another former dock now converted into high-end property. It was a stark contrast to the rest of the neighbourhood to the south of the stadium, where the charming, old two- or three-storey houses were tightly packed together.

Naturally, Bruno and I spent a lot of time chatting about football, regaling each other with stories of our two clubs. I was impressed by his level of English. It would take me years of living in Argentina, immersed in the language and culture, to get my Spanish up to a similar level. After an hour or so of football chat, we took our seats. We weren't sitting together so I had to go find my seat in a different section, before making my way over to the divide where he met me to get the membership card back. I had to hand him the *carnet* very slyly while he kept an eye out for the stewards.

The location was decent: a seat in the corner, about ten metres from the corner flag, with a good view out over the terracing behind the closest goal. Next to me was a father with his five-year-old son, a bit bemused to see a gringo sitting next to them. There was a long time to go until kick-off but by no means were we amongst the first to take our seats. The stadium was pretty much full already, some 90 minutes and a whole football match ahead of kick-off. The two terraced sections behind each goal were already in full swing – singing, jumping, chanting, extended arm-fanning-and-flailing. The game hadn't even kicked off yet and there was already a better atmosphere than any Premier League game I had been to.

As we were waiting for the game to begin, plastic shopping bags full of ripped and shredded paper were passed up from the front row and each *bostero* was encouraged to grab a handful before sending the bag on its way. For around 45 minutes I stood with a handful of paper, not quite sure when I would need to launch it. As the teams exited their individual inflatable tunnels and entered the pitch, a snowstorm of this improvised ticker tape filled the air. For about ten seconds I could barely see two feet in front of me, zero visibility as if it were a snowstorm.

It was a mouth-opening reception. The referee tried to initiate a minute's silence for someone's passing, and around me I heard a few people trying to shush people around them. But after that amount of energy welcoming the Boca Juniors heroes on to the pitch for this massive game, trying to bring it all to a sudden halt was impossible. Not once, in six years in South America, did I see a successful minute's silence.

In fact, on this occasion Boca fans made ghouly ghost sounds. *Oooh, oooooooh!* They weren't distastefully mocking the passing of a notable figure. The noises weren't related to the minute's silence. The *oooooh*s were for River Plate and the stain of their 2011 relegation that they couldn't erase. The 'ghost of the B', the ghost of the B Nacional.

The ghost of relegation is a sinister presence. It threatens to kill a club's status as a top division team and drag them into the underworld of the lower divisions. If a club has a bad start to the season, the ghost's presence grows. No team is safe from the ghost. No team is immortal, as River Plate found out in 2011. Their relegation and the subsequent riots that led to El Monumental burning gave their rival fans a lifetime of ammunition.

The *ooohi*ng and the booing ended, the game started, and the initial nerves set in. It's this nervousness, this fear of losing to your greatest rival, which sees many a *clásico* or *superclásico* end 0-0. Not until the tension is broken by a significant event on the pitch does the atmosphere reach its full potential. A goal, a red card, a shocking tackle, an injustice, perceived or real – people are not released from their shackles until something happens. The atmosphere is akin to the skies rumbling before a storm. It begins with short, isolated rumblings. You know it's coming, and you want the heavens to explode and the drama to unfold in front of you. But sometimes you're left with the what-could-have-been, the rumbling continuing without ever relieving itself of the built-up pressure, like a tickling sneeze that never quite forces its way out.

River Plate scored first. Without away fans, the hour-long rumbling became a momentary grumble before the singing in support of the home team intensified. Now wasn't the time for whinging and whining, the home players needed a push. It helped – Boca equalised within ten minutes. Juan Román Riquelme – one of *the* iconic cult figures of Boca Juniors and Argentina, greater than even Maradona to many fans – scored a superb free kick. To the left of the penalty area's D, favourable for a right-footed genius, Román sent it over the wall and into the goalkeeper's top-right corner. It went in off the bar, as if it weren't already perfect!

It was the lightning strike that made the earth shake and the stands rock. The water in the harbour a few hundred metres away was rippling from the vibrations. The pressure had been released, an explosion of joy but also relief at having equalised. Of having cancelled out their rival's opener. Four years earlier I had seen Román miss a penalty against Arsenal de Sarandí in this same stadium. Riquelme didn't exactly need to make up for anything where Boca Juniors were concerned, but his legend was certainly intensified with this free kick. Whether or not Boca would go on to win the game remained to be seen. But that wasn't important now. Live in the moment. Live it up, breathe it in.

On any other day and at any other game, I would have been tempted to film the free kick, even if I had expected it to hit the wall or fly over the crossbar. I could have easily spent half the day hiding behind the screen of my phone. We know it's stupid and we even criticise others who do it at football matches or concerts. But it's easy to get caught up in the moment and want to try to savour the experience for ever. Only because of the borrowed paranoia of going to La Boca for a Boca-River game had I left my phone at home. Each moment had to be lived there and then.

In future games I would feel comfortable taking my phone and I would always end up wanting to record the free kicks, penalties, the reception of the teams. My brother nor my mates from home were there with me and they would never understand the moment I was experiencing. I wanted to show them and share it with them. But the video never truly conveyed the experience.

Piel de gallina, the Spanish for goosebumps. *Gallina* fittingly being the nickname given to River Plate and their fans. Watching the goal online will always give me *piel de gallina* at the expense of *las gallinas*. I didn't hear the television commentator's inflection as the free kick was flying in until I watched the highlights the next day. Maybe *bosteros* in the crowd listening to their transistor radios had heard something similar. Would it have added to the experience there and then? A world-class free kick from a world-class player in a *superclásico*.

The atmosphere reached fever pitch. Frozen in the moment, I was standing gazing out on to the pitch. I didn't really have anyone to share the moment with. Everyone around me was embracing someone – a father, a son and/or daughter, a brother, a sister, a friend. I tried to look for Bruno to give him a nod of appreciation, but I couldn't see him.

I could see 50,000 ecstatic *bosteros*. The sight of that multitude of blue and gold celebrating a goal of that quality wasn't to be the highlight. Clearly a winner would be even better, but it wasn't forthcoming. Had it finished 1-1 I would have been happy with my day out at the football. But we were only halfway through the spectacle. Within three minutes of the equaliser came *the moment*. It was a moment that I would retell again and again on many a beer-fuelled evening of football talk across South America.

Inevitably, people would ask about the *superclásico* and whether or not I had been. A disappointingly small number of people would get the Spinal Tap reference I would use. It was a pity; Argentines in particular would love the film. I thought we were at fever pitch. Little did I know that the dial went up to 11. The noise in the ground after Román's stunner was already at a level that I thought was maximum. Ten out of ten, full capacity, full intensity. How could it get any better? The dial only ever goes up to ten, right? But what if the sound level of the La Bombonera went up to 11, which is, after all, one more than ten?

Fans were still getting over the equaliser when a passage of play unfurled in front of us. Having just conceded, the wounded white-shirted, red-sashed *enemigo* went on the attack and got a shot off, which Boca's goalkeeper, Agustín Orion, parried. Boca picked up the loose ball and went forward down their own left-hand side. Fans were off their seats; they hadn't yet sat down from the equaliser. The self-imposed restraints had disappeared. It was now finally unfettered devotion from the *Xeneizes*. The sequence of events ended with Boca's left-back Emanuel Insúa unleashing a powerful shot from 25 yards. River Plate's Marcelo Barovero took it cleanly and held on to it, giving everyone a chance to breathe. It wasn't a goal, but a second River Plate goal had been averted and a decent shot from distance had seen Boca threatening to take the lead. Buoyed on by the equaliser and now this energetic counter of a counter-attack took the atmosphere to 11: 11 out of 10!

Overwhelmed by the intensity of it all, tears appeared in my eyes. I couldn't help it. I was taken aback by the level of noise, by the sheer glee and excitement of these intensely passionate football fans. I was hoping for an unforgettable game, but how could I have prepared myself for this? I just stared out on to the pitch, trying to catch my breath while everyone around me sang another Boca anthem, jumping up and down, arms extended back and forth at the elbow, limp wrists flicking out.

The *locura* wasn't over. Inexplicably, fireworks were set off over La Bombonera's main stand, the thin little side of the stadium that contradicts the three steep sides of a bowl. It seemed like a premature celebration. It was only 1-1. Whoever was responsible for the display could be excused for getting carried away. But it was the 78th minute. Boca had equalised ten minutes previously but there was a sixth of the game yet to play, and by no means had the game been decided one way or the other. Crashing into the sky above was a cacophonous sound of explosives, not lightning strikes but a Riquelme strike. Maybe it was in celebration of the free kick. Sod the result.

One thing was sure; the fans fed off the display. It gave them energy. The songs became a little bit louder, a little more intense. As the ball went out of play, the referee momentarily stopped the game. But without any sign of the fireworks stopping, he let the players continue, and more than five minutes passed under a yellow and blue and green and pink and silver sky. I wondered for a second whether the fireworks counted as *mufa* against the home team.

It was the visiting team who ended up celebrating the victory. Late on, a corner was awarded to River Plate. Ramiro Funes Mori scored and his *gallinas* took all three points back across Buenos Aires. (Both of River's goalscorers that day would end up in the Premier League within a few months, with Funes Mori going to Everton and Manuel Lanzini to West Ham United.) The corner shouldn't have been given. It's known as the 'ghost corner'. Having teased the away team with the ghouly *oooohs* at the start, La Bombonera was now ghostly silent from having the arch-enemy snatch a late win. Without visiting fans, the away goal was met by a few milliseconds of silence before the crowd moaned at the referee and then began to sing in encouragement to go again. That silence, however long it might last, is magical for the opposing fans. It's something they will reference again and again. 'Remember when we turned the sound down to zero,' they might say.

It almost seems unfair that those 11 players who walked out on the turf that day wearing white should have to bear all of the hatred accumulated through 100 years of intense rivalry alone. Without away fans, 50,000 *bosteros* in attendance could focus all their rancour on the opposing players. Not that that seemed to bother the River Plate players on this occasion. Nor does it seem to put off many Argentine players. They seem to revel in it. Somewhat protected by fences, glass screens – in Racing Club's case, a moat circling the pitch – players are not afraid to get stuck in when contesting a 50/50, to celebrate goals, or antagonise the crowd. *Somewhat*; despite the protection, police officers with riot shields, often two or three at a time, are required to protect players taking corners as objects hurled from the stands rain down on the corner flag. Not only is there little room to take a run-up, to make it harder police officers crowd around the corner-taker to make the squeeze tighter still.

All the same, River won this one from the 'ghost corner'. The derby defeat is bitterly rejected by *bosteros*. I wanted to beat the rush leaving the ground but was a little unsure how best to get out and away. I wouldn't have Bruno to guide me, I was alone. Darkness was falling, and as the final whistle blew I set off for *El Caminito*, a very touristic area that I was familiar with, and where I knew the 152 bus set off from. The streets were eerily quiet, only a handful of others had ventured out at the same time. I walked quickly, keen to get to the bus stop. Once on the bus I could relax and reflect on what had been a crazy day. One I would never forget. I never wanted to forget it.

Only a few months later I was offered a chance to watch the corresponding fixture at El Monumental, a semi-final second leg. But in between these two fixtures, I had a World Cup to attend.

My new home, Buenos Aires.

The neighbourhood of Colegiales in northern Buenos Aires as seen from Chacarita.

Where football is omnipresent. A River Plate flag hangs from a balcony in the Buenos Aires neighbourhood San Telmo.

Arsenal de Sarandí looking resplendent in their light-blue and red kits.

Las Islas Malvinas/the Falkland Islands. The disputed islands are to be seen everywhere in Buenos Aires and Argentina, no place more so than at football grounds.

Racing Club de Avellaneda's El Cilindro (left) is only 300 metres from rivals Club Atlético Independiente's Estadio Libertadores de América.

El Cilindro on matchday. Diego Milito's No. 22 shirt is almost as iconic as Racing's light-blue and white striped kit.

Defensores de Belgrano fans enjoying a game in the Markitos Zucker stand at Estadio Juan Pasquale in northern Buenos Aires.

The loft at ESMA. On 25 June 1978 Argentina beat the Netherlands 3-1 (aet) at El Monumental. Less than a mile from the stadium, opponents of the military junta were held at the clandestine detention centre.

25 June 1978: General Jorge Rafael Videla attends the 1978 World Cup Final.

Las Madres de Plaza de Mayo. The mothers of Argentines who disappeared during the 1976–83 dictatorship protest outside the presidential palace in Buenos Aires.

The barra brava arrive at games hanging out of the windows and open doors of decommissioned or borrowed school and city buses.

Vatican City. San Lorenzo fan Pope Francis receives visitors from Buenos Aires.

Argentinian Wembley. A mural of the former home of San Lorenzo – El Viejo Gasómetro – in the Buenos Aires neighbourhood of Boedo.

La Bombonera. Estadio Alberto J. Armando, also known as the chocolate box, is one of the most iconic football stadiums in the world.

THAT goal. Juan Román Riquelme scores a free kick in the superclásico at La Bombonera, 30 March 2014.

Maracanaço. Brazilian goalkeeper Moacyr Barbosa is unable to stop Uruguayan Alcides Ghiggia's winning goal in the final group game and de facto World Cup Final in 1950.

World Cup quarter-final. Gonzalo Pipita Higuaín scores the winning goal against Belgium at the 2014 World Cup in Brazil. Argentina went on to lose in the final.

Copacabana beach. It is estimated that 200,000 Argentines flocked to Rio de Janeiro in Brazil for the 2014 World Cup Final.

Rocinha. Some 100,000 people live in Brazil's largest favela, situated within 30 minutes of Rio de Janeiro's Zona Sul.

'Brazil's Hiroshima'

MY WORLD Cup 2014 began on my mum's sofa nine months earlier. I was in the UK for a couple of weeks before the big move to Argentina. Travelling up to Brazil for the Brazilian World Cup was baked into the plan of moving to Buenos Aires – the allure of this tournament was too much to pass up. And it was impeccably timed.

When I logged on to FIFA's website to apply for tickets, only a handful of teams were guaranteed their place. But that didn't matter as I wouldn't be applying for tickets to follow a country, nor could I apply for specific games as the draw hadn't yet been made. I was applying by host city. A good friend from my university days was from São Paulo and he had encouraged me to visit him. Guto said I could stay with family members of his wherever in Brazil I might need to. He had a cool aunt in Natal, he said.

Along with Natal, I applied for tickets in Salvador da Bahia. It was a place I wanted to revisit despite nearly getting robbed on my very first day in the country and on the continent on my first trip to South America five years earlier. Rio de Janeiro and São Paulo were other cities where I would have free accommodation, so I tried for tickets there, too. When the email came through confirming three tickets for the World Cup, the first two games would be in Natal.

The city called Christmas had called. Founded on 25 December 1599, the city's name sounds better to a foreigner than it does to a local. Guto's sister assured me that Natal gets 360 days of sun a year. I spent nine days there and it rained for seven of them. So much for the guarantee; I wanted to ask for my money back.

Even before the 24-hour flight from Buenos Aires to Natal, via Santiago de Chile, I was wet. But not from the rain. I was on the bus from the centre of Argentina's capital to Ezeiza airport when I felt my ankle getting wet. The litre bottle of Fernet Branca that I was travelling with had smashed and was gushing out into my backpack. It was a regular city bus out of Buenos Aires city centre. Rather than paying for a taxi to the airport, I had jumped on the No. 8 bus, which cost about 15p. It did take two hours rather than the 40 minutes a taxi or *remís* would take, but I had loads of time and enjoyed travelling like a local.

I had loads of time to try to salvage some of my clean clothes before they were all marinated in Fernet. Sticking my hand into the bag to find the bottle, I stabbed my finger on a shard of glass. The cut wasn't deep, but it was big enough to be inconvenient. It wouldn't stop bleeding. With one hand in my mouth, I had one free to root around to try to save some of the clothes that were still dry. Little by little the bus was filling up as we left downtown Buenos Aires and headed through the suburbs.

I managed to separate about half of my belongings into two halves: some dry and others drowned in Fernet. At the airport I grabbed some paper towels, some plastic bags and cleaned up as much of the spillage as possible before sending my bag through. It had been a bad start to a long trip, but spirits were still high. I was going to the World Cup after all.

My host in Natal was my mate's aunt. Nancy was a very friendly lady in her early 50s. She had taken all my clothes and put them straight into the washing machine. By the time I woke up they were already hanging to dry and breakfast was on the table: toast, jams, coffee and lots of fresh, tropical fruit. Maracuya was a new fruit to me and the smell of it, even before it had been sliced open, permeated the flat. The smell will always remind me of Natal and Nancy's little flat.

The next day, the World Cup began. We would spend the day at the house of Guto's family. Another of my friend's aunts was hosting and the whole family were expected. A small buffet had been prepared and the excitement for Brazil's opening match was building. There were about 15 family members there across four generations. Guto's cousins were there and we immediately started talking about football. I immediately pulled out my favourite trivia question: 'Only one footballing nation has never lost to Brazil, who?' They guessed Norway straight away. Correct! (Since 2014, Senegal have added themselves to this illustrious list after a 1-1 draw in a friendly in 2019.)

Brazilians don't know much about Norway. And why would they? But maybe the people of Natal knew more than the average Brazilian. A lot of connections seem to have been made here. Wandering around the city I stumbled across a Norwegian bar on a square near the centre, tucked away from the beach behind a hotel. Carambar was a place of intrigue for me, some 5,300 miles from home. In Oslo I knew a man married to a Brazilian girl from Natal. He was in his 50s while she was half his age and younger than I was. Sitting in the bar with a watery beer, I saw similar relationships and got the impression the city was a popular place for Norwegians to come to find love.

Not necessarily looking for love myself, I did meet a Norwegian Arsenal fan who had made his way out to Brazil for the World Cup. Leif Åge also had tickets for the following day's group game between Mexico and Cameroon. Despite the promise of sun, the heavens had opened, and before leaving the flat I had found a big, long, yellow rain poncho to borrow. Being in the tropics, it wasn't the type of rain I was used to. It was bucketing it down in vast amounts. It was difficult to understand that so much water existed. There was no wind, so it wasn't a storm as such. It was just a run-of-the-mill release of pressure, and life went on as normal.

My host drove me to the stadium. It took longer than expected and I was nervously checking my watch as kick-off was approaching. At the Arena Das Dunas there were extensive security measures to get into the ground. It was a lot like going through an airport, but for the rain. I missed the national anthems.

The game ended 1-0 to Mexico in an entertaining encounter. My seat ticket was high up in the corner of the stadium and I found myself sitting with a big, round German and a friendly Brazilian (aren't they all friendly?!). Next to the German was Bjorn, a Belgian fan who had travelled out to Brazil on his own. He was a bit overexcited and wouldn't stop talking about how much he was enjoying Brazilian prostitutes while his girlfriend was seven months pregnant at home. We were glad when Mexico scored to drown out this idiot Belgian.

It was only the second game of the tournament. Everyone in the ground had been anticipating their first World Cup 2014 game, and the moment had finally arrived. The sound of the stadium was a general rumbling of excitement at the commencement of the Brazilian World Cup. The Mexican fans had travelled in great numbers and created an incredible atmosphere. It wasn't like being at a club game, where fans sing or chant in unison, but the block of Mexican fans was big enough to be heard.

At half-time I went to join the queue for the toilet. There were dozens of Mexicans in green and white, when an American wearing his USMNT top walked in. He looked uneasy when he saw the multitude of Mexicans, but he needn't have worried. The atmosphere was carnivalesque. The gringo was treated to a chorus of *U-S-A, U-S-A* from his neighbours to the south waiting in line to relieve themselves.

I was enamoured with the Mexicans. The same couldn't be said of the USA fans who I came across a few days later, however. I was heading back to Arena Das Dunas for Ghana versus USA. Walking to the ground with a friend, we were surrounded by Americans in fancy dress, faces painted, seemingly high on too much sugar. The chant they were singing the whole walk to the ground was one of the most egregious ever heard. 'I believe that we will win' was repeated again and again like a mantra. No melody, no wit, no creativity. And no repertoire. It was going to be a long game.

The Ghanaians provided a lot of colour and a little more humility. Having got into the ground and found my seat, I was desperate for Ghana to smash the Yanks. But it wasn't to be. It had been another decent game, though. A 2-1 victory to the States. I would meet them again later in the knockout phase, but not by design.

After nine days in Natal I was back in Salvador da Bahia again. The journey between the two cities took 22 hours by coach. I hadn't really planned my accommodation for this part of the trip and ended up forking out a fair bit for the first few nights in hostels in the touristic Pelourinho area. The World Cup had pushed up the prices significantly, but at least staying in hostels was a great way to meet fellow football-backpackers.

I was travelling with my best friend from school, a petite Greek girl whose first desire was to go to the beach the moment we arrived. As a pasty and pale Norwegian/Brit, the beach didn't appeal. But spending time on Brazil's beaches would be inevitable. On our first day in a new country on a new continent, unsure of what to take with us, we ended up with backpacks full of towels, clothes, sun cream, cash, passports, pre-smartphone cameras, and more. We had read in our guidebooks that being on an empty beach wasn't wise, but my friend was determined.

We found a little bar to sit and have a drink at, me positioning myself safely under the parasol, while Danáe tanned her already brown legs in the searing sun. Little did I know then that I was already burnt to a crisp. We had walked about an hour along the beach, the morning sun barely bursting through the heavy cloud cover. It was hot and I had taken my T-shirt off. I got burnt despite the lack of sun. For the next week I was sleeping on my back without being able to turn on my side. My shoulders were red-raw, and I was in pain.

But the sunburn hadn't set in yet when we were approached on the beach by a local. After we left the bar and walked back to the bus stop, a man in his 20s approached us with his jumper over his hand. He had a gun. At least that's what he was intimating. There were no other people on the beach, and we had found ourselves in a spot of bother within 12 hours of landing in Brazil. Luckily for us, this would-be mugger was an amateur. He put his supposed gun into my stomach. It wasn't a gun at all. 'That's your hand,' I muttered, hoping he would understand English. I was a little slow in grasping the situation. He panicked and tried grabbing the strap of my backpack, but I just pushed his hand away. Being small, he wasn't especially intimidating. He went for the strap again, but it wasn't a struggle to deflect his grab. He walked away and we carried on, a little uneasy and now desperate to get back to the safe, touristic neighbourhood of Pelourinho where we – and all the other tourists – were staying.

But the ordeal wasn't over. We walked up to the main road and tried flagging down a taxi. It was rush hour, and they were all full. Unsure of where the buses stopped, we just kept walking, trying our luck with a cab. Ten minutes later, I turned around to see our new mate was following us, this time with company – a bigger mate. They were unarmed but now there were two of them against my tiny Greek friend and me.

As the bigger of the two confronted me we heard a car's horn tooting. A man, who was waiting at the traffic lights, got out of his car to shout at the assailants as he was leaning in to press the horn. His shouting was enough for the two local lads to leave us alone. They left, trying to shake our hands, pretending we were the best of friends. They split up, and as one of them was crossing the road, the man who had intervened sped up, trying to run him over. We had been saved, but seemingly by a vigilante who was willing to kill for us.

We kept walking. Doubly shaken now and doubly desperate to get on a bus. We found a surfer walking with his surfboard under his arm. We started talking to him, hoping he would look after us. He spoke no English, we spoke no Portuguese, and when our mates came back for a third time, he was no use. Without waiting for help, we ran across the street, jumped on the back of a bus and headed back towards the part of Praia do Flamengo where the ordeal had started. The two wannabe muggers tried jumping on the bus, but I shouted to the driver and the conductor that we weren't too keen on them getting on, so he drove off. A five-minute drive later and we were back near the bar. We found a taxi and were driven back to the touristic part of the city.

Salvador da Bahia is a big city, Brazil's fourth largest with three million inhabitants. From 1549 to 1763 it served as Brazil's first capital city and has beautifully colourful colonial architecture, especially around the historical, cobblestoned centre, the Pelourinho. Michael Jackson's They Don't Care About Us music video shows the city in all its splendour (ignoring the image of Rio's Cristo Redentor statue at the start).

Bahia is a region that became the main base for the Portuguese slave trade to their new colony in the Americas. Everything about the city reminds visitors of its African heritage, from the inhabitants' dark, African skin tone, their dress, food and music, to *Candomblé* ceremonies. The neighbourhood's name, Pelourinho, means 'whipping post' and was where slave auctions took place.

I had seen *O Pelo* before. And the colourful buildings. And the churches. And the *capoeiristas*. This visit to Salvador was supposed to be quick. I had only been allocated one ticket at the Arena Fonte Nova and I didn't know where I would be travelling to after the game. The options were endless – Brazil is a big country. In the end, I stayed nearly two weeks and caught three games at the spectacular new stadium.

Switzerland against France turned out to be a great game. The French won 5-2 with seven different scorers across both teams. *Les Bleus* were rampant and even a scoreline of 5-2 flattered the Swiss. Coming into the game, Switzerland were ranked as the sixth-best team by FIFA, France 17th. It looked like France were out to prove a point. Or maybe Didier Deschamps' team were just very, very good.

Before the game I sat down for lunch with a handful of members of Arsenal Brasil. From the Pelourinho it was a ten-minute walk to the ground, and as everyone was coming from the same area, the streets were full of people walking together with many different kits on display. The Group E game was an Arsenal-tinged affair, with former, current and future Arsenal players on both teams. Senderos, Djourou, Xhaka and Lichtsteiner were no match for Koscielny, Debuchy and the stand-out player, Olivier Giroud. Bacary Sagna looked on from the bench. The Arsenal link gave me lots to talk about to French and Swiss fans alike.

It had been a good day and an excellent game. I wanted more. The FIFA website showed available tickets for the Iran versus Bosnia-Herzegovina clash five days later. The ticket set me back £55 but I figured that I was only going to have a limited number of chances to experience a World Cup, with the next two scheduled for Russia and Qatar. Anyway, the game could have been a classic. It wasn't. Despite the four goals in a 3-1 win to Bosnia, I had been hoping for a more entertaining game. Iran, after all, had a chance of going through to the knockout stages. It wasn't a big chance, but with a win it was possible. Argentina and Nigeria met in the other game and that result did go Iran's way, but nothing about their body language or urgency suggested they felt they had anything to play for. Much like the spectators in the Arena Fonte Nova, the players seemed to realise that the world's eyes were on Messi's Argentina and it detracted from the spectacle.

By now I had met some locals from the city and been invited to stay at a flat in the so-called lower part of the city. It was back at Praia do Flamengo where I'd had the finger-gun incident five days earlier. But I wouldn't dwell on that. It would save me a lot of money and give me a chance to see how the locals lived. Luciano lived with his mum and sister, but with French Mika and Polish Marek, a FIFA volunteer, already staying, there wasn't room for his sister, who went to stay with their grandmother. There wasn't really room for me either. I ended up sleeping in a hammock on the balcony for the next week, grains of sand still lodged between my toes from having played beach football a stone's throw from the flat.

Luciano's dad, Antonio, lived in a seaside resort town 200 miles north of Salvador. Visiting Aracaju, his old man would ply us with beer and food and would bring friends around to show off the foreign guests. If he wasn't bringing people over, he would take us to what constituted a pub. At the simple restaurant with plastic chairs, we sat outside eating and drinking. At any given opportunity he would introduce a friend, acquaintance or random passer-by to us. We were being paraded as a fashion accessory, a status symbol we had unerringly agreed to be part of.

But I couldn't complain. Here I was, staying for free in a town I would never otherwise have visited, with new mates, watching football and drinking watery beer by the sea. After a couple of days we returned to Salvador and got back to the Arena Fonte Nova for one more game. First up, however, the hosts were due to play in the knockout stages.

Brazil against Chile in the first of the last-16 games had been a high-octane, 120-minute affair settled on penalties. With two friends from Buenos Aires who had also made the trip north, I went to the FIFA Fan Fest, an outdoor screening of all World Cup 2014 games. Watching with thousands of Brazilian *baianos*, the atmosphere was tense. A penalty shoot-out was a treat for the neutral, although few neutrals could say they didn't want Brazil to win. There was the issue of Neymar, of course. But to see Brazil win the World Cup on home soil and to avenge the *Maracanaço* of 1950 was what we were all here to see. Wasn't it?

Zizinho's Brazil were expected to win the 1950 edition, the first Brazilian World Cup. And *O seleção* were poised to do so with only one match left of the final round of games. In the first round, four groups harvested four finalists who played each other in a final group of four. (There was no knockout round or final to be contested until the World Cup in Switzerland four years later.) In the second group phase, Brazil brushed aside Sweden 7-1 and Spain 6-1. Brazilians were already celebrating having won the 1950 World Cup. In the week leading up to their last game against Uruguay, a Brazilian player is said to have joked: 'This will be a tough game. We might only win 4-0.'

A year earlier, in 1949, Brazil had won their third South American championship (now named the Copa América). As hosts they annihilated visiting teams, their results reading: 9-1, 10-1, 2-1, 5-0, 7-1, 5-1, 1-2, 7-0. The 1-2 reverse came against Paraguay, who three days later were beaten 7-0 in the final. An eight-team group saw Brazil and Paraguay finish on 12 points apiece – seven victories, one loss. The unplanned final – a play-off because of the parity at the top of the table – was played at Vasco da Gama's ground, Estádio São Januário, in the then-capital city Rio de Janeiro. The Maracanã was still being built and was due to be opened in time for the 1950 Copa do Mundo.

A year later, it was the same host but this time it would be Uruguay who would be final-fodder for the champions-elect. And the game would be played in the Maracanã, the world's biggest stadium with a capacity of 160,000, although over 200,000 spectators are thought to have crammed into the ground. Brazil had beaten Uruguay 5-1 in the Copa América of 1949, but only needed a draw in this final match. Uruguay had been drawn in Group 4 (a group consisting of only two teams after France's withdrawal from the finals) and dispatched Bolivia 8-0 to qualify for the final group stage without breaking sweat. But in the final group stage they drew with Spain and only just beat Sweden 3-2 with a late goal, coming from behind.

The date was 16 July 1950. Was it a de facto final or was it a closing ceremony exhibition match? The day before the game, a Brazilian newspaper printed a front cover showing the Brazilian players under the heading 'Here Are the World Champions'. Uruguay's captain subsequently bought 20 copies of the paper, which he threw on the floor of the toilets of the hotel where his national team were staying. Obdulio Varela encouraged his team to walk over and urinate on the newspapers. Adding insult to injury, Rio's

Mayor, Ângelo Mendes de Moraes, gave a pre-game speech inside the ground.

'You Brazilians, who I consider World Champions, who in less than two hours will be crowned champions by millions of your compatriots. You have no equal in this hemisphere. You are superior to any opponent, you who I already address as conquerors.'

What could possibly go wrong? Leading 1-0 after Albino Friaça's opener just after half-time, everything was going to plan. But the 200,000 Brazilians in attendance were jolted when Peñarol's Juan Alberto Schiaffino equalised, then stunned into silence when his club and country team-mate Alcides Ghiggia scored the winner in the 79th minute. 'It was the first time in my life that I heard something that wasn't noise,' Schiaffino said years later when talking about the game.

The loss was 'Brazil's Hiroshima', according to Brazilian playwright Nelson Rodrigues. Nine-year-old Edson Arantes do Nascimento (Pelé) saw his father burst into tears as the final whistle was blown. Pelé would never wear white for his country. After losing in the South American championship final of 1953 to Paraguay in Perú (down 0-3 by half-time, losing 2-3 after 90 minutes), the white shirts were deemed to bring bad luck and a competition was launched to design a new national kit. The *Correio da Manhã* newspaper demanded the use of the colours in the Brazilian flag. Five World Cups were won between 1958 and 2002 wearing the iconic yellow-and-green kits.

Shirts don't have feelings, but players do. As Brazil's goalkeeper on that fateful day, Moacyr Barbosa was the only Brazilian not wearing white. Beaten at his near post for the winner, Barbosa received much of the blame for the defeat, the hammer blow dubbed the *Maracanaço* by newspaper *O Globo*. 'Warning: Contains Scenes Some Brazilian Viewers Might Find Disturbing' read the subheading. In the racially divided Brazil of the 1940s and 50s, Barbosa was scapegoated for the defeat along with the two other black players in the starting line-up. Two weeks before his death of a heart attack in 2000, Barbosa lamented on his 79th birthday, 'Under Brazilian law the maximum sentence is 30 years. But my imprisonment has been for 50 years.' To a friend he cried, 'I'm not guilty. There were 11 of us.'

'Look at him, son, he is the man that made all of Brazil cry,' a woman was overheard telling her son as Barbosa walked around a supermarket 20 years later. After retiring from football aged 42, he got a job working at the swimming pool at the Maracanã complex. When stadium management had to change the famous stadium's goals, Barbosa asked if he could have *that* goal, the two posts and crossbar where the two Uruguayan goals had been scored. He took them home and burnt the woodwork. Up in flames went 'Ghiggia's Goalpost', as it had been dubbed. As Barbosa watched the flames flickering, he hoped that his curse would burn away, too.

Maracanaço in Portuguese. *Maracanazo* in Spanish. The two words have a very different meaning. For Brazilians, it means *catástrofe*. But to Uruguayans, it can mean miracle or overcoming adversity. Brazil had hoped that the 1950 World Cup would allow them to show the world that they were a nation on the up, that problems of the past were in the past. The building of the Maracanã itself was supposed to show this new pride in all its glory. But the loss seemed to confirm many people's fears that the new Brazil was all fiction, their self-worth brought down a peg or two and back to reality.

Maybe the Americans' 'I believe that we will win' chant originated from the Rio mayor's infamous speech in 1950. They were equally sure in their proclamations. In one regard, the Yanks were right to believe. They had at least got out of their group, more than the Englishman in me could boast. Belgium in Salvador were next up for the USMNT. By now I had been in Salvador for nearly two weeks. My next stop was supposed to be Rio de Janeiro, but I didn't want to get there too early; I still had a month left in the country. I had played around with the idea of going to Manaus in the Amazon or to the gaucho south, but was enjoying where I was.

Without a ticket I walked up to the ground with a group of people who did. I wanted to take in the atmosphere. I was particularly looking forward to hearing *that* chant for hopefully the last time, at the same time as I feared bumping into an STD-ridden Bjorn. Whilst I didn't miss him, I was wondering how he was getting on.

As we were walking up the hill towards the ground, a Russian man walked past offering tickets. Russia had been knocked out of Belgium's group and he had a dozen tickets to get rid of. I was hesitant to buy a ticket off the street like this, but the tickets seemed legit and the seller seemed trustworthy. His back story checked out: his national team were already on their way home. I went for it. £60 face value and a chance to see a knockout game.

The last-16 game between Belgium and USA turned out to be one of the best of the tournament. It was the best 0-0 I can remember, albeit vaguely, having seen live. The Belgians made the US goalkeeper work hard, with Tim Howard setting a record for the number of saves in a World Cup game with 16. His heroics were enough to take the game into extra time, but the Belgians' quality told, and they won 2-1 after 120 minutes played.

I wanted Belgium to win, but the result would work in my favour more directly. After the game I met a disappointed and emotionally drained American. In his early 40s and travelling alone, he was slumped on a hostel sofa. He had a ticket for the quarter-final, but wanted to go home. Rather than the US, it would be Belgium who would face Argentina in Brasília. I snapped up the chance to buy his ticket, despite the £200 price.

A 20-hour, 1,000-mile bus ride later and I was in Brasília, the new capital of Brazil. I had spent a long time in the beautiful Salvador, but I wanted to see more of the country. Brasília was built in the 1950s with the intention of moving the capital away from Rio de Janeiro, which had served the role since 1763 (having replaced Salvador da Bahia). Much like Salvador, Rio was vulnerable to attacks from the sea. It was also overpopulated, with little room for expansion, something that caused endless tensions across the city. Deep inside the sparsely populated centre of Brazil, a plot of land was put aside, and a modern city was designed. The layout of the city centre takes the shape of an aeroplane, and all the major avenues are wide enough to land a plane, should it be necessary in time of war or otherwise, I was told by my new host.

Another Arsenal Brasil member, based in Rio, gave me some advice on Brasília. He put me in touch with another Arsenal fan who offered to put me up. The Brazilian hospitality was exceptional. I felt a little uncomfortable being treated like a special guest, but was in no position to turn such a generous offer down. Luan and his girlfriend, Gabriela, came to pick me up from the bus station. They were incredibly friendly and took me on a tour of the city.

In the middle of the city, a huge artificial lake was created by damming the river Paranoá. It was a nice place to go for a stroll. The lake now is where embassies are housed, posh restaurants sit and regatta clubs row, with the former village of Vila Amaury submerged under water. The tour continued to downtown Brasília and the Monumental Axis, an open space contrasting the tall buildings surrounding it, much like Central Park in New York City. The main architect of the new capital, Oscar Niemeyer, built a stunning cathedral here (despite being a non-believer), as well as Complexo Cultural, housing the national library and national museum.

The ground in Brasília, the Estádio Nacional Mané Garrincha, named after the Brazil legend of the 1950s and 60s, is located near the centre in the multisport Ayrton Senna Complex. This ground wasn't new for the World Cup; it was originally built in the 1970s, but underwent redevelopment for 2014. A significant capacity increase, from 45,000 to 73,000, made it the second-biggest stadium in Brazil behind the Maracanã. It's an aesthetically pleasing stadium, comparable to the Olympiastadion in Berlin, with its tall concrete pillars running all the way round the circular structure.

Garrincha was, of course, not from Brasília – no one was really *from* Brasília. It was a new city and people had to move from other parts of Brazil. With the capital having been relocated from Rio de Janeiro, most of the new inhabitants were *cariocas* moving from the old capital. With them they brought their football teams. Brasília today has a team in the third tier of Brazilian football. Brasiliense, founded in 2000, have a cheap-looking club crest showing a smiling cartoon crocodile standing with a football. The only top-flight football the capital gets to watch is when the big teams from Rio play matches there.

The biggest Brazilian teams often play their home matches in other cities throughout Brazil. Flamengo, the most popular Brazilian team, occasionally play games in other states, having such a huge following across the whole country. As South American football expert Tim Vickery explains, when radio first became accessible to the majority of Brazilians, the dominant team were Flamengo. Without extensive coverage of football, the one team that was featured on live games, and the team who got the most focus, became the biggest team in Brazil. Those foundations have solidified their status as the biggest team in the country.

The other teams from Rio also enjoy popularity outside their home city, particularly in Brasília. It's not uncommon for Flamengo's bitter rivals Fluminense, Barbosa's Vasco da Gama, or Garrincha's own Botafogo to play Série A games in the Estádio Nacional Mané Garrincha.

But the stadium was about to host a World Cup quarter-final. I was among my adopted Argentines. Although I still didn't speak much Spanish and had only lived in Buenos Aires for seven months, I massively enjoyed the build-up to the match, standing on the concrete steps outside the ground among the *albiceleste* fans. Belgium didn't have too many fans at the game (no, I didn't bump into him here, either), certainly not when compared to the Argentines, a country four times bigger and significantly closer in terms of travelling to the finals. Supporting the underdog and to antagonise their visiting neighbours, the locals bought up tickets and came out in force. Before the game, one could be excused for thinking it was Argentina versus Brazil rather than Argentina versus Belgium. If only.

The Argentine fans were singing their famous and very catchy 'Brasil, decime qué se siente' song, a rework of Creedence Clearwater Revival's 'Bad Moon Rising'. It references their Round of 16 meeting at Italia 1990, a 1-0 win that saw Argentina go through to the quarter-final. 'They have been crying since Italy until today,' they sang. It concludes with the assertion that 'Maradona is better than Pelé'. It was a song I couldn't get out of my head and that took many weeks to learn the words. The two crowds goading each other was mainly in a well-mannered, good-natured way, but some minor fighting did break out and the police had to have their wits about them to stay on top of the banter.

With the rivalry of the different tribes outside the ground, I was a bit confused to be sitting next to a Brazilian wearing an Argentina shirt. Diego was from Rio Grande do Sul, a southern state closer to Buenos Aires than to Rio de Janeiro. His father, who did support the *seleção*, had named his first born after Diego Armando Maradona even before *El Diez* had raised one arm above Peter Shilton's head, or later two arms above his own head, hoisting aloft the 1986 World Cup trophy.

In this tournament hosted by Brazil it was *selección* over *seleção* for Diego. I found out that people from the south of Brazil often feel they have more in common with the Argentines and Uruguayans than they do with people from other parts of their own country. Also called *gauchos*, southern Brazilians live rural lives: they farm cattle, produce milk and eat steak. They produce red wine. They drink *chimarrão*, a drink similar to the yerba mate drunk in

Argentina and Uruguay (as well as Chile and Paraguay). More importantly, Diego told me, on the pitch teams from the south of Brazil have a similar style to those of Argentina: physically tough and *poniendo huevo* (literally 'putting their eggs into it' but figuratively meaning fighting or having balls).

As was the case in Argentina and Uruguay, immigrants came to this region of Brazil from Italy and Germany (and, of course, Portugal), forming a more European culture compared to the north dominated by the slave trade. For many reasons, some southern Brazilians feel that they have more in common with their neighbours to the south rather than the rest of the vast, multicultural nation that is Brazil. To meet an Argentina-supporting Brazilian blew my mind and taught me a lot about the complexities of life in such a big country.

Enormous country and an enormous game. It would be the biggest game I would go to in terms of the hierarchy of world football. Whether or not I will ever make it to a World Cup semi-final or final (or third-placed play-off) remains to be seen. Yet, despite the enormity of the stage, the match was easily forgotten. Maybe I would have remembered more had it not been for the pre-match beers. An early Gonzalo Higuaín goal was enough to see Argentina through to another semi-final. Messi, with the weight of a nation on his shoulders, picked the ball up deep after Vincent Kompany had lost it bringing it out of defence. *La Pulga* (the flea) turned Kevin de Bruyne and Marouane Fellaini, both twice his size, holding off the sharp-elbowed giant to send the ball on to Ángel Di María. *El fideo* (the noodle) tried playing the ball in behind captain Kompany's backline to Zabaleta but the ball ricocheted and landed in front of Higuaín just inside the box. *El Pipita*'s half-volley finish into the bottom corner was worthy of being a match-winning goal. Having scored in the 118th minute of their last-16 match against Switzerland, Argentina had scored within eight minutes against the *De Rode Duivels*. And it was enough. The son of 'the big nose' had scored his first World Cup 2014 goal (Gonzalo's father, Jorge Higuaín, was nicknamed *El Pipa* for his impressive snout, hence Gonzalo's diminutive version of the same moniker).

The goal came to our left, at least 200 metres from our vantage point high up in the stadium. We were halfway inside the Argentinian half in the first period. Decent seats, as could be expected for the whopping £200 I laid out on the ticket. The second half became a tennis-head-shaking exercise. Leading 1-0 and holding on, Argentina set up to counter-attack and had a couple of chances in the second half. Higuaín hit the bar after a marauding run, and Messi was thwarted by Thibaut Courtois when through one-on-one. Belgium created one chance towards the very end, but the Argentinian defence kept them out. It was a defence that only conceded four goals in the whole tournament, two of which were against Nigeria in a meaningless – for Argentina, at least – game.

All in all, it was a drab and scrappy game. It might have been the World Cup quarter-final but if I were to have £250 burning a hole in my pocket again, I would much rather spend it going to a *superclásico* in Buenos Aires. World Cups, it turned out, were fairly sterilised and the knockouts overly tense games.

I spent only a couple of days with my hosts in the new capital before making my way down to another old capital, Rio de Janeiro. We were now at the semi-final stage and the final, thereafter, would of course be held at Estádio do Maracanã. Accommodation was still obscenely expensive. To sleep in an eight-bed dorm at a backpackers' hostel, one could expect to pay what a hotel room would normally cost. Paying hotel prices wasn't an option for a seven-week trip. A Danish-Sri Lankan friend from Buenos Aires was by now also in Rio and we found a hostel in the *favela* Rocinha, Brazil's largest 'slum'.

The idea of staying in a *favela* wasn't initially very appealing, but at the same time we had heard and read a lot about the so-called 'pacification' of the infamous Rio shanty towns. We took a taxi out to Rocinha. The scenery changed rapidly. We left the rows of tall, colonial buildings lining streets in the expensive neighbourhoods of Zona Sul and drove through a tunnel under one of the city's big hills. Coming out of the other end we saw the box-shaped red-brick housing with hundreds of electricity cables exposed. The heavens had opened, the rain was rushing out of the sky. As our taxi stopped outside the hostel, Nimalan and I looked at each other. We were considering dropping the idea but decided to check it out. We could always get a taxi back to Copacabana or Leblon or Botafogo if we continued to feel uneasy. We got out of the car and ran up the stairs to the first floor where we checked in.

The police and military had essentially waged war with the gangs who ran the *favelas*, and extrajudicial killings had been commonplace, with civilians caught up in the crossfire. It had been an effective way of ridding the area of the bad guys. *Favelas* are otherwise a good option for working-class people who can't afford to live in Rio's centre. They are often referred to as urbanised slums, areas that have basic amenities as well as banks and other businesses one might expect to see in any South American town.

Rocinha also had two bus lines serving it, linking the neighbourhood to the touristic Zona Sul, and we could get to Copacabana beach within 30 minutes. Lots of people had had the same idea and we met several of a similar age with a similar story. There were two French lads who had tickets for every game of the tournament. Whether or not France made it to the final, they would be there. There were Brits, Brazilians, Peruvians, South Africans, even a New Caledonian. Matthieu was this incredibly laid back, handsome 20-something from the tiny Polynesian island off New Zealand. We might have been at the *World* Cup, but many nations hadn't been invited. In this hostel, everyone was welcome. The whole world was represented.

Having helped support Argentina to victory in Brasília, I was excited about their semi-final with the Netherlands. Most people growing up in the 1980s and 90s have a soft spot for the Dutch. The iconic orange kits and bucketloads of stylish players. My last game in the UK before leaving for Argentina had been to see Edgar Davids turn out in the orange of Barnet FC at The Hive in north London. (Davids was Barnet's player-manager and captain, and he even wore No. 1 on his back.) And however much I loved Dennis Bergkamp, the prospect of a Brazil versus Argentina World Cup Final *in* Brazil was almost too much to imagine.

First up, however, were Brazil and their semi-final against Germany. We jumped on the 537 bus headed for Copacabana beach. FIFA had their alcohol-free fan zone area there. The other FIFA fan zones had sold alcohol, but for some reason this one didn't. It was fenced in and ID had to be shown to enter. The long queues put us off. Luckily, the screen was big enough to see from either side of the Fan Fest's fences, so most people stationed themselves on the sand flanking the designated area.

The atmosphere was tense before the game, as one would expect. The World Cup Final was at stake for a host nation that prides itself on being the most successful team in the tournament's history. Within 30 minutes of the game starting, however, many people had left the beach and gone home. All Brazilian plans for 13 July had quickly been shunted forward to the day before, the day of the third-place play-off. Germany were leading 5-0 by the 29th minute. Small groups of Brazilians did stay, in shock and bemused by what they had seen. The only thing to do was laugh, and yellow-clad locals began celebrating German goal after German goal with irony and self-deprecation. These weren't the serious, most fanatic fans; they had already stormed off to dress their wounds.

As a result, the atmosphere wasn't one of anger, luckily. There had been many locals wanting Brazil to win, there were pockets of Germans supporting their *Mannschaft*, but the rest of us were neutrals. At half-time, our little group also considered knocking it on the head. The party atmosphere had died a quick death and the mood was sombre; it wasn't easy to know whether it could turn ugly. Brazil had been desperate to make up for the 1950 *Maracanaço*. But somehow they had managed, in spectacular fashion, to eclipse the pain of 64 years earlier by losing 7-1.

The next day it was Argentina's turn. We made our way back to Copacabana via the supermarket. Booze had been sold on the beach the day before, but we had paid well over the odds for a homemade *caipirinha* or can of beer. There was no guarantee that the beach cocktails included all the ingredients – we had been sold *caipirinhas* without *cachaça*. It was an expensive error. This time we walked down the hill of the *favela* to the main road where there was a huge supermarket serving the neighbourhood. A lot of military police were stationed there. It was a buzzing, energetic area with the traffic whizzing out of the motorway tunnel and lots of people milling about, selling phone chargers, clothes and foodstuffs. We picked up a bottle of the sugarcane rum *cachaça*, as well as six-packs of beer and snacks for the day's game. We would have to get there early to get a good spot, so our provisions had to last around four or five hours.

Arriving at Rio's Zona Sul, we walked past the entrance to the fan zone and made our way as close to the big screen as possible. Around three hours before kick-off, the beach was already filling up. We managed to find a spot huddled in amongst the estimated 100,000 Argentines on the beach that day. Upon the *albiceleste* making it to the latter stages of the tournament, thousands of Argentines had made their way to Brazil, by hook or by crook – some spending extortionate amounts of money on flights, many more driving the nearly 1,800 miles from Buenos Aires.

It was another tense game, which ended 0-0. There had been surprisingly little entertainment in the knockout stages of this World Cup. There had only been four goals in the four quarter-finals, 18 in the eight round-of-16 games. The previous day's semi-final went some way to making up for the few high-scoring games before. But with 120 minutes unable to separate the Dutch and the Argentines, more penalties were lined up.

Watching Brazil-Chile being decided on penalties with thousands of Brazilians had been fun. But I was now amongst 100,000 Argentines. The time between each penalty felt like a week the elation felt when *my* team scored indescribable. When Maxi Rodriguez scored Argentina's fourth penalty to send them to the final, Copacabana beach exploded with a mass of people jumping up and down, hugging random people, throwing beer into the air. I got a bit carried away with it all, certainly aided by several hours of drinking, but also by the sheer emotion of the occasion.

The three or four minutes of jumping around were enough for someone to run off with my backpack. We had made a little base for ourselves in a patch of sand, which would be ours for the next several hours. Our belongings were in a pile around which we stood. With the celebrations, we strayed a little from base and when I got back my rucksack had disappeared. Copacabana beach does have the reputation for theft and many who have visited Rio tell of the sweeping raids young kids do of the beach on a daily basis, World Cup or no World Cup. A friend of mine had seen it from one of the rooftop bars of a hotel looking down on Copacabana beach a few years before and described it as a swarm of 100 young children looking like little bugs from his high vantage point. We had seen it the day before prior to the kick-off of the first semi-final, with a ten-year-old stealing a solitary flip-flop. But there is little you can do when caught off guard in that situation. It all happens within 60 seconds and the kids will grab anything.

As for my rucksack, I had only used it to bring our food and drink. I also had sunglasses, sun cream and a cheap Casio watch in it. They took my flip-flops, too. Both of them. The most valuable thing was the backpack itself. My phone and wallet I had on me. It was inconvenient, especially seeing as I now had to walk barefoot to and from the bus. But that aside, it had been a good day.

Back in Rocinha, on one of those days between the semis and the final where the football suddenly stops, we explored the neighbourhood. We now felt safe walking around and hiking up the hill, and on one of these forays we stumbled upon a new artificial pitch with a little clubhouse. From the pitch there was a great view of the rest of the *favela*.

The pitch was fenced in but there was a little gap where we snuck through. The first time Nima and I went there, we watched some local kids playing football for a while until eventually we dared to ask if we could join in. The next day we dragged almost the whole hostel up there. The four armed police officers guarding the facility barely acknowledged us. Their shotguns and huge, dark-grey sub-machine guns were a bit daunting. We muttered an *oi* ('hi' in Portuguese) but got nothing back.

The night before the World Cup Final, 12 of us wanted to go up to play football. It was already late, around 11pm, when we set off from the hostel and arrived to find the pitch without lights. It probably shouldn't have surprised us. Disappointed, we hung around for a bit. There really wasn't much to be done. Just as we were about to head back down, tails between our legs, a local came up to us. We had a Brazilian amongst us who could do the talking, and the Peruvians understood enough of what he was saying. We were being invited to play football somewhere else. We were in the middle of Rocinha, it was nearly midnight and we were now being led through the backstreets.

Up until the pacification of the *favelas*, the only foreigners to enter Rocinha were tourists on appalling, distasteful *favela* tours, which looked more like human safaris. Back in 2009, my friend and I had seen a poster for such a tour but thought better of it. In 2014, walking down the *favela* streets eating and drinking among the locals, I saw the tour operators' vehicles cruising down the high street. As if we were in Kenya spying lions and giraffes, tourists were crammed on to benches on the open back of 4x4 Jeeps. The 537 bus served the same purpose for anyone curious, the Jeeps seemed excessive.

Eventually our very conspicuous group of foreigners made it to an indoor football pitch several blocks into Rocinha from the main road. The main road, where the buses took us into town, was a reference point, and wandering down the backstreets I felt it would be easy to get lost. We had a guide anyway, a local leading us, so it was just a case of trusting and following. At the indoor pitch were a group of local footballers already playing. They were aged between 18 and 24 and got distracted from their game at seeing a dozen foreigners with an array of random kits and colours walk through the door.

The standard of the football was high. And they were fiercely competitive, as you might expect. We were looking for a friendly kickaround. As you might not expect, Matthieu the Micronesian was the best player among us. We also had others who were less useful up against these amateur Romarios and Ronaldo *Fenomenos*. It was suggested that we mix the teams. A good idea. Although I couldn't match the speed or the skill with which they played, I felt I held my own, at least. We were playing futsal rather than football. The surface was harder and the ball heavier. It was great to be kicking a ball around after having only watched a lot of football over the past few weeks. We played for a few hours, until past 3am, before going for some beers at a little kiosk on the street. The evening lasted until 6am and the next day we had the World Cup Final to get ready for.

Up until the day of the game itself, I had been looking and asking around for a ticket to the final. The prices were unsurprisingly astronomical, but I was still surprised at just how much tickets were going for. I had met an English guy in Buenos Aires a year prior to the World Cup and we were in touch during Brazil 2014. His trip was financed by the buying and selling of tickets and he seemed to be doing alright for himself. When I was offered two tickets for the World Cup Final for £3,000, I got on to him to see what he thought. Just one ticket was going for that price, he said. It got me thinking. Maybe I could buy the two tickets, sell one on for £3,000 and keep the second one? I spent the rest of the day trying to figure out how it would work, but there was so little time before the game. What would be harder would be finding a few thousand dollars at short notice and getting it out from a Brazilian bank. It was a fun project to daydream about but not particularly realistic. I would have to remain content with the quarter-final I got to attend and be happy with another day at the beach.

We had the same routine for the final as we'd had for the semis. But this time more people would join us. At Copacabana beach we found twice as many people than four days earlier. Estimates suggest that there were now 200,000 Argentines in Rio de Janeiro. There was a lot less space and it took us a long time to find a decent spot, even a few hours before kick-off. Walking through the dense crowd was only made harder as we had a Brazilian wearing a Germany shirt with us. Nervous Argentines felt he was antagonising them and we regularly had to stop to explain that this guy wasn't really a big football fan. He hadn't really thought through his choice of outfit. At some point during the first half he disappeared.

By the time the game had started, going to the toilet was a problem. We weren't more than 20 or 30 metres from the sea, but it took more than 15 minutes to get there and back through the vast number of bodies and around the encampments of foldable chairs and cooler boxes. It was too far to go for most. Rather than using the sea as a urinal, a little hole in the sand was dug and the toilet-goer went down on one knee as if they were proposing to the person in front's backside. It was revolting standing on wet, warm sand but after drinking beer for several hours on the beach, I also had to go. At least it was my own wet, warm sand.

The game came and went without anything notable happening, the eventual winning goal for *die Mannschaft* aside. To have watched it there with so many Argentines was probably better than having been in the ground. Had I been given a ticket I wouldn't have thought twice about going to the Maracaná for a World Cup Final. My ticket-touting mate had flown back to Buenos Aires to watch the game there, as had many Argentines who couldn't get tickets for the final. Instead of watching the final in Brazil, they wanted to be with their friends and family for a potentially generation-defining game. But it wasn't to be.

We hung around Copacabana for about an hour after the final whistle. Many Argentinian fans were crying. We consoled the *albiceleste* and watched all the comings and goings of people and police before jumping on the bus back to Rocinha. We had seen a few Brazilians goading Argentines after the game, but they had been smart enough to stand next to a police van while doing it. On the bus, seeing that we had Argentina and Boca Juniors shirts on, the bus driver held his fingers up to show the final score. 1-0! He was trying to provoke and upset us, but none of us were Argentines so we just laughed it off. Disappointed that we hadn't bitten, he kept doing it. He kept taking his hands off the steering wheel to mock us. Getting a bit fed up, we all put seven fingers up symbolising their semi-final defeat. He seemed to get angry. We had gone too far.

By now I had already spent six weeks in Brazil. I had been lucky to catch a few matches live and many more on TV in bars, restaurants, hostels or at local Brazilians' houses. Once the World Cup was over, I headed to São Paulo to visit my mate, where I spent a week detoxing from football. It was nice to wind down, to not have to think about football, to be free of the daily schedule of games. Guto took me out on the town and his family made me feel welcome in their home. They took it in turns to entertain me. Guto's brother-in-law took the day off work to drive me to the Museu do Futebol at Palmeiras' old stadium, Estádio Pacaembu. The huge museum housed exhibits from Brazilian football throughout the decades since their first international game against Exeter City in 1914. The museum was fantastic – an impressively large area over three floors dedicated to all elements of the game. Maybe I hadn't had enough of the sport, quite yet. It was a thoughtful excursion.

My flight back to Buenos Aires was from Rio de Janeiro. The Brazilian league season had already begun. I managed to squeeze in one last game. Nima had by now recovered from two weeks of the potentially fatal dengue fever and was keen to go to Estádio Maracanã. Botafogo were hosting Flamengo, the same fixture I attended back in 2009. The stadium had been redeveloped since then. But she still hadn't seen Brazil lift the World Cup trophy on home soil and would have to be content with Brazilian league fixtures and the occasional *seleção* game for the foreseeable future.

Flamengo's red and black horizontal stripes against Botafogo's black and white vertical stripes. Former Arsenal player Eduardo da Silva was on the bench for Flamengo, but wouldn't get on. The game promised a lot following a shot from 25 yards just four seconds after kick-off. It was Éverton who fired off the shot and it was Éverton who curled in an inviting cross for Alecsandro to head home after 33 minutes. One goal would be enough, and Flamengo took all three points, winning 1-0 (just as they had done in 2009). We were standing amongst Botafogo fans holding aloft a black-and-white Bob Marley flag. But the away fans *were* worried. Their team ended up finishing second to bottom in Série A that season and would have to spend 2015 in Série B, which they subsequently won.

The stadium was 70 per cent full and there were a lot of empty yellow-and-light-blue seats. But a return to normal, everyday football seemed appropriate. My holiday was over. It was time to get back to reality and in Buenos Aires a new teaching job awaited me. As did a few new grounds and more *fútbol argentino*.

Semi-finals and UFOs

IT HAD been a good year so far. At the end of March I had shed a tear at the enormity of a *superclásico* at La Bombonera. In June and July I travelled around Brazil watching football, drinking beer and meeting a lot of new friends. But 2014 still had a lot to offer.

At a hostel in the Rio neighbourhood of Botafogo, I had met a group of hardy River Plate fans. The majority of the guests were European backpackers wearing the same clothes and speaking the same tongue. The four *porteños* from Buenos Aires, with their sleeveless River Plate training tops, tracksuit bottoms and *mate* gourds stood out. To say they looked like four *barra bravas* would be typecasting them as something nefarious, which wasn't the case. They were very friendly, offering food and drink whenever I walked past them in the kitchen. They had prepared a *picada* and were drinking *Fernet y Cola*.

My Spanish wasn't up to the conversation. The biggest, burliest and gruffest of the group was the friendliest. Despite our very limited chats, Sergio insisted on adding me on social media. But he didn't know how to do it and seemed perplexed when I said I couldn't log him in for him because I didn't know his password.

He phoned his son back in Villa Soldati and the son fixed the problem.

Four months after meeting Sergio I received a message. Would I know anyone interested in two tickets to River Plate versus Boca Juniors in the second leg of their Copa Sudamericana semi-final? The price was steep: over £125. Initially I decided it was too pricey for me, but I asked a friend. Josh was 20 years old and living in Buenos Aires on a one-year university work placement. He had grown up a stone's throw from where my English family came from and we got on well, playing football and, the subsequent food and beers we would treat ourselves to after a good game. Upon hearing about the ticket, Josh got excited. He was very keen. His enthusiasm spread, and little by little I found it harder to find a reason not to accept the ticket.

I replied to Sergio that I wanted the tickets. We were to meet Sergio and his *Pibes de Soldati* on a street corner in Barrio Chino, a few blocks from El Monumental. We would pay for the ticket there and follow them to the ground. The deal was done: we were going to go to a Copa Sudamericana semi-final.

Whilst the Copa Libertadores is the South American cousin of the UEFA Champions League, the Copa Sudamericana correlates with our Europa League. However, before 2018, the Libertadores was played in the first half of the calendar year, with the Sudamericana taking place from August to December. Teams could qualify for and win both tournaments in the same season. In 2015 River Plate won the Copa Libertadores and reached the semi-final of the Sudamericana, where they lost to fellow *porteño* side Huracán.

In 1992 a secondary continental competition was created to complement the Copa Libertadores. Inspired by the

UEFA Cup, the Copa CONMEBOL saw clubs who didn't quite reach the league spots to qualify for the Libertadores play in the secondary competition. Between its inception and 1999, the precursor to the Copa Sudamericana was shared between Argentinian and Brazilian clubs.

After 1999, and for only four years, the Copa CONMEBOL was split into two separate competitions. The Copa Merconorte was contested by teams from Bolivia, Perú, Ecuador, Colombia and Venezuela (as well as teams from Costa Rica, Mexico and the US in 2000 and 2001). Seven of the eight finalists over four seasons were Colombian, the eighth team from Ecuador.

1998: Atlético Nacional beat Deportivo Cali over two legs.

1999: América de Cali beat Santa Fe after penalties.

2000: Atlético Nacional winning again, beating Millonarios on aggregate.

2001: Millonarios going one better, beating Ecuadorians Emelec on penalties.

The Copa Mercosur saw teams from Argentina, Brazil, Chile, Uruguay and Paraguay fight, it out with the Brazilian league dominating, again with seven finalists out of eight. Whilst the Copa Merconorte teams played two-legged finals, aggregating the score and having a penalty shoot-out should scores be level after two games (no away goals), the Copa Mercosur had a different format for the final for the first three years. Three points were awarded for a win in the final, one point for a draw and nothing – naturally – for a loss. After two games, if the teams had the same points, they would play a third game. This happened twice over the three seasons, namely in 1998 and 2000. In 2001, they reverted to the normal two-legged format, penalties deciding the tie in case of a draw.

In 1998 Cruzeiro beat Palmeiras 2-1 in the first game, with Palmeiras winning the second 3-1. Both teams had three points. Palmeiras were drawn as the home team for the third game, which they duly won 1-0 to finish with six points to Cruzeiro's three.

The four Mercosur Final ties looked like this:

1998: Palmeiras overcoming Cruzeiro over three games.

1999: Flamengo beat Palmeiras in the first leg, drawing the second leg (Flamengo won 4-1 on points – and, technically, on aggregate, too).

2000: Vasco da Gama beat Palmeiras 6-3 on points over three games, the third game finishing 4-3 to Vasco away in São Paulo.

2001: San Lorenzo breaking the Brazilian monopoly on the competition by beating Flamengo on penalties after two draws.

Ahead of the 2002 campaign, the *Merconorte* and *Mercosur* were merged back together and named the Copa Sudamericana, the secondary competition for teams from all the continent's ten nations. For four seasons between 2005 and 2008, CONCACAF teams – Central America, the Caribbean and North America – were invited to join, with Mexican teams reaching the final the first three years, winning once when Pachuca lifted the 2006 edition. In the final of those four seasons, Guadalajara made it to the semi-finals.

On this Wednesday night in late November it would be an all-Argentine affair. The English institute where I worked was only a few blocks from China Town, where we would meet Sergio and his friends. November is the end of the Argentinian school year so, without classes on, I left the institute earlier than normal and went to meet Josh. Just as Josh and I found each other on Avenida Libertador, an old pickup truck drove past. Sergio was leaning out of the window waving at us, a big River Plate flag flapping out of the back window. We followed the plume of smoke trailing the truck and got some cans of beer from the local *chino* supermarket.

El chino is a big but simple convenience store owned by immigrants from China or Taiwan. Naturally I was hesitant to use the word *chino* to talk about a shop owned by Asians – it seemed politically incorrect. But political correctness doesn't exist in the same guise in Argentina. Yes, Argentines are a people who fight for the downtrodden with a strong activist soul, but the discussion about such words has not yet been had. Maybe it will happen one day.

The use of the word *chino* and similar phrases was explained to me in a footballing context: when a club has a black player, he is referred to as *el negro*. The word doesn't carry the same connotation as in other cultures. Within a group of friends, the one whose eyes are slightly narrower than the rest will be called *el chino*, even without Asian heritage. The chubby friend, *el gordo* (fatty), the Italian, *el tano* (Italian) and the Jew, *el ruso* (the Russian).

We had an hour or so to kill so we stood on the corner of the street drinking our cans, trying to converse. My Spanish wasn't noticeably better and I was having the same communication issues as I'd had in Rio. Josh, on the other hand, was studying the language at university and was already pretty much fluent. He consistently used to mock my poor Spanish, and rightly so. I had, by now, been living in Buenos Aires for over a year – albeit seven weeks of those 12 months had been spent in Brazil – but I struggled to get by.

It has to be said, though, that Argentinian Spanish is tough to learn. With its Italian words, harsh-sounding accent and *lunfardo* slang, *argento* or *castellano rioplatense* is much harder than learning the same language in Bolivia, Perú, Ecuador, Colombia or Venezuela. There is a good reason why many backpackers tend to start their Spanish classes in these countries, rather than in Argentina, Uruguay or Chile. *Olvidalo!*

I had many other excuses for why my *castellano* was *una mierda*. Firstly, my job. I was paid to speak English. Working with other Brits and a handful of people from other English-speaking countries, we would exclusively converse in English when getting a beer after work. As a new teacher I spent a lot of time planning classes and had little time or energy outside of work to study another language. It was painfully ironic. The little spare time I did have, when my head wasn't buried in an English-grammar-for-idiots book or marking my students' essays, was spent playing football.

Ideally, I would have been playing football with locals. But the locals had their well-established football groups and first you had to meet locals to be invited to play. To meet locals you had to speak the language. It was a catch-22 situation. I ended up playing so-called pick-up games with other expats up to four times a week. The lingua franca was English but at least I met people and my network expanded rapidly.

I was also occasionally meeting girls. The Argentine girls I met tended to speak excellent English. It was another contradiction: I wanted to meet *argentinas* to improve my Spanish but could only connect with those who wanted to speak English. The Argentine *pibas* who didn't speak English weren't frequenting the same bars as the expats. What was the point? Anyway, why should they speak English?! I was the one living in a foreign country. But naturally communication was much easier in a language that both spoke rather than in a language that I spoke to the level of a three-year-old.

Josh served as my translator and the hour passed quickly as we drank our cheap cans of Schneider beer and watched people funnelling off towards the stadium. Sergio suggested we had a picture taken together and we held up their *Pibes de Soldati* flag – 'the lads of Villa Soldati', a working-class neighbourhood towards the south-west of the city. Soon it would be our turn to set off and with it the heart raced a little faster. We knew that we were going in on someone else's membership card and that, more worryingly, we stood out as gringos.

Getting closer to the stadium and being amongst a flock of thousands going towards the various checkpoints, all memories are blurry. Without remembering specifically, I almost definitely needed to go to the loo as beer tends to go straight through me. It all went very quickly, even if we had to pass through several police barriers. On a big matchday there could be up to seven or eight checks. We managed to lose Sergio in one of these checkpoints. He didn't get in. I'm not sure if he was even expecting to get in. Maybe he had planned to rush the gate, taking advantage of the number of people and just sliding through behind someone else. But he was a rotund man so this wouldn't have been an easy task. It obviously didn't work; he was nowhere to be seen.

He missed quite the spectacle. As with any River-Boca/Boca-River game and any important match, the *recibimiento* of the players was spectacular on the night. It was not only the deafening noise, but the fireworks and thousands of flares made the stadium look as if it was on fire. Flags hung from every naked bit of concrete or from every metal *paravalancha*. The white-and-red seats were covered with people wearing white-and-red shirts, jumpers, jackets and bucket hats.

The first leg finished 0-0. Within only 30 seconds of the second leg, Boca Juniors were awarded a penalty. It broke the seal on the emotions bottled up inside all 70,000 people in El Monumental. League games are tense, but a winner-takes-all semi-final second leg needed an icebreaker, otherwise we would very possibly have been heading for another 0-0 draw. (I wouldn't have turned down penalties, though.)

It took three minutes from the awarding of the penalty to its taking. An early penalty awarded; an early penalty missed. We were sitting beneath *Los Borrachos del Tablon*. River Plate's hardcore fans call themselves 'the drunks of the terraces'. The penalty was all the way down the other end, but there was no doubt that it had been saved by the River goalkeeper Marcelo Barovero. Boca's No. 9, Emmanuel *El Puma* Gigliotti, was complaining about a laser pen being shone in his eyes. Watching the replays he had a case. But regardless of the green light shining down from above, a decent penalty saw a very decent save by Barovero: 'It's celebrated as if it were a goal [for River],' the commentator shouted. Just over ten minutes later River Plate scored down our end. Cue pandemonium. Goal celebrations seem as if they will never end in these situations. Celebrating a goal against the eternal rivals should last as long as possible and the initial roar was dragged out by River fans desperate to eternalise the moment. From sheer ecstasy to a rumbling of gleeful conversation and the reliving of the goal. Then comes the revitalised support. For an indefinite period of time after the goal, every anthem is sung with exaggerated vigour in order to repay the glory of the feat. *Piel de gallina* in the stadium of *las gallinas*.

The goal was enough. A 1-0 River Plate victory sent them to the final of the Copa Sudamericana 2014, where they would face Atlético Nacional of Medellín, Colombia.

River Plate fans were delirious. More so for having beaten Boca Juniors than for having reached the final. With a couple of litres swishing around in my gut, my delirium set in and I saw a UFO hovering above the pitch at El Monumental. It was a spectacular sight that I felt only I saw. For every year that passes without evidence of its occurrence, the more I doubt its happening.

At some point during the second half, a drone was flown into the stadium. From outside the stadium and over the huge stands of the monumental concrete bowl. Suspended from the drone was a white sheet with the letter B written on it. It was the ghost! *El fantasma de la B* had paid a visit to El Monumental. The same drone was flown over La Bombonera six months later in their infamous Copa Libertadores last-16 match.

It was a heroic piece of inter-rivalry piss-taking. The range of a 2014 drone couldn't have been more than a few hundred metres, meaning that a hardy *bostero* must have parked up as close to the ground as possible to fly this not-so-friendly gesture over the 20-metre stadium wall. With roads closed off and a heavy police presence, the tennis courts adjoining the stadium would have been their best bet for such a prank. Few fans of the home team would ever admit to having seen it. If pictures were taken, they certainly weren't disseminated on social media for retweets, comments or likes. They would have been printed off and burned, or even the whole mobile phone thrown in the toilet to erase the horror.

Leaving the stadium I received a message from Sergio. He was inviting us to celebrate the game back in Villa Soldati. It was already 11pm and I had to work the next day. Lots of Fernet and one-litre bottles of beer was to be expected, with an *asado* put on in celebration miles across town. I wasn't even sure where Villa Soldati were. I had no idea how I would have got home. In later years, with better Spanish and feeling an even greater connection with the Argentinian people, I would have jumped at the chance to spend an evening enjoying the occasion, but in late 2014 I bottled it, using work as an excuse. It was the thought that counted, and I was touched to have been invited. The invitation showed how friendly, open and genuine Argentines are. Maybe I had been a walking dollar sign initially, a foreigner willing to pay daft prices to attend a *superclásico*. And even despite the lack of intelligible Spanish, we had connected through football. But it was beyond our shared enthusiasm for going to *la cancha*. Maybe it was a shared enthusiasm for everything that was Argentinian. And it was the reason I ended up staying so long in Argentina: I had fallen in love with the Argentinian people.

The *superclásico* of international football

A YEAR after the River-Boca semi-final, I returned to El Monumental to catch another major footballing rivalry. If Boca-River is the *superclásico*, Argentina-Brazil must be the international *superclásico*. The two superpowers of South American football going head to head is another heavyweight bout most football fans keep an eye out for. I say most – I was unaware of it happening at all. International breaks tend just to come around uninvited.

The game was meant to be played on a Thursday evening in November 2015, but torrential rain put a stop to that. The game was postponed. With the Brazilian players already in town, and with the inevitable complexities of rescheduling a game like this in an already packed fixture list, the authorities pencilled the game in for the following evening. Sometimes they would just play the fixture regardless of the weather because it's more convenient to have the game played, even if the conditions are less than ideal. This was the case with a Primera División *superclásico* shortly before their Copa Sudamericana semi-final clash at the end of 2014. With my girlfriend at the time, we found a nice *parrilla* to watch the game but, with a downpour unrivalled by anything I had seen before, the game was expected to be called off. But it wasn't. The game went ahead even though the ball could barely roll two metres without stopping dead in the water. The game was a farce, but to the authorities a lot of planning had already gone into it. It was simply more convenient to get it over with.

After the postponement of Argentina-Brazil on the Thursday night, I received a message from a French friend offering me a ticket. Because of the postponement his friend's ticket was available. I had met Guillaume through playing football in Buenos Aires. We found a good chemistry on the pitch and enjoyed grabbing beers together off it. Unlike many of the other French people I met, Guillaume was also keen to stay after the football (regardless of the result), grab a beer and have a chat. He preferred to speak Spanish, so I really needed to throw myself in the deep end, however uncomfortable that was. I wasn't going to learn the language by speaking English.

Guillaume was an interesting character. He worked as a musician and producer in a cumbia band and never stayed very long in any one place. He travelled the world and travelled freely, with mates and girlfriends wherever he went. I hadn't seen him since he was last in Buenos Aires the year before, so it was nice to catch up. I got the bus over to where he was staying, walked three blocks still wet from the night before, and we had a few beers before setting off for Argentina's national stadium, El Monumental.

It wasn't to be the rendezvous we had been hoping for. Already two blocks after leaving his friend's flat, Guillaume got a text message from France. Something had happened at the concert hall and theatre, The Bataclan, in Paris.

It was unclear exactly what had happened, and accurate information was hard to come by. Nonetheless, he was unsettled and continued trying to find out what was going on back home. As a musician Guillaume had played at The Bataclan and knew many people on the French music scene. Without knowing exactly what had happened or where, there was no talk of dropping the game, but we both frantically looked for information online as we walked towards the Buenos Aires metro with a can of *cerveza* in our hand.

Riding the metro the six or so stops towards the Belgrano barrio, we were trying to get a signal. With free wi-fi at the metro stations, each time we approached the next stop we began trying to connect to the internet to look for the latest news from Paris. As we exited the Subte, Guillaume started making phone calls. I walked solemnly by his side, unsure what to say and understanding little of the French spoken. I understood enough to know that it wasn't good news.

The events in Paris overshadowed the game. The gravity of the attacks wasn't yet clear, so I tried to enjoy the game. The players lined up for the anthems under a clear but dark sky and the Argentines hummed along to the wordless tune of theirs. Their national hymn is so long that at football matches only the first minute or so is played. The small travelling contingent of Brazilians dared to sing during the Argentinian anthem and *un argentino* sitting in front of us began shouting *filho da puta* across to the visiting fans who were sitting over 250 metres away. After screaming this several times he sat back down and lit another cigarette. He would smoke a whole packet during the game.

Other than that, it was a little surprising how civilised the game was. I was expecting more fight, the kind of petty squabbling rival players engage in just to show that these games mean a lot to them. Fighting for the sake of fighting. But it was a fairly cordial affair with polite applause from the local crowd when Argentina came close, followed by chants of *Argentina! Argentina!*

Maybe I had been spoiled by the much more partisan and slightly rougher crowds at the local matches. Maybe I had to sacrifice atmosphere for the higher quality of football on show. Either way, I suspected that the players had been aware of news from France and that might go some way to explaining the friendlier atmosphere.

David Luiz – then at Paris Saint-Germain – saw a late red card, receiving two yellow cards in the space of a minute. Messi was absent for the hosts, but the visitors had their main man. Neymar, sporting a cotton headband (a trend that thankfully never caught on), was involved in a lot of the Brazilian attacking play. It was an end-to-end, entertaining game that ended 1-1. Another PSG player, Ezequiel Lavezzi, scored for Argentina in the first half and Santos's Lucas Lima equalised in the second half. It had been a decent enough spectacle, despite the circumstances.

I caught up with Guillaume about a week later. We stayed around for some beers after having played football. After the Argentina-Brazil game he had stayed up all night following the harrowing events back home. He told me that he had been relieved that none of his friends had been injured or worse but that he did know victims indirectly. It was a sobering conversation.

Three days after their 1-1 home draw, Argentina beat Colombia 1-0 in Barranquilla. It was a much needed win in *las eliminatorias*, the South American qualifiers for the 2018 World Cup in Russia. In the previous round of fixtures, *la albiceleste* had lost at home to Ecuador (their first home loss in 40 qualifiers) and drawn in Paraguay. To finish in the top half of the ten-team South American qualifying tournament, no nation could afford to drop points like Argentina had done in October 2015. The four points gained in November represented an improvement, but they still only had five points from the first four games.

South American qualification for the World Cup is far from straightforward. It has been argued that the ten-team league is the most competitive league in world football. Since 1996, South American nations have competed for 4.5 places at the World Cup finals. Playing each other home and away over a period of two years, four countries qualify directly. The team finishing fifth plays a two-legged play-off game against a nation from another confederation's qualifying setup (in 2018 it was between Oceania or CONCACAF, as drawn by FIFA). A 45 per cent chance of qualifying may seem like decent odds, until you consider the quality of the teams involved.

Unlike in Europe, all South American nations are guaranteed to meet at least twice every qualifying campaign. And nearly every fixture is a derby. Argentina-Brazil is an obvious one. As the two major powers on the continent – in terms of football but also in terms of economics and military might – the two have a natural rivalry. It's a rivalry that can be traced back over half a millennia when Spain and Portugal fiercely competed to gain territory in the Americas. Fast forward to the 19th century, between 1822 and 1825 the two nations fought a war over what is today Uruguay. Some 190 years before Argentina's 1-1 draw with Brazil at El Monumental, the Cisplatine War also ended in a stalemate. Then came the Platine War of 1851–52. In more recent times, Argentina had compulsory military service between 1945 and 1995, and inevitably Argentines were indoctrinated to consider Brazilians as the greatest threat and most likely enemy in possible future wars. Territorial wars have been replaced by battles on the football pitch.

But what about Argentina-Uruguay? The two nations are culturally very similar. The footballing rivalry stems from the early days of the international game when the two countries were vying to be labelled the best in the world. Before the World Cup, Olympic football was the tournament that determined the world's best footballing nation, and it was Uruguay, as champions of the 1923 Copa América, who travelled to compete at the summer Olympics in Paris 1924. Five games, five victories and 20 goals later, Uruguay had won the championship and were crowned de facto world champions.

Bitter at having to watch their brothers across the *Río de la Plata* getting all the plaudits, Argentina invited Uruguay to a two-legged friendly upon returning home. They had played each other before the Olympics, playing two games on the same day, 25 May 1924. The first game in Buenos Aires ended 4-0 to Argentina in the Copa Newton, a 'friendly' cup, before both teams travelled across the River Plate to Montevideo, where Uruguay triumphed 2-0 in the Copa Lipton and were presented a trophy donated by the tea mogul, Sir Thomas Lipton. (It wasn't the last time they would play two games in two different countries on the same day: in 1929 and 1944 they would repeat the feat.)

Three months after the Paris Olympics, the two nations played the first leg of the friendly that Argentina so desperately wanted to win. The match ended 1-1 in Montevideo on 21 September 1924, with the Argentinian media commenting that 'having been so unfancied against supposedly superior rivals, a draw is like a win to us'. A tense return fixture had to be abandoned at the first attempt with overexcited fans encroaching on to the pitch. Uruguay refused to continue under the seemingly threatening circumstances. When the rearranged second leg came around, a four-metre-high fence was in place to protect the players (and it has been in place ever since). Unsurprisingly, a very physical game was played out, with Argentina winning 2-1 (3-2 on aggregate), and with it they could claim a moral victory from the Olympics in which they didn't take part.

The first goal in this 2-1 victory was a special one as it was (probably) the first-ever goal scored directly from a corner. Less than three months earlier it had been decided that such goals would now be allowed. Huracán's Cesáreo Onzari whipped in a corner that went past everyone and into the Uruguayan goal. From then on, a goal scored directly from a corner has been called a *gol olímpico*, the first having been scored against the Olympic champions.

Uruguay defended their Olympic football title in Amsterdam in 1928 by beating Argentina in the final. After a 1-1 draw, Uruguay won the rematch 2-1 three days later on 13 June 1928. Two years later they would meet again in a final, this time at the first World Cup Final in 1930. On home soil Uruguay prevailed again, winning 4-2. A pre-match disagreement over who should provide the match ball gave the Belgian referee, John Langenus, a headache. Eventually he decided that Argentina's ball would be used in the first half and Uruguay's in the second. Argentina led 2-1 at half-time but Uruguay scored three second-half goals with their own ball to win the tournament. A real game of two halves.

From the *Río de la Plata* to the Andes *cordillera*, Chile seem to be disliked by all their neighbours. The Argentina-Chile border is the third longest in the world and border disputes haven't been uncommon, with tensions from time to time, particularly in Patagonia (a region which spans both countries). Despite animosity, the two countries have never fought a war against each other. But Argentina-Chile relations suffered a blow when Chile's dictator, General Augusto Pinochet – a friend of Margaret Thatcher – supported British troops during the Falklands/Malvinas war of 1982. The fact that Chile beat Argentina in successive Copa América finals in 2015 and 2016 has added spice to an international fixture previously dominated by Argentina.

Bolivia and Chile don't get on either. In 1879, more than a hundred years before the Falklands War, Bolivian dictator Hilarión Daza Groselle went after Chilean-owned mining companies in the Litoral state by the Bolivian Pacific coast. Chile reacted by going to war and occupying the area. It was a five-year war that Chile won. They kept Litoral, resulting in Bolivia becoming a landlocked country and losing an area rich with resources. These would eventually include football resources: Alexis Sánchez was born in Tocopilla, a city that would have been a part of Bolivia had it not been for Litoral's annexation. (Bolivia's flag has ten stars: an *estrella* for each of its nine states, with the final star for the fallen state of Litoral. They also have a navy, in the hope that one day they will recover their Pacific coast and unlock their landlocked status, literally becoming littoral once more.) On the pitch, like during the War of the Pacific, Chile dominate the fixture.

There is more *antichilenismo*. Perú resent their neighbours to the south, too. Having signed a secret defence pact with

Bolivia in 1873 to protect each other from attackers, Perú joined Bolivia in the war with Chile. They subsequently lost a state called Tarapacá to the victors. Post-war treaty negotiations eventually returned the city of Tacna to Perú after 50 years of being a part of Chile, but Arica stayed south of the Perú-Chile border.

The derby between Chile and Perú is billed as the *clásico del Pacífico*. Its significance has increased over the last few years. They have faced each other in two recent Copa América semi-finals (2015 and 2019), winning one apiece. Bus attacks in qualifying for the 1998 and 2002 World Cups, in Santiago de Chile and Lima respectively, added to the tension and mutual loathing. Worst of all, cuddly toy monkeys wearing Peruvian kits were hanged with a noose around the neck in view of the visiting players.

The resentment goes deep. Perú is the only Spanish-speaking country to use a different word for the overhead kick. *La chilena* is used universally, but Peruvians, denying their neighbours the credit for inventing the most beautiful goal there is, use the word *chalaca*.

But most importantly it comes down to what happens on the pitch, and with Argentina, Brazil and Uruguay particularly strong, Chile and Perú (along with Colombia) are often left to fight it out for the last spots. That said, Paraguay have qualified for eight World Cups and Ecuador three, so they are not to be underestimated either. Of the ten nations, only Venezuela have never reached the World Cup finals.

For every campaign, there are several compelling events and stories. Qualifying for Russia 2018 was no different. After Chile and Bolivia drew 0-0 in Santiago de Chile in September 2016, the Chilean FA appealed the result, having discovered that Nelson Cabrera had played 13 minutes for the visitors. Centre-half Cabrera was Paraguayan and had played one friendly for his home nation, but after living and playing for four years in Bolivia had switched to play for *la selección boliviana*. The problem was that he was a year premature – five years of citizenship is what FIFA demand in order to switch allegiance. Chile's appeal was successful, and they were handed a 3-0 win in lieu of the misdemeanour. They had turned one point into three after the final whistle.

However, only five days before Chile-Bolivia, Perú had lost 2-0 at 3,600m altitude in La Paz. The 34-year-old Cabrera had played all of eight minutes in his adopted country's victory. The result was overturned, 2-0 became 0-3, and zero points became three for Perú. At the end of the qualifying process, Perú and Chile finished on the same points, the former in fifth place and the latter in sixth, goal difference separating them. Had it not been for the Chilean appeal, it would have been Chile facing New Zealand in the play-off over their Pacific rivals Perú.

Chile and Perú were at it again in the final round of games. After 90 games and 242 goals in the CONMEBOL qualifying campaign, it all came down to the final minutes of the last game. Perú were facing Colombia in Lima, and with Brazil leading 3-0 against Chile in São Paulo, *los Incas* knew a draw would be enough for them to take fifth spot. Colombia took the lead but Perú equalised when Colombian goalkeeper David Ospina made a lazy attempt at stopping a Paolo Guerrero free kick. The free kick was indirect, and without Ospina's touch it wouldn't have counted. Colombia were sweating. They had been in second spot in the qualifying group for several weeks and could have qualified for the World Cup with a round to spare. Leading 1-0 lead at home to Paraguay, two signature Ospina gaffes in the dying minutes saw Colombia lose and fall into third, tantalisingly close to losing out on Russia 2018 altogether.

Upon Guerrero's goal (credited as an Ospina own goal because Guerrero couldn't technically score from an indirect free kick), Radamel Falcao was quick to tell his Peruvian counterparts that a draw would be good enough for the hosts and that trying to score again wasn't necessary. To play out a draw with 14 minutes remaining on the clock was in everyone's favour and would see the hated Chileans miss out. (Although, had Perú scored they would have avoided a play-off game.) The Chilean media cried foul and called it the Lima Pact (in reference to Colombian football in the 1950s). The 2017 Lima Pact was a prime example of *chilenophobia* at work. Perú were lucky all the same: had Paraguay beaten the bottom team Venezuela at home in Ascunción, they would have taken fifth and the play-off place. As it was, they bottled it, losing 1-0.

The final round also saw more Argentinian drama. *La albiceleste* started with a home loss to Ecuador and began their final qualifying game going 1-0 down to the same opponents in Quito. Romario Ibarra (born in 1994) scored after 38 seconds. Romario was the name on the back of the yellow Ecuadorian shirt. It was a game Argentina had to win whilst hoping other results went their way. Lionel Messi – without a name on his back, the Argentinian shirts modestly only carrying a number – stepped up and scored two by the 20th minute, sealing his hat-trick in the 62nd minute. Messi was involved in all eight of Argentina's goals in the second half of World Cup qualification. Over 18 games, Argentina had Messi available for ten, from which they harvested 21 points. In the eight games without him, only seven points. Despite a poor qualifying campaign, Argentina won their final game 3-1 and leapfrogged Chile, Perú and Colombia to take third place.

All this was unfolding while I was sitting with some friends in a bar full of yellow-shirted Colombians in Medellín. We could only sit at one of the tables by the outdoor screen on Carrera 70 if we bought a 750ml bottle of Aguardiente Antioqueño, a popular Colombian liquor. I was happy to go elsewhere but a German mate of mine was entertaining a local girl and desperately wanted to sit at this particular bar. The game began, Ospina bumbled and fumbled as goals were flying in across the continent. I was the only person celebrating Argentina's goals. Argentina winning was inconvenient to Colombia, but I didn't care, I was in a rebellious mood. The game was on almost in the background as we chatted about football and some of the more outrageous footballing stories from our new home, one of which featured Argentina's opponents that evening, Ecuador.

Chile were again involved, albeit indirectly, in the infamous and mind-boggling Enner Valencia story of game week nine. Ecuador were hosting Chile, and West Ham United's Enner Valencia, on loan at Everton at the time, was in a spot of bother. As the Ecuadorian national team's coach arrived at the Estadio Olímpico Atahualpa in Quito, police attempted to arrest Valencia for unpaid child maintenance payments, apparently amounting to about US$15,000. His team-mates convinced the officers to allow one of their star men to play the game, and within 19 minutes Enner had set up Antonio Valencia (no relation) to score the opener. Ecuador scored two more and the game was essentially over by the 46th minute with the score at 3-0.

Knowing that he was to be arrested after the game, Enner went down 'injured' and received treatment on the pitch. It must have been serious because he was given oxygen by his national team's medical staff. The golf cart-esque buggy used in South America drove on to the pitch and off again, racing along at a maximum speed of 10 mph towards a waiting ambulance. Worthy of a Benny Hill sketch, policemen chased the buggy along the running track, but Enner got away, taken to Quito hospital. He ended up fleeing the country without facing the authorities.

It has to be said that Enner Valencia did subsequently come out to tell his side of the story, and convincingly so. But the footage remains etched in the memory as another anecdote from the wonderful world of *las eliminatorias* – the best and most ridiculous football competition in the world.

Santiago de Chile:
the atrocities at Gate 8

IT WAS approaching the end of the school year and the ridiculously hot Buenos Aires summer was looming. Students at the institute were getting excited about their holidays: they would be off to the US, two months of backpacking around Europe, or heading to Japan. Earning Argentinian pesos at a time when the local economy was on its knees, I could barely afford to go on holiday. But I had to get out of the city. Nearly 40°C temperatures weren't something I would choose to have to live through if I could avoid it.

I decided to get the 20-hour long-distance coach to Chile. It was supposedly cooler there and their football season would kick off in the middle of January. New Year's Eve in Valparaíso was also meant to be worth the trip on its own. It was an unoriginal idea. After 18 hours traversing Argentina from east to west, our bus approached the Chile-Argentina border. Sitting in the front row of the second floor of the double-decker, I had a good view of the hundreds of cars heading into Chile for the turn of 2016.

There had been a mudslide on the Andes crossing and I had already had to wait ten hours at the bus station in

Mendoza on the Argentinian side, trying to sleep on the cold, hard floor. We had another ten-hour wait at the border. It had taken nearly two days to get there (but that was nothing compared to the drama that was to unfold a month later when returning to Buenos Aires after a more severe mudslide).

Finally I had arrived. It was time to let my hair down after a busy school year and a stressful trip. It was estimated that over one million people would visit Valparaíso, a port city with just 300,000 inhabitants. It was a historic city. Up until the opening of the Panama Canal in 1914, the 'Jewel of the Pacific' had been the major port along the west coast of Latin America, with ships heading for western cities across North, Central and South America forced to round Cape Horn, the southern tip of the Americas. As a result of the shortcut that the Panama Canal provided, *Valpo* lost business and fell on hard times.

Yet it was a charmingly beautiful city one hundred years later. It's built on nearly 50 steep hills that look out into the Pacific Ocean, 14 of which are served by creaky, old cable cars running uphill along tracks. The remaining hills have long, steep concrete staircases, with colourful graffiti throughout the city. It's a training studio and art gallery merged into one. But it needs tidying up a bit; the streets were dirty and there was a smell of urine at almost every corner. The one million partying visitors and hot summer temperatures probably didn't help.

Along the shoreline going north there was a posher town called Viña del Mar. Viña is home to Everton FC, one of (at least) six clubs of the same name in South America. Four Argentinian clubs and one Uruguayan club took inspiration from the English Everton's tour of the two countries in

1909. On the other side of the Andes a group of British expats formed their own Everton in Valparaíso. In 1943 the club moved the six miles up the road from *Valpo* to Viña.

The novelty of seeing the Chilean Everton was too much to resist, and I made my way by train along the coast to Viña del Mar. I was one of 2,500 people at their pre-season friendly match at the 23,000-seater ground, the Estadio Sausalito, a ground that had hosted eight games during the 1962 World Cup. Now, 54 years later, rather than a World Cup semi-final, second division Everton lined up against top tier Unión Española. We were treated to a goal fest, 3-2 to the visitors. Not bad for £3. Despite the entertainment, it definitely had a pre-season feel, with few fans and little by way of matchday atmosphere.

I would come across Unión Española a week later, this time in the first round of Primera División fixtures. Colo-Colo, one of Chile's big two teams, had won the 15-game Apertura season towards the second half of 2015. They started the 2016 Clausura with a 1-1 draw against Española. It was a disappointing experience. Only 10,000 people attended the game at Estadio Monumental David Arellano, a 47,000-capacity stadium. With the summer holidays in full swing, many people were out of town when the season started. Many more stayed away in protest at high ticket prices.

Expecting a bigger crowd, I arrived four hours before kick-off to get a ticket. I had set aside the whole day for the game, but with a ticket easily obtained I had a lot of time to kill. Disappointingly, there was nothing around the stadium other than a shopping centre. With air conditioning and a food court, it turned out to be the perfect place to escape the 35°C midday sun.

But my four hours in the shopping centre nearly got me denied entry to the ground. Entering the ground, I wasn't surprised to have my bag checked, but was dumbfounded when the army officer confiscated two pens I had just bought across the street. He took out the fancy four-colour Bics – handy for marking English students' essays – and pointed towards a big, empty water butt serving as a bin. Dressed in sandy-brown army fatigues in the ridiculous heat, the army officer looked bored. Patting down a gringo wasn't the activity he had dreamed of spending his Saturday doing. I felt he was trying to antagonise a reason to dropkick me to the ground. Not really understanding what he was asking of me, playing (and being) the fool helped avoid a confrontation. The situation was diffused, and he went to try again with the person behind me.

But once safely in Estadio David Arellano, fireworks were being set off from behind the one goal, whilst a group of Colo-Colo fans my age were snorting coke in the family section. Yet it was two pens that signalled the greatest danger to the local crowd.

The ticket had only cost 6,000 Chilean pesos, some £6. It was a relatively boring 1-1 draw, but the Estadio Monumental David Arellano was a ground I had wanted to visit for a long time. Not only are Colo-Colo an iconic club and one of Chile's most successful, but also the story of their founder and first captain Arellano is a tragic one.

Initially part of another Santiago club, Deportes Magallanes, a 23-year-old Arellano left to form a new club. He and his contemporaries would choose to name the club after the tribal leader Colo-Colo, who himself got his name from a species of wild cat native to Chile. The Mapuche chief Colo-Colo had fought in the Arauco War against the Spanish, a war of independence that lasted for nearly 250 years. The modern club badge is of the legendary *cacique* under a horizontal black ribbon in honour of another fallen hero.

The stadium bears the name of the founder and first club captain of Colo-Colo. But David Arellano would only live for another two years after helping to create the club in 1925. The club quickly gained a reputation, having won the amateur Liga Metropolitana without losing a game in their very first season in existence. In 1927 *los invencibles* went on a six-month international tour on which they played 42 games, winning 25 and scoring 126 goals (W25, D4, L13). The tour started in South and Central America before heading for France, but the players wanted to visit Spain so they changed course for La Coruña. From the north-western coast of Spain and then into Portugal, the 20-man squad arrived a month later in Valladolid.

After a 6-2 win against Real Unión Deportiva (now Real Valladolid) on 1 May 1927, the two sides met again on the following day to play out a 3-3 draw. The second game is remembered for a collision between David Arellano and an opposing player, resulting in the Colo-Colo captain having to leave the pitch. Having received a mighty blow to his stomach, Arellano got medical treatment back at the Hotel Inglaterra. But his internal bleeding wasn't caught, and he died on 3 May.

Amazingly the tour continued for another month, taking in 13 games, albeit with some of these organised to raise funds for Arellano's mother. The team had made quite the impression in Spain, with Arellano showing the Europeans, probably for the first time, the overhead kick created by fellow Chilean Ramón Unzaga in 1914. The local press dubbed this creative piece of acrobatics *la chilena* in honour of the team who brought it to their shores.

In the middle of June 1927 Colo-Colo headed back across the Atlantic to face teams in Montevideo and Boca Juniors in Buenos Aires, losing all four games heavily. But ultimately the tour had been a success on the pitch. Off it, it had been a disaster, with the passing of the club's most important figure. Arellano scored eight goals in six games for Chile and was top goalscorer at the Copa América of 1926. The whole nation mourned.

Two days after paying my respects at the stadium named after Arellano, I was heading to southern Santiago again. This time it was to watch Palestino versus Audax Italiano in the two clubs' Clausura opener. The game is billed as a *clásico de colonia*, one of three such derbies between Palestino, Audax Italiano and Unión Española. Apart from all three being from Santiago, the clue as to the origin of this triangular derby series lies in the clubs' names.

The 12,000-capacity ground, the Estadio Municipal La Cisterna, was in a dusty suburb of the city, a far cry from the bustling Ñuñoa neighbourhood where I was staying. The area was flat, offering views of the snow-capped Andes in the distance. The bowl-shaped ground was also flat, fitting in with the surroundings. It was a modest ground and only 1,000 spectators attended the Monday evening game. I assumed they were all still on holiday.

Los Árabes went behind early on but by the 33rd minute were 2-1 up. There were no more goals, but it was an entertaining, energetic *clásico*. The fact that it had been a good game was a bonus, but again I wasn't there for the football match itself. Rather, I was keen to see a team and club who had gained notoriety over the past few years. First and foremost I was intrigued by the name. Founded by Palestinian immigrants in the southern city of Osorno, the club started its life in the southern amateur leagues. Thirty-two years later, in 1952, they were integrated into the new, professional second tier of Chilean football and had now moved to the Chilean capital. They won the Segunda División (then the second tier but now the third tier of Chilean *fútbol*) and were promoted to the Primera. Professionalism forced the club to scout players from outside the Palestinian community, which up until then had served them well.

Sixty-six years in the Primera División have harvested two league titles (1955 and 1978), as well as three Copa Chiles, the latest having been won in 2018. The club has a modest title haul, but has been on the up in recent years, with regular appearances in both the Copa Libertadores and Sudamericana since 2015. But their white, green and red kits stirred up controversy with the numbering used on the back.

From the turn of the millennium, the club has had a lot of support from the Middle East, with their games being broadcast on many sports channels across the Arabic world. Palestino have visited the Palestinian territories and refugee camps, playing games against the West Bank Premier League champions as well as the national team of Palestine. In 2014 Palestinian leader Mahmud Abbas called Palestino the 'second Palestinian national team for a Palestinian people'.

Around the same time, the club changed the No. 1 on their kits to show the outline of Palestine as she was before 1947 (when the UN Partition Plan for Palestine was approved). The historical outline of the country lends itself perfectly to replace the No. 1 and players wearing shirts No. 1, 10, 11, etc. would be showing their solidarity with the Palestinian cause. However, it was to the consternation of those who spout the cliché that 'football and politics shouldn't mix'. The shirts with this numbering were banned from the pitch, but replicas were still sold in the tiny club shop. They all had the No. 11 on the back. I had to get one.

Three games down, one to go. Four games in a month in Chile was a modest haul in terms of groundhopping. Throughout my time in Chile I was in contact with a Dane who put my groundhopping commitment to shame. Nicolai was backpacking around South America. In six months he visited 65 grounds. When I finally met him back in Buenos Aires a month later, I was ticking off only my 65th ground. I realised then I was an amateur.

There was one last ground I wanted to visit. It was my 31st birthday and The Arsenal were playing Chelsea in the Premier League. I had met a Chilean Gooner in Argentina, watching Arsenal beat Liverpool a couple of years before in a bar in Buenos Aires. Sebastian had a tattoo on his forearm of The Beatles at Abbey Road, and we got talking. We stayed in touch. He was from Santiago and we agreed to meet up to watch the Arsenal game with some beers before heading off to the Estadio Nacional Julio Martínez Prádanos. Club Universidad de Chile were hosting O'Higgins from Chilean Patagonia and, as a local, Seba would sort out the tickets.

The game ended 8-1 to the home side! A cracking *goleado*, which we wouldn't end up seeing. We had hoped to be able to get tickets online a few hours before the game, but failing that we wandered the few blocks to the ground. No tickets were sold at all on the day for security reasons and we were turned away whilst watching blue-clad home fans walking past us on their way to find their turnstile. Just 23,000 fans would get into the ground, which could hold 47,000. The rest were probably still on holiday.

Qué decepción! I had been to three grounds, each of which had history either in the crumbling stadium walls or in the fabric of the club's shirt. In some cases both. The Estadio Nacional was no different. During the 1962 World Cup in Chile, the stadium witnessed one of the most violent games of football ever seen. With 66,000 fans in attendance, Chile's 2-0 Group 2 victory over Italy was nicknamed the Battle of Santiago. The game kept English referee Ken Aston – who had fought in the Second World War – busy. Too busy, in fact. The official needed the help of armed police on three separate occasions to break up the fighting on the pitch. Aston expelled two Italian players and they finished the game with nine men. It was this game that inspired referee Aston to invent the yellow and red cards, which first saw daylight in the 1970 World Cup eight years later.

Eleven years later a different battle was being fought in Santiago. On 11 September 1973, democratically elected socialist President Salvador Allende was toppled in a CIA-backed coup d'état. Army General Augusto Pinochet – in coalition with the air force, navy and police force – led an attack on the Presidential Palace, La Moneda. Cooped up inside, Allende refused to step down. At 10.15am on 11 September, barricaded in his office with two machine guns, three rocket launchers and a handgun given to him by Fidel Castro, Allende gave a final speech to the Chilean people: 'This will surely be the last opportunity I have to address you. The air force have bombed the towers of Radio Postales and Radio Corporación. Surely Radio Magallanes will be silenced, and the quiet metal of my voice will no longer reach you. It does not matter. My words don't contain bitterness, only disappointment. May they be a moral punishment for those who betrayed their oath … I will not resign! I will pay back the people's loyalty with my life … These are my last words, and I am sure my sacrifice will not be in vain. I am sure that, at least, it will be a moral lesson which will punish the crime, the cowardice and the treason.'

Hawker Hunter planes, tanks and snipers surrounded La Moneda. Allende committed suicide in his office. Pinochet ruled the country for the next 17 years. Democracy died with Allende and a brutal repression and persecution of political dissidents and potential subversives followed. The stadium, which was (and still is) home to *la selección chilena* and Universidad de Chile, was used to detain suspected subversives with torture chambers set up on site. Within a week, 7,000 Chileans and 250 foreign nationals were held at the stadium and 40,000 were said to have passed through Estadio Nacional.

For ten weeks the stadium was used for this terrifying purpose. Prisoners were placed on the terraces with the guards watching over them. To keep spirits up, detainees would scream *GOOOL* whenever the groundsman pushed his lawnmower between the posts and over the goal line.

The pitch was being prepared for a World Cup qualifying match. CONMEBOL qualifying for Germany 1974 saw eight teams split into three groups. Brazil qualified as 1970 champions and Venezuela had been banned by FIFA for 'irregularities', leaving two groups of three and one group of two. Grupo 3 consisted solely of Chile and Perú after Venezuela's exclusion. Perú won the first Pisco derby 2-0 in Lima's Estadio Nacional. Chile won their home game at Santiago's Estadio Nacional two weeks later. A play-off before the play-off was needed. Chile beat Perú 2-1 in Montevideo, Uruguay.

Two weeks after the coup, Chile travelled to Moscow and played out a 0-0 draw against the 1970 quarter-finalists.

Chile had gone from being a socialist country and friend of the USSR to becoming a fascist dictatorship overnight. Tensions were high and the Chilean players were unsure of what to expect upon landing in Moscow. There is no television footage, no radio coverage nor photographs from the game as no journalists were invited to cover it. Only player testimonies – Russian and Chilean alike – attest to an onslaught from the home team. The USSR had already decided that they weren't going to travel to Chile for the second leg and wanted a 3-0 win in the home leg, knowing Chile would be awarded a 2-0 walkover home victory. The Chilean defence stood firm and kept them out.

The second leg was scheduled for 21 November but, despite the 0-0 draw in the first leg, the USSR still refused to play the game. 'We will not play on a pitch stained with the blood of Chilean patriots.' FIFA sent delegates to inspect the stadium but 'only seemed interested in the condition of the pitch'. By now, most detainees had been moved to a detention centre in the Atacama Desert in northern Chile, but some remained in the ground. Prisoners said they had seen the delegates. They shouted to the inspectors, but FIFA's report stated that life in Chile was 'back to normal' after the military coup.

The game had to go ahead, with or without the opposition. Somewhat ironically, it would be without opposition as the Soviets opposed what was happening to Pinochet's opponents. So, 17,000 spectators entered the stadium and saw 11 Chilean players running on to the pitch alone and waving to the crowd. They took their positions to start the game. Luckily the home team were awarded the kick-off (anything else would have been inconvenient for FIFA) and *La Roja* walked the ball into the back of the

Soviet net. It would have been a good team goal, ten mostly one-touch passes (a hint of offside for each pass), had it not been for the lack of opposition.

And had it not been for the blood of the political opponents in the stands. Forty-one people died in the stadium complex according to official records. Nearly 50 years later a section of the stand at Gate 8 is left untouched, identical to how it looked back in 1973 during the first days and weeks of Chile's last military dictatorship. With paint peeling from the concrete, a few rows of wooden benches are fenced off with the words: '*Un pueblo sin memoria es un pueblo sin futuro*' – 'A people without memory is a people without a future'. It's a powerful dedication to the 41 lives lost and thousands detained and tortured at Estadio Nacional. Had it not been for the farce of the World Cup play-off second leg, many more would have lost their lives at the stadium. They most probably met the same fate in their new detention centre.

The Estadio Chile, an indoor arena used for futsal, as well as other indoor sports, was also used for the detention of opponents. The folk singer Víctor Jara, who was a member of the Communist Party and had antagonised right-wing conservatives with his socialist songs for years, was one of the first political activists detained. He was tortured at the arena and shot 40 times in one of the changing rooms. The stadium's name was changed to Estadio Víctor Jara in 2003.

The Estadio Nacional Julio Martínez Prádanos (named after a sports journalist who died in 2008) saw Chile's first international trophy success when *La Roja* hosted the 2015 Copa América. 'JM' would have loved to have been commentating on the final. Facing Argentina in the final, the game ended 0-0, and with Argentina having missed two of their first three penalties in the shoot-out, Alexis Sánchez went forward to Panenka his winning penalty past the *albiceleste* goalkeeper, Sergio Romero. Chile's golden generation had a trophy to boast about.

A year later the same two teams met in the 2016 Centenary edition of the Copa América, inexplicably held in the US. Again the final finished 0-0 and penalties were needed. And again Chile won the shoot-out and were crowned champions for a second time in two years and for only the second time in their history.

My visit to Chile came in between these two trophies when Chilean football was at its zenith ... After a month in the country it was time to leave. I arrived at the bus terminal an hour early and sat down to have some *medialunas* and coffee. There was the normal movement of people and noises of all sorts. I tried to find a quiet area to relax before the 20-hour return journey. Ten minutes before the coach was due to leave, I went to find the platform. I had been blissfully unaware of the cancellation of most of the buses leaving the Terminal Alameda that Wednesday morning. There had been a huge landslide on the same border crossing as a month earlier when I had entered the country. The early prognosis was a 48-hour wait but it could be a lot longer, they said. I had to get back for the new school year starting after the weekend. I went to find the bus company's booth and found the tail of a long queue.

The girl in front of me was from Switzerland. I asked her briefly whether she had any information, but she had just been told to get in the queue for a refund. She had already decided to rush off to the airport and was buying a flight on her phone as she waited in the queue. I decided to tag along. In a worst-case scenario, I could just return to the city and spend another few days.

Arriving at the airport 90 minutes before the KLM flight to Buenos Aires was due to depart got my heart racing. Normally I would get there much earlier. I still had to get a ticket and I joined another queue. My card wouldn't work at the counter. But there were ATMs. I rushed over to that corner of the airport. No cash available. There were now three more people in the queue. Would there be any tickets left? It was taking a long time and the next queue for security was getting longer, too.

The Swiss girl was near the front of the queue snaking slowly towards airside. 'Have you bought a ticket?' she asked. I told her my card didn't work and that I had no cash. Without having known me for more than an hour, she handed me 100,000 Chilean pesos (£100). I gave her my email address in case I couldn't get a flight. But luckily, I did! It took another 20 minutes and now I only had 40 minutes to get to the gate. I had no other choice but to jump the security queue and run to the gate. I arrived at a deserted gate and ran down the ramp towards the plane. I was the very last person on. The contrast between my blood pressure and the atmosphere on the plane as I dashed on was so marked that I felt like a being from another planet or alternative dimension walking down the cabin.

When I found my seat, I saw the Swiss girl. I had been given the seat next to her. We asked for a Heineken from the stewardess and chatted throughout the two-hour flight. The next day we went for dinner in Buenos Aires. To repay her trust in me and the loan, the least I could do was act as a guide for a couple of days.

A short excursion to Excursionistas

I HAD been struggling to learn Spanish. My month in Chile had only increased my frustrations. I regularly felt like a four-year-old child listening to a discussion about politics, stunned into silence at the complexity of the conversation. I was disappointed and embarrassed that it was taking me so long to get anywhere with the language. It was advancing, but slowly. And I definitely didn't feel confident having conversations with random people, unless it was about football. Somehow, I managed to get by talking about football. I was now entering my third year in Argentina and finally things would begin to fall into place, and I could begin talking about other topics.

Not that I wanted to talk about other things. One thing I felt was needed was to find a football team of locals who I could play with, have beers with and talk football with. For two years I had been playing 'pick-up' games with foreigners. English was inevitably the language of choice. But with time I got to know more people and was asked to join an 11-a-side team made up of people from all over the continent – Chileans, Colombians, Peruvians, Venezuelans, a couple of Argentines – as well as a couple of Europeans who already spoke the language fluently. Finding a team of locals wasn't easy, but one that exclusively spoke Spanish would do the trick.

The standard of football was decent and I was excited to be playing proper, full-scale football again after two years of only playing five- or six-a-side. The league our team, Internacional, had entered was played at the ground of a fourth-tier team called Excursionistas. The pitch was in Belgrano, close to China Town, three blocks from the school where I worked but, more importantly, walking distance from the flat I was renting. Playing in a semi-professional ground with concrete terracing, tall fences and barbed wire added to the anticipation. Naturally, the green-and-white seats were empty but for a couple of girlfriends who came along to watch. I got the impression that the girlfriends were there to keep tabs on their partner rather than to watch the football, but that was just a hunch. Maybe it was the other way around.

Playing football in Argentina was definitely a culture shock. As was to be expected, having seen the way South Americans play in the big leagues and in the Champions League, there was a different intensity to their game. The locals never took their foot off the gas; it was 100 mph, 100 per cent of the time. They really lived the game. Unfortunately, their game did involve a lot of histrionics, too. I have only ever received two red cards in my playing 'career', despite enjoying the physical side of the game. The first red, in Oslo, was for a handball on the goal line where I had run behind our goalkeeper to try to block a shot, the ball inadvertently hitting my arm. It was certainly *not* a Luiz Suárez versus Ghana type of intervention. My second dismissal came at Excursionistas when their winger conned the referee into believing I had elbowed him in the face.

I was playing left-back. On our team there was a clear divide between the Latin Americans and the northern Europeans. It was obvious who fancied themselves as attackers and strikers and those who didn't mind filling in as defenders. I was already annoyed at missing Manchester City versus Arsenal, which was being played at the same time as our Sunday early afternoon kick-off. As their right-winger played the ball down the line, I put my arm across his chest to slow him down. Naïvely. There was no swing of my left arm and certainly no explosive impact to his body, that could explain the flop to the artificial turf, arms flailing. The screaming was embarrassing. Platoon, sniper in the empty stands, etc. I was shown a red card. I could have stood there remonstrating with the referee, but I knew it was hopeless. For the histrionics to work at all, the referees have to buy into the culture and either ignore the utterly pathetic behaviour of an adult or play along and be part of its drama. Even a 12-year-old watching WWE wrestling knows it's all a lie, but they get really into it. Referees at this modest level (all levels) must consciously evaluate cheating and decide that these conniving practices are part of the entertainment. And the word entertainment is used very lightly in our case, especially as there were only about eight people watching our games, mostly either oppressed or distrusting girlfriends.

Whilst I might not have got many red cards, I did get several yellows, often for poorly articulating to the referee that there were zero people in the crowd there to watch him. It never went down well, but it was always paramount to make that fact clear. It was, nonetheless, good practice for my Spanish. Had the referee not understood me, he wouldn't have booked me.

I hated the cheating. A younger, more stubborn me would have stayed as long as I could to show how hard done by I felt. But I was older and wiser, and to some extent it was for me to accept their footballing culture, right? However much I disagreed with it, I had chosen to live there and play their *fútbol*. The red card and figurative 'early shower' allowed me to grab a litre-bottle of beer and sit and watch the Arsenal game in the little pitchside café/ bar under the main stand whilst my team-mates fought out the second half.

Playing *fútbol* was an interesting cultural experience. There were entertaining language barriers: shouting *man on!* on a pitch with Spanish speakers invariably sees most stop dead in their tracks. Handball in Spanish is *mano* and every handball is given, regardless of how, where and why. The classic Sunday league concept of 'time' (an example of ellipsis where the full version equates to 'you have a great deal of time on the ball young sir/madam, please make the right decision') also sees most players stop dead in their tracks. It will be interpreted as time's up, game over.

When we Europeans use words to express ourselves on the pitch, South Americans use noises. It took me a few months to accept the noises coming from a player wanting the ball. I would hear mouths clicking as if I were a dog or horse, or kissing noises as if a Jamaican Londoner was disapproving of something said. While I was speaking English or trying to speak Spanish, it sounded like everyone else was communicating in a long-lost African tribal language.

After a few months of putting up with these noises during games played at the 7,000-capacity Estadio de Excursionistas, a group of us decided we should go to watch a game there. Seeing as I lived close, we had a little *previa* at my flat. There were six of us – English, Irish and Dutch – in the big, open front room. By now I was living alone, having first shared with an American former colleague of mine who got kicked out, before a Swedish girl had made my flat her home.

Fanny had found me on an expat group on social media. I had posted a picture of a handwritten note in the entrance of our building. It stated, with all the authority a handwritten note can muster, that the building's gas had been cut off. Fanny saw the message and sent me a message. It had nothing to do with gas or heating of any kind, but saying she had just arrived in the city, and using the Scandinavian link, she suggested getting a beer.

It was the end of the Buenos Aires winter. It can get very cold in the city. A humid 10°C is too cold a temperature in which to be having cold showers. It wasn't a fun time, but my work fixed a temporary solution: an electric shower. It was a bucket in which, once filled, the water is heated like a kettle. About five minutes' of hot water was the result. It was good enough. But it wasn't something a child could be trusted to operate. It was exactly this that finally led to my American housemate having to move out. He had turned the electric water butt on to have a shower. Either he had forgotten or changed his mind about showering, but he left the flat without switching the contraption off. When I came home in the early hours of the morning after some beers with Fanny, I slipped on the wet bathroom floor. The 20 litres of water had been boiling for several hours and the bathroom had become a steam room. There was no water left to evaporate and had I not come home when I did the shower would have caught fire. I was seething. The Yank could have burned the whole building down.

Metrogas was the name of the infamous company operating many buildings in Buenos Aires. They had a reputation for cutting off people's gas for extended periods of time and there were rumours that a little bribe was all it took for them to turn the right key to let the gas flow again. I had been told that it was common for people who were moving out of a block of flats to report the smell of gas in the building as a way to inconvenience former neighbours they might not have got along with. Unfortunately, everyone else in the building would be victims of these petty feuds happening throughout the city. Metrogas would cut the gas to the whole building before investigating. It could take over a year before the gas was turned on again. So infamous are Metrogas that people won't even report a problem even when there is one. 'Wait until summer' to report the smell of gas, someone else advised. It was too late; we were now without gas. We had to cook on a small electric cooker, and shower with an appliance that I didn't fully trust nor trust my housemate to use capably.

A couple of days after chatting online, Fanny and I met for dinner. That was Sunday. On Monday she had moved in. It was a temporary arrangement while she found a new place to rent. She had only just arrived from Sweden and was staying in a hostel that wasn't up to her standards. The Yank and I had loads of room and I had blurted out that she was welcome to stay. She wasn't my first Swede. Patrik had stayed with us for a few weeks at the start of the year (although he had slept on the sofa).

Patrik was another excellent footballer I had met at the five-a-side pitches. Typically laid back with a cheeky smile, we had a good connection on and off the pitch. And much like French Guillaume, Patrik led a nomadic existence, playing poker online, only entering tournaments when he needed to add funds to his travel budget. Living the expat life, one often met really cool people, characters with special personalities to spend time with, only to see them disappear as quickly as they had appeared.

Maybe Fanny was a way of replacing Patrik. She ended up staying from Monday to Sunday while looking for a flat to rent. We were now seeing each other, and she would come over regularly. That was until she fell out with her landlord six weeks later. The Yank had moved out and I said she could move in.

The relationship didn't last very long from that point on. But Fanny had already invited her parents to use the flat when they were visiting. I was now living with a Swedish girl who I had had a short fling with and subsequently broken up with, but she seemed to have no intention of finding a new place to stay. After her parents left, I asked her to leave too. She collected her things when I was at work and I never saw her again.

With the flat to myself again, I could have who I wanted over. It was late November and the summer had definitely arrived, so a few beers on the balcony were in order before heading down to Estadio de Excursionistas. It was a local derby against Platense. Five kilometres separated the two humble clubs in the northern part of the city. This game had been on my list for a while. We didn't want to go to any *Excursio* game. A fixture between two clubs from the same part of town would make it more interesting, even if there were no away fans.

Platense had always appealed to me because a former student of mine supported them. Guido was the one positive kid who was always smiling in a class full of depressed and depressing 13- and 14-year-olds. This young sunbeam made my job a little easier. He was now a young man I could have beers with while chatting about football. Platense stood out as one of the few teams who wore brown, as well as being where David Trézéguet, curiously, took his first footballing strides. They were also so close to where I lived that it was near the top of the list of teams to visit before leaving the country. But for now, Platense would be the away team, Excursionistas would be hosts.

There were about 1,000 people in the main stand, with another 500 dotted around the other sections. It was fun to see the ground with spectators for once, albeit far from full. The club and its supporters had the reputation of being a bit sketchy, even though the ground was located amongst some excessively expensive real estate in the rich part of Buenos Aires. Most lower league clubs tended to have the same reputation.

A famous Spanish documentary from 2012 about Argentina's *barra bravas* starts at Excursionistas. It begins with the Canal+ host interviewing a sword-wielding fan showing his moves to the camera. Akin to a six-year-old playing out their Teenage Mutant Ninja Turtles fantasies, but being a grown man, the video is a bit unnerving. This *barra* is clearly unhinged and desperate for the attention of the camera. And probably desperate for any money he might have received for his appearance. For the production team, it's TV gold. They were grateful for Alejandro *Chiquitona* Flores. But the interview was cut short after *Chiquitona* took out a loaded gun and pointed it – in a dramatisation – at the presenter. 'He was uncontrollable. And continued to talk without even one coherent sentence about football and passion,' the narrator explained. They interviewed him at just the right time; a week later he was found murdered in his flat. Even though *Chiquitona* wouldn't be at the game we were attending, we were a little apprehensive about what to expect from Excursionistas.

We certainly weren't expecting a good game, we never really were in Argentina. It was interesting watching better players playing on the same pitch we had played on many times. The pitch seemed much smaller. It seemed much tighter with players moving quickly and organised from side to side to press the ball. That seemed obvious. What wasn't immediately obvious was the reasoning behind the colours on display. Never again would I be exposed to such a ridiculous ensemble. Excursionistas, traditionally green and white, lined up in a purple away shirt with green shorts and white socks. Platense, went for light brown shirts, with dark brown shorts and socks.

Once we had recovered from the catwalk disaster that was the teams entering the pitch, we settled down to enjoy the anthropological masterpiece unfolding in front of us. Some 80 per cent of the game was spent people watching rather than paying attention to the action being played out on the pitch. Behind us and seemingly on his own, there was a nine-year-old child wearing the green of *Excursio*. As people were walking in and out of the toilets below him, he would slyly spit down. He didn't seem to be watching the game. Sending a little ball of spit towards an unsuspecting victim, he had found his entertainment for the afternoon. Seeing something landing in front of them, some would look up, but he was already looking out towards the action, feigning his interest in the game. Credit where it's due, he was quite good at it. And brave. I wouldn't have wanted to bring unwanted attention unto myself from the people in that crowd.

Spitting was obviously part of the game here. A group of four mothers standing by their prams were next. At pitch level there was a two-metre-wide walkway between the fenced-off pitch and the ten levels of concrete steps that made up the terracing. These lactating ladies were chatting to each other, rocking their prams occasionally, until the play came towards our end of the pitch. That's when the fearsome four sprang into action. They would leave their buggies unattended to run to the fence and spit at the linesman. Several times this happened before one of them hit her target, receiving high-fives from her *compañeras*.

The Argentinian matchday experience was just as much about watching the crowd as watching the game. I had missed large chunks of the match, but at least we had been treated to three goals, one of which came for the home team, providing the home roar we had hoped for.

After this third division match, the crowd flocked off home and left the *gradas* empty for our next match. I played a few more games for Internacional de Buenos Aires, the last of which came in December. The summer had most definitely arrived, and temperatures were soaring. We had been scheduled to play at midday in 35°C heat. It was punishing. Whenever the ball went out of play or a player was down injured (which seemed to happen a lot), I would walk over to the shadow cast by the floodlights. Even 60 seconds of respite in the shade helped, but I finished the game feeling unwell. I got home with a terrible heat rash on my legs and a pounding headache. It was bad timing because I had a Brazilian friend coming over to stay the night. There wasn't much left in the tank that evening.

The next week we had another early-afternoon kick-off but refused to play, asking the league to reschedule for an evening. Playing in that heat and humidity wasn't worth it.

La Paz: the gringo trail

AFTER MORE than three years in Buenos Aires, I decided that it was time to leave. I had spent the last three years working hard, earning a local salary, yet seeing my students and the backpackers I came across in the city's gringo network travelling far and wide. I had got to know Buenos Aires and her inhabitants well and had fallen in love with both. But I was restless, knowing what the rest of the continent had to offer.

Teaching English online gave me the chance to get extra classes and save money. By the start of 2017 I was ready to see more of South America. I wanted to move to Medellín in Colombia. So many good things had been said about the city from the backpackers I had met. Nobody had a bad word to say, it seemed. But I wasn't going to fly directly between Buenos Aires and Medellín – there was so much in between I wanted to see. I budgeted a month or two in each of Bolivia, Perú and Ecuador on my way to Colombia. It would give me a chance to travel slowly. The gringo trail, as it's known, is a very well-trodden path, but there are a lot of gems if you have time to stray off it.

A common backpacker's mistake in South America is the time/distance-optimism. In four to five months the majority can tick off a lot of the biggest, most famous sites. Upload a picture to social media and consider it *done*. This is how I travelled back in 2009. Yes, a lot can be seen and done in a short space of time and not everyone has several months to travel freely. But when do you have time to reflect on what you're experiencing? Do you take time to read about the sites you have visited? What about just sitting in a café or restaurant (or food court in a marketplace) and talking to the locals or even just people watching? These were the things I wanted from my second backpacking trip in South America, having experienced the first way. I had time, I had enough money saved up and I wanted to experience the true *América del Sur*. In the places where I felt at home, I would stay longer. In the places where there wasn't much *onda* (vibe), I could move on.

My first stop, however, was Bolivia. Having sorted out some visa issues in Buenos Aires and paid the fine for overstaying my tourist visa, I found my seat on the long-distance bus headed north. Thirty-six hours later, the coach arrived on the Bolivian border and the town of Villazón. The journey was *only* supposed to take 24 hours, but a landslide in the northern province of Jujuy kept us from progressing for another 12. It was just a case of sitting and waiting. I got off the bus and stepped into the desert landscape and the dry, 35°C heat to stretch my legs, but would never last more than five minutes at a time. I had nothing against sitting and waiting in the air-conditioned bus. What I enjoyed about being on these long-distance journeys was being forced to relax. In order to save battery on my mobile, flight mode was on, so there was no needless swiping on the phone's screen to keep me entertained. Besides, there was no phone signal to be had in the desert.

The train could have been an alternative. I had heard of a train going from Buenos Aires to Tucumán in the north of the country. I looked into the prospect of making this the first part of my journey. The tickets were ridiculously cheap but, counterintuitively, it would take longer than the bus. Argentinian trains are probably not as comfortable, anyway. The coaches are not the same third-class journey we took from the UK to Italy on a school ski trip back in 2001. The long-distance *micros* in Argentina serve whisky, albeit cheap whisky – pronounced *wiki* – and the seats recline beyond that of an economy seat on an aeroplane.

Getting a train ticket would involve queueing one morning several months before the journey at a ticket office somewhere in the centre of town. Tickets couldn't be bought online. I got the impression it was like queueing for centre court seats at Wimbledon, people camping the night before. It was a train that served poorer communities when they wanted to travel to their hometowns in the Andean north of Argentina, or maybe beyond that further into Bolivia, the same trip I had hoped to make. I gave up on the train without really trying and resigned myself to taking the bus.

Unfortunately, trains in Argentina have been allowed to go into such a state of disrepair that they are not a viable option when travelling around the country. Argentina is the world's eighth largest country in terms of area and the landscape is mostly flat. Trains would serve the country so well. Compare the landscape to those of Bolivia, Perú, Ecuador and Colombia, for example, where a train network would be prohibitively expensive.

The British constructed most of the nearly 30,000 miles of railways from the mid-1800s. The network was nationalised and privatised several times before Perón – an

Anglophile – brought it back under government control. After his death, and during the anti-Perón military dictatorship of 1976–1983, the train network was deliberately sabotaged by the junta. They ripped up thousands of kilometres of tracks so that trains would never be able to run again. According to Daniel Tunnard, an English expat who wrote a book called *Trainspotting on the Argentine Railways* (as well as a novel about Scrabble), there were 25,000 miles of tracks at the start of military rule, yet just 15,000 miles seven years later. Today, there are some networks that work well enough, but these are mostly in the city of Buenos Aires and her conurbation than nationwide.

The old railway network influenced Argentinian football. Many of the clubs in the city of Buenos Aires started at or close to a train station. Many clubs were created by the workers of the railways. Some even carry the name of the company, such as Ferro Carril Oeste. Comparing groundhoppers to trainspotters, we are not too dissimilar – maybe the groundhopping subculture should be renamed 'groundspotting'? Would it sound less cool?

I'd had a lot of time to think on the bus journey. With football on my mind, I walked over the Argentinian-Bolivian border at La Quiaca and reboarded the bus for another five-minute drive to the town of Villazón. Uyuni was meant to be my next stop, but I had just missed the last bus of the day. Buses were still going to the town of Potosí, but I would have to wait three hours. I was flexible and I was in no rush. Which is just as well because I had a seven-hour journey ahead of me.

I arrived in Potosí 48 hours after leaving Buenos Aires. I was keen to find a hostel and relax. There was a lot to see and do in the historic town, but first I wanted to rest.

The first people I ended up hanging out with were three Argentines who worked in the Casa Blanca hostel. We sat drinking yerba mate and I was getting a lot of good inside tips on the town and the country as a whole.

I also met a German from Dresden. Torsten was a Sankt Pauli fan and that immediately piqued my interest. I didn't really know much about the club, only that they had a cult following for their political leanings and activism. We chatted a lot about football but suddenly he had to leave; he was off to watch a game. I had only been in the country a few hours and was still acclimatising to the 4,000-metre altitude. I hadn't yet even thought about local games to catch. But he was off to a game now and if I wanted to tag along, I was welcome.

We were off to see Nacional Potosí. Arriving at their Estadio Víctor Agustín Ugarte, I thought I had been transported straight back to Buenos Aires. The club badge was identical to that of Club Atlético River Plate. Plagiarism is a feature of South American football. Badges, kits and even names are copied across the continent. Ecuadorian Barcelona SC from Guayaquil use an almost identical FC Barcelona badge, complete with the English Saint George and the Catalan flag, and the *blaugrana* stripes beneath the two. Their home kit, however, is yellow. There is an Everton in Chile, a Liverpool in Uruguay, an Arsenal in Argentina. Moreover, in Argentina, the top teams have copies further down the Argentinian pyramid. It can get a little confusing.

Nacional Potosí and their neighbours Real Potosí are two such examples. While Nacional have ripped off River Plate's badge and kit down to a tee, Real have a logo based on that of Real Madrid, as well as purple and white home kits, reversing the white and purple of the Spanish giants.

Milling around outside the 30,000-seater municipal stadium, we watched the fans arriving. The ticket cost no more than 20 bolivianos (£2.50), although on the ticket the price was listed as 10Bs. The thin air and bus-lag from the journey suffocated any strong sense of injustice I felt. There would be plenty more instances of paying the infamous gringo tax along the gringo trail and lots of opportunities to complain. It gave me a good chance to practise my Spanish, anyway.

We took our seats on the concrete steps of the Curva Sur as a *chola* lady walked past selling popcorn. She had two tightly weaved braids flowing down her back, typical of the indigenous people. Equally typical were the black dress and bowler hat she wore. Her dark skin was weathered by the harsh environment: the cold, the strong sun, the lack of air and a tough life. It was impossible to tell whether the little girl following her was her daughter or granddaughter.

There were only about 1,000 people in the ground. The 29,000 empty seats revealed a Bolivian flag painted on to the seats in the main stand, which normally would have been covered by backsides. Unsurprisingly, as with so many of the games I had already attended in South America, this game ended 0-0. Two mouths yawning in Bolivia. As you might expect of the Bolivian top division, the quality was low. On this occasion, maybe the altitude can take some of the blame. But then the home team should be acclimatised. The opponents, Jorge Wilstermann, come from a city called Cochabamba, which has an altitude of 2,500m. It's not an insignificant altitude, but certainly more comfortable than 4,000m. And maybe more conducive to playing football.

There are several clubs in South America named after important people. Jorge Wilstermann was a *cochabambino* and was Bolivia's first commercial pilot. Initially the club – created by workers of the aviation company Lloyd Aéreo Boliviano in 1949 – were called Club Deportivo LAB. But four years later the name was changed to bear the name of the company's and the city's prodigious son who had died in 1936 in a plane crash, aged just 25. The city's international airport is also named after him.

Only six months after seeing Jorge Wilstermann – the club – playing in Potosí, I watched them again on TV. In the Copa Libertadores quarter-final first leg, they recorded a stunning 3-0 home win against Nacional Potosí's badge-sakes River Plate. The return leg didn't quite go to plan, however. River came out on top, winning 8-0 to go through 8-3 on aggregate. Former Sunderland striker Ignacío Scocco scored five, the first three of which were within 19 minutes to level the tie on aggregate. (River, in the semis, would charge into a 2-0 lead away to Lanús from southern Buenos Aires, only to lose the first leg 4-2. They won 1-0 at home but went out. Lanús then lost twice in the two-legged final to Brazilians Grêmio, 1-0 away, 1-2 at home.)

At altitude, the footballing cliché of 'a shot that stays hit' has more credence than it would otherwise have. A shot from 30 yards (or any yardage, for that matter) isn't subject to as much resistance as there is less oxygen in the air, and the velocity is maintained for longer. The ball is lighter and doesn't move as much. It might be like playing football on the moon (time will tell). However, in this very worldly game, shots that stayed hit only hit Row Z. Only one of the 15 speculative long-distance shots hit the target, confirming that shooting from range in and of itself isn't enough, despite the supposed advantages of playing at altitude. We realised early on that we were in for a goalless draw.

People watching became a viable alternative. The crowd was mostly *mestizo* or indigenous and everyone was chewing on coca leaves. Once the game had finished, I went straight to the market to buy myself some. Chewing the leaves helps your body deal with the altitude. I figured that if the locals, whose bodies have evolved to adapt to living at altitude, need coca leaves, then I definitely did. I grabbed 15 of the leaves out of the big bag and a pinch of baking soda. The bicarbonate of soda activates the coca alkaloids, and without it the effect is fairly limited. After a while I noticed that the side of my mouth and my tongue went slightly numb. Whilst cocaine comes from coca leaves, chewing the leaves provides no high other than a slight rush similar to caffeine. It also helps with oxygen circulation in your bloodstream, amongst other things.

I would need the oxygen circulating. Potosí is a hilly town. I was quickly out of breath exploring the pretty streets. It was a charming town. But with the already oxygen-less air being polluted by buses spewing out a thick, black smoke, breathing was doubly hard.

The town is most famous, historically, for the Cerro Rico hill, or *Sumaq Urqu* in the indigenous Quechua language. The translation of the two names gives an indication of two very different cultures and worlds: the Spanish *Cerro Rico* translates as 'rich mountain', whereas the Quechuan name would translate as 'beautiful mountain'. For the Spanish occupiers, the silver mined here would fund their empire in Bolivia, neighbouring Andean countries and back in Europe, empowering their king, their banks, and providing wealth for generations to come. For the local indigenous populations, the mountain was holy, a part of the goddess of the earth, Pachamama, and subsequently of farming, fertility, crops and harvests. She was to be respected and protected.

Whilst having written a wonderful football book, Uruguayan Eduardo Galeano is most revered for his book about the colonial history of Latin America. *The Open Veins of Latin America (Five Centuries of The Pillage of a Continent)* was published in 1971. Galeano estimates that up to eight million people died working as slaves in the mines at Cerro Rico. It was the 'mountain that ate men'. Legend has it that so much silver was taken from the mountain that a bridge made entirely of the sought-after metal could be made linking Potosí with the Spanish capital 5,750 miles away. This is chillingly countered by locals, who say that a bridge made entirely of the bones of the people who died mining the silver could be made coming back the other way. Picture a bridge in the off-white of the silver, shining guiltily, pretending not to be dirty, whilst the glorious and true bright white of the bone shamefully marks the tragedy of the building of both bridges. It was an image that stuck in my mind.

At the time of Spanish rule and at the height of the silver mining at Potosí (throughout the 16th century), the city was estimated to be home to some 200,000 people. Potosí was as big as London at the time. Due to the altitude, however, most of the Spanish arriving to the area would settle in nearby Sucre. At an altitude of just under 3,000m, the air was still thin but, comparatively, Sucre was a much more comfortable place to live. The colonial architecture on display in the city shows where some wealth ended up going.

Today, there is no more silver in Cerro Rico/Sumaq Urqu. Yet the mines are still full of workers looking for tin and other metals. A part of their income comes from tourism and I signed myself up for a tour of the mines. I wasn't sure whether this was an ethical excursion. On the surface, it was similar to the 'people safaris' I had lamented in Rio de Janeiro. We were going to visit a historic site but also gawp at locals grafting down a mine. They were a people who had a very tough life and a low life expectancy. I asked travellers who had been in the region longer than me, and those who had been to similar places, but found no definitive answers. I signed myself up.

The mine guide was a very charismatic local and had been recommended to us by one of the Argentines working in the hostel. I was both edgy and excited about going down into the belly of the beast, into a mountain that eats men and whose collapse has long been predicted. The mountain's peak drops a few inches every year. It's only a matter of time, they say.

My disquiet was compounded as the guide was handing out the protective equipment we had to use. I was handed a miner's suit, a headtorch, goggles and a helmet with the number 33 on it. Up until that point I had never been one for superstition but maybe time spent in Argentina increased my belief in the occult. I had recently seen the film about the Chilean miners. Thirty-three people had been trapped underground for 69 days in 2010. The film was called *The 33*. I asked for a different helmet.

Entering the mine was terrifying. A ladder led us down into a tiny hole in the wall of the mountain. I was expecting to walk straight in, as if it were the entrance to a big, open cave. Once inside the mountain, it was rumbling as explosions were going off. The air was thinner still inside. We spent about 90 minutes in the mine's adits and tunnels, bumping into a few of the workers for whom we had bought coca leaves and alcohol as gifts. We visited and paid our respects to the devil who the miners had built a shrine for. His big, red, erect penis had been adorned by confetti. Empty beer bottles were strewn at his feet. Pachamama represented fertility but it had been the devil who had impregnated her to create this mountain, our guide explained.

Walking into a dead end, my claustrophobia reached a point where I started to feel uncomfortable. Nerves and caution were replaced by sweaty palms and a racing heart. But I was just visiting for the length of a football match. Locals had to spend their lives down here. It had been a humbling experience, but I was very pleased to see daylight and to get out of the mountain.

Before leaving Potosí, I wanted to visit the countryside. About 40 minutes from the town was a natural thermal pool called El Ojo del Inca. 'The Eye of the Inca' was a perfectly round pool surrounded by hills and where the Peruvian Inca Túpac Amaru spent time bathing in the summer. However, it was now closed. Only two weeks prior, two tourists had been sucked into the earth's core, never to resurface. That was enough to put me off thermal pools. The last couple of days had hammered home my dislike of being inside the planet when we thrive best on its surface.

I was enjoying the open skies above and I wasn't alone. Another backpacker – a French lady in her late 60s – had the same plan, so we joined forces to find the little lake together. As we walked around the thermal pools, we came across a group of Argentines who were camping. They had commandeered a swimming pool where the thermal waters had been channelled in. One couple were having sex in the pool, while the others drank their Fernet y Colas and talked loudly at the other end. It was all *Che boluda* this and *Ey loco* that – it made me reminisce about the country I had just left. I realised I already missed it. That was until we got closer. As I walked past with my 60-year-old travel companion for the day, a girl shouted, 'Ah, how sweet, he's travelling with his grandma!'

Having paid my respects to both Túpac Amaru and the two deceased tourists, and staved off the taunts of hippie Argentines, I was leaving for Sucre. I had my eye on an international fixture and had lots to squeeze in before getting to the Bolivian capital, La Paz.

Two and a half weeks later I met up with Torsten the German again. Our trips had taken slightly different directions but, like me, Torsten had also been aiming to be in the capital for the World Cup qualifier between Bolivia and Argentina. *La albiceleste* had found this fixture tricky before. Playing at altitude wasn't a breeze.

Infamously, at least from an Argentine's point of view, *la selección argentina* with Diego Armando Maradona as manager, lost 6-1 to *los altiplánicos* in La Paz. It was their joint biggest defeat, having lost 6-1 to Czechoslovakia at the 1958 World Cup in Sweden, and then again to Spain in a friendly building up to the 2018 World Cup in Russia.

Only a year before that heavy defeat in 2009, Maradona had visited the Estadio Hernando Siles for a charity match organised by Bolivia's first indigenous president, Evo Morales. FIFA had, throughout the 1990s and 2000s, threatened to ban games being played at altitude. Grounds above 2,500m or 3,000m wouldn't be able to host World Cup qualifiers or Copa América games according to the proposed new rules. Bolivia's national stadium was at 3,600m and the altitude was considered a significant home advantage.

The 2008 charity match was organised to raise money for 80,000 victims of a storm, La Niña. Evo Morales and Friends versus Diego Maradona and Friends allowed the two protagonists to show FIFA that playing at altitude was easy. Maradona, giving a speech before the game, said: 'You have to play where you were born. You can run here! Not even God can stop you from playing here, let alone [Sepp] Blatter.' He concluded by saying: 'We Argentinians are not scared of the altitude.' Thirteen months later, his Argentina crashed to a 6-1 loss in the Estadio Hernando Siles.

Playing at altitude was something that did make teams worry. I was panting just walking up the steep hills of the capital; I couldn't imagine playing football at an international level at nearly 4,000m above sea level. Daniel *El Káiser* Passarella, legendary Argentine defender and coach, said in 1997 as manager of Argentina: 'It's inhumane to play at altitude!' His team had recently lost 2-0 against Ecuador in Quito (2,800m) and they had a trip to La Paz at 3,600m coming up.

That game at Hernando Siles was on the verge of being abandoned in the dying minutes of the *eliminatoria* for the 1998 World Cup. With Argentina down to nine after a fractious encounter, the 22-year-old River Plate striker Julio Cruz went to retrieve the ball from the Bolivian bench. Cruz got into an altercation with the Bolivians and was punched with a left hook. The Bolivian coach then hid behind the military police, who had conveniently been watching the game from the wide running track, on hand if anything other than a football match were to kick off. All hell broke loose, with Argentinian players rushing over to get involved, pushing and shoving military police who had riot shields.

Their dark green uniforms were not too dissimilar to the green kits of the Bolivian national team.

A slain Julio Cruz was peeled off the ground by Argentinian backroom staff and carried into the changing room. The game eventually resumed with Argentina lining up with eight men for all of a minute before the Brazilian referee blew for full time. But the drama wasn't over yet.

The fallout is more stuff of legend from a continent famed – or *in*famed – for providing football stories. The Bolivian left hook landed on the debutant Cruz's right cheek. Footage shows Cruz holding the right side of his face with no marks whatsoever on the left cheek. However, once Cruz had been taken to the changing rooms and attended to by Argentina's medical staff, a cut appeared on his face – on his *left* cheek, close to his eye. The picture of Cruz laid flat out, blood pouring from his face, was plastered on the front page of newspapers across the continent. Conspiracy theories abounded, but Cruz denied any accusations.

On the front page of *El Gráfico* – Argentina's number one sports magazine – the image of Julio Cruz is accompanied by the title 'Qué bochorno', 'What an embarrassment'. Alongside the image of a bloody Cruz there was a list of bullet points detailing why they had lost:

- because we played badly
- because of our indiscipline
- because we remembered the altitude and forgot the football
- because of Bolivian aggression
- because worse than losing is not knowing how to lose

The Argentines were ashamed of their team's attitude, having received two red cards before their goalkeeper headbutted the Bolivian striker. The commentators watching the game live – unaware of what was to come seven minutes later – were lamenting the attitude of the already red-carded Zapata, who was rolling around on the floor feigning a Bolivian punch, and the goalkeeper Nacho González. The goalkeeper was lucky to escape reproach for his headbutt during the game but was suspended retrospectively and left out of the Argentina squad that travelled to France a year later.

The Julio Cruz incident was reminiscent of a similar, if not more dramatic, incident from a decade earlier. Brazil and Chile met in a World Cup qualifier in Estádio do Maracaná in September 1989. Chile had to win to have a chance of qualifying for the 1990 World Cup in Italy. With Brazil leading 1-0 in the 70th minute, time was running out for the Chileans. That's when a flare was thrown on to the pitch from behind the visitors' goal. The Chilean goalkeeper Roberto Rojas sensed his opportunity and threw himself to the floor holding his face. Whilst writhing around on the ground, he cut himself on the cheek with a razor blade he had hidden in his sock.

The Chilean players – and it's difficult to know how many were in on it – were indignant and insisted on carrying their bleeding team-mate from the field. They had signalled for a stretcher, but it wasn't forthcoming, so instead six players carried him. When the stretcher-bearers came on, they were pushed aside by the Chileans, who went straight down the steps into the underbelly of the stadium. Enough melodrama befitting of a Latin American *telenovela*.

Chile refused to continue the game and it was abandoned. They had hoped that the game would be awarded in their favour for the supposed attack on their goalkeeper, but they were found out. The game was awarded to Brazil 2-0, and Chile, therefore, had no hopes of qualifying for Italia '90 and were subsequently banned from the 1994 World Cup in the USA for their troubles. Rojas received a lifetime ban from football, which was pardoned in 2001 (once he was too old to play). He now works as a football coach in Brazil, apparently without any aggro for his crime. The infamous and shameful game is referred to as '*Maracanazo de la selección chilena*' or '*Bengalazo*' (flares are called *bengalas* in Spanish). Personally, I like the third nickname the best: *El Condorazo*, taken from Roberto Rojas's own alias *El Cóndor*.

The condor sat proudly on the Bolivians' chests as they ran out on to the Estadio Hernando Siles pitch in 2017. There was no such drama to expect from this World Cup qualifier, not on the pitch at least. Torsten and I met in town and wandered over to the ground. It was raining heavily, and the plastic poncho sellers delightedly took to the streets. Outside the ground, people were mingling in the rain, beer in hand, covered in plastic sheets of different colours. I went for a green one, Torsten yellow and his Northern Irish mate a blue one. Had we got hold of a red poncho rather than a blue one, we could have made the Bolivian flag. Although with the flag's horizontal stripes we would have had to have laid on top of one another. I didn't know either of my new friends *that* well yet.

As we were congregated outside the ground, rumours spread that Lionel Messi had been banned by CONMEBOL for swearing at a linesman in the last round of international fixtures. Apparently, Messi had already boarded the plane for La Paz when the ban was issued. It was a shame not to see the world's greatest player playing at altitude, but maybe even he was relieved. Landing at La Paz's international airport shortly before kick-off was one of many tactics utilised to avoid the disadvantage of playing at altitude. And Argentina looked the more energetic, although they were chasing the game after half an hour. The Bolivian Juan Carlos Arce headed home a cross from Pablo Escobar (no, not that one), and in the 52nd minute Bolivia scored again. It finished 2-0 to the hosts and Argentina once again suffered defeat in La Paz. In the crowd, a Bolivian fan was dressed up as a ghost with the word 'altitude' scrawled across his white bedsheet. *El fantasma de la altura* was present to taunt the Argentines again.

Other than the Halloween costume in March, the worst insult heard from the stands was 'Andáte al semáforo' ('Fuck off to the traffic lights'), which was being shouted to the Argentines in the upper tier. *Argentinos* travelling in Latin America are extremely resourceful and find many ways of working while on the road. One gig is circus juggling at traffic lights. They can spend hours standing amongst the cars stuck at a red light. Clearly, some *paceños* (the people of La Paz) have typecast all Argentines as circus entertainers. In all fairness, Bolivians living in Argentina receive a lot worse, so this, in some ways, was a chance for them to be the aggressors for once.

This was the last game I saw in Bolivia. I spent a few days in Cochabamba, but my time there didn't coincide with a Jorge Wilstermann game. I didn't make it to the football-mad city of Santa Cruz, either. In La Paz, I missed the derby match between The Strongest and Bolivar, the two biggest clubs in Bolivian football. But there had to be time for non-footballing tourism, too. Before leaving La Paz, I visited the infamous San Pedro prison. I had picked up a copy of *Marching Powder* by an Australian called Rusty

Young. It was one of those books most backpackers in Latin America had read.

Near the centre of the city sits the Plaza San Pedro in one of the nicer parts of town. On one side of the square is the former monastery-turned-prison. The San Pedro prison functioned in many ways as its own mini economy, a microcosm of the outside world. It was a prison where one had to buy or rent accommodation. The richer inmates – the corrupt politicians and the drug lords – had nicer flats with a separate entrance from a side street. They were five-star 'prisoners' who had Jacuzzis and other luxuries. For the rest of the prison population, they either lived relatively comfortably or on the street. That is, the street within the prison walls. Inmates could be homeless within the prison.

Prisoners who had family would be joined by their wives and children, who had no way of sustaining themselves on the outside. Every morning the prison gates open to let some 150 school kids leave to attend school. Some of the prisoners' partners leave to go to work, but most work in shops or restaurants inside the prison. Worse still, some work in the cocaine labs in the prison. It's said that the children are often used to smuggle the drugs out.

The presence of children in the prison also provided an opportunity for an inmate with dwarfism, who dressed up like a school pupil and simply walked out of the prison amongst the other primary school children. It was his mother who had hatched the plan on behalf of her prisoner son.

Whilst some people were trying to leave the prison, tourists started entering the prison to spend time with inmates. With cocaine being produced on site and with corrupt guards at the gates, taking a tour of the prison became popular. A visit would turn into a party, and tourists spent the night inside the prison walls, which housed some of Bolivia's most hardened criminals. At one point, the *Lonely Planet* guidebook included a tour of the prison as one of the must-dos in the city.

The government cracked down (excuse the pun) on these tours in 2009 but I heard rumours that it was still possible. I wasn't too keen. Instead I settled for a 'tour' with a former inmate taking place outside the prison's wall. Every day the American, Crazy Dave, went to the plaza at midday to see if any gringos had come to hear him talk. Without shoes and wearing tatty old clothes, he admitted that he lived under a bridge nearby.

Crazy Dave had spent 14 years at San Pedro prison. He said he was on parole, couldn't leave the country and that he was serving out his last few months giving tours. It was a 90-minute theatrical performance rather than a tour. I preferred the 90 minutes of a football match. His performance was surreal. It was awkward having this American loudly shouting the voices and playing the roles of various characters of his own story. We were standing in a public park where Bolivian office workers were enjoying some sun on their lunch break, and where older citizens were sitting on park benches enjoying their afternoon. After 30 minutes I was keen for it to be over.

We cringed for another hour before the theatrical performance art finally ended. Our little group of randomly assembled tourists – a couple of Irish lads and a couple of Norwegians, coincidentally – gave him his tip and off he went to one of the *kioskos* on the corner of the square. Ignoring the prison and the history it has, the rest of the neighbourhood seemed legitimate, until it became clear what it was Crazy Dave was buying from the newspaper stands on the corner.

Lima: Foals to the slaughter in deepest, darkest Perú

I HAD overstayed my welcome is what the border guard at the immigrations office was telling me. Upon entering Bolivia, I had been given a 30-day tourist visa. Thirty-five days later I was trying to cross the border into Perú from Copacabana on the shores of the famous Lake Titicaca. The border officer was happy for me to pay a little fine, as long as I didn't come back, he said. I said I was heading for Mexico. He seemed to believe me. The money I handed over definitely didn't find its way into the Bolivian government's coffers, but rather a cotton coffer by this officer's pistol. Passport stamped and wrist slapped, I was back on the bus to Puno in Perú.

I knew nothing about Peruvian football before entering the country, just as I had known nothing about Bolivian football. I hadn't been too enthused about watching football outside of Argentina because, frankly, nothing would live up to the level of football culture or romanticism there. Even Colombia didn't inspire much, although clearly there would be more to see there than here.

The altitude was still 4,000m above sea level. From Potosí to La Paz, I had only occasionally gone below

3,000m. There was no professional football in this part of the world. Not yet anyway. Not long after my visit to Puno, Deportivo Binacional of the neighbouring town Juliaca were promoted to the Peruvian top tier, straight from non-league football. In their first season in Perú's Primera, Binacional won the league. But how did they get there?

The Copa Perú. With only two professional tiers (consisting of 20 and 12 teams, respectively), the Copa Perú is an innovative way of keeping the rest of Peruvian football motivated. Teams from the top two tiers don't participate in the Peruvian cup. It's a tournament that gives the best of the rest a chance to join the professional leagues.

Perú is a country of nearly 35 million inhabitants spread over an area bigger than any European country and most African countries. The British Isles would fit into Perú all of five times. What's more, the terrain is dramatic: rolling and rugged and in many places inhospitable. Getting from one part of the Andean nation to another is inconvenient and prohibitively costly for most Peruvian teams. Many European countries have the wealth and infrastructure to support several tiers of national competition (without the mountainous landscape to boot). Perú simply does not.

With only 32 professional teams, the rest of the nation's clubs have to fight it out in the Copa Perú starting at a district level. This bottom tier of Peruvian football might only consist of two or three teams in the case of the most rural places. In the cities, there are up to 30 teams competing at the first stage. In 2019 some 22,000 teams started at the first stage: mini-leagues at a district level. The winners of each of the thousands of district leagues funnel into provincial mini-leagues, from where they qualify for the state level. By now teams have reached the third tier of Peruvian football where 50 teams compete on a national level for 16 spots. The last 16 becomes a knockout cup tournament, the equivalent of tier two or the second division.

After the quarter-finals, four teams remain. But instead of continuing the knockout structure (semi-finals and then a final), yet another mini-league is played. The winner is promoted straight into the Primera División. Previously, the runner-up would go straight into the Segunda División, but recently changes have been made so that the winner enjoys the top tier, whereas the second- and third-placed teams in the four-team mini-league play off to decide who goes into the Segunda. Fourth place gets the wooden spoon and a few weeks to lick their wounds before it all starts up again.

This whole process of filtering from 22,000 teams to a last 16 happens over a calendar year. The Copa Perú starts in March and, if your team reaches the final stage, finishes in December. It's a long journey soaring through the divisions in nine months. Wimbledon FC's meteoric rise from the English non-league football to the old First Division (now Premier League) took many years, including several years waiting to be elected to the football league, before promotion/relegation between non-league and the Fourth Division came about. More recently AFC Wimbledon have emulated their forerunner and namesake. But had the Peruvian system existed, both Wimbledons might have done it much quicker.

It's a fair way of organising 22,032 teams in a poor country with poor infrastructure over the mountains and through the rainforests. The system also allows an investor to have a team in the professional divisions relatively quickly. If a local businessman wanted to establish a team in a football-loving town or city with the resources to sustain a team, club directors would have to convince players to support the project for nine months and, assuming the players assembled are of sufficient quality and get the results, the top division will open its arms to the club. Before long the new team will be hosting the big boys of Peruvian football, namely Alianza Lima and Universitario, amongst others.

Binacional from Juliaca were one such success story. Not only did they get promoted to the Primera, but they went on to win it in 2019, beating giants Alianza to the title. The Copa Libertadores might be their limit, however. They beat São Paulo FC at 3,800m in their first-ever Libertadores game, but went on to lose 8-0 to River Plate at El Monumental at sea level in Buenos Aires. Home advantage might see them get some decent results in Juliaca, but away games might show them up. (Unfortunately for Binacional, the resumption of the Copa Libertadores after the novel coronavirus pandemic of 2020 saw all games in Perú played in Lima. Binacional lost their remaining four games, 1-0 in Lima to LDU Quito, 6-0 in their 'home' tie with River Plate, 4-0 in Quito and then 5-1 in São Paulo.)

I spent a few days in Puno blissfully unaware of the football story brewing down the road. Cusco would be my next stop and one of the highlights of my travels. So much did I like it that I spent about a month there. Machu Picchu was on my list, as it was everyone else's. Unashamedly so. With the draw of the mystical Incan citadel perched atop a mountain, I was expecting Cusco to be a small town unable to cope with the sheer number of tourists flocking there each year. But what I found was a charming town with an awful lot to offer. I almost didn't want to leave.

Cusco also had a recent Copa Perú winner. In 2012 Real Garcilaso won the tournament and finished second in their maiden Primera campaign, qualifying for the Copa Libertadores. The following year they came second again, and another season in the Libertadores. At the end of 2019 the club changed its name to Cusco FC.

Unfortunately for me, football wasn't on offer in the city. I was visiting during the winter holidays and other cultural festivities took centre stage. The streets were more colourful than normal, which takes some doing in the Andean highlands. Colourful colonial buildings are surrounded by green hills and the streets are walked by indigenous peoples wearing *aguayos* of the rainbow. Every restaurant table is adorned with the same festive colour scheme and the rainbow flag – the flag of Cusco – flaps and flutters with pride.

I was a year too late to see Ronaldinho playing for the other local side, Cienciano. They won the Copa Perú in 1973 and are the more traditional of the two Cusco sides. One of the first images I came across while walking the streets of Cusco was of the legendary Brazilian in the red of Cienciano. It was a poster hanging in the window of a sports shop. I knew he had played for many clubs since leaving Europe, but I was pretty sure this medium-sized Peruvian club wasn't one of them. Either way, I wouldn't be seeing Ronaldinho playing in Cusco, nor would I be catching a game at the Estadio Inca Garcilaso de la Vega.

My first visit to a Peruvian ground would be in Arequipa to see FBC Melgar: Foot Ball Club Melgar, nicknamed *El Sangre Y Luto* (the blood and mourning). The club is named after Mariano Melgar, a Peruvian revolutionary born in Arequipa. He fought and died in the Peruvian War of

Independence. Melgar was 24 in 1815 when the Spanish Empire lined him up in front of their firing squad. FBC Melgar were formed 100 years later. *El Sangre Y Luto* has to be up there as one of the best club nicknames.

Perú would defeat the Spanish at the Battle of Ayacucho nine years after Melgar's martyrdom. It was fitting, then, that FBC Melgar came up against Ayacucho. Their 2-2 draw in the Primera División was enjoyed by no more than 5,000 spectators. Only 10 per cent of the municipal Estadio Monumental de la USNA's seats were occupied. Melgar use the big municipal stadium (47,000) as well as their more modest Estadio Mariano Melgar (15,000). It was a shame they didn't use their own ground with so few turning out to watch them.

A Dutch Granit Xhaka lookalike was keen to come along to the game. Ties was in Arequipa on a university exchange year, working in the alpaca wool industry. He was expecting it to get cold during the game, so put on his new, woollen sweater and we set off walking from the centre of town. It wasn't far to walk and it would give us a chance to stop off at shops along the way to pick up a can of Arequipeña or two.

The main street around the sports complex was busy as we arrived. It appeared to be one of only two main entrances to the ground. We hung around people watching for a while before going through security. As we were padded down, we were asked to take our belts off. *How bad could the football be?* I thought. But it wasn't for our own safety. The stewards pointed us to a local man who had laid out a blanket. He promised to guard the belts whilst fans were at the game at the cost of one Peruvian sol. The ticket itself only cost S/8 (£2).

A week later I was heading back to the ground, this time without Xhaka's doppelganger and without a belt. A former colleague of mine from Buenos Aires was passing through on her travels. She wasn't a football fan but Melgar were coming up against River Plate in the Copa Libertadores group stage. For both of us it was a link back to Buenos Aires and a chance to hang out with travelling Argentinian football fans. Two days before the game I went to a supermarket to pick up tickets in the away end. Any opportunity to see Argentinian teams playing abroad had to be taken, and all the better that we could sit with the visiting fans.

I had hung around in Arequipa specifically for this game and it was one worth sticking around for. River Plate won 3-2 in a meaningless game for them as they had already won the group. But Melgar had to win if they wanted to progress from Group 3. A second-string River side raced to an early 2-0 lead, but the hosts pegged them back. A 70th-minute winner kept my football-sceptical friend sufficiently entertained. It also helped that the ground was almost full this time, with around 40,000 having left their belts at the door to enjoy this goal fest. Not bad for S/15 (£4). (River Plate would get to the semi-final and be leading 3-0 on aggregate just before half-time of the second leg against fellow Argentinian side Lanús, only to lose 4-2 in greater Buenos Aires.)

Arequipa was a nice city to hang around in waiting for a football match. The sun shines all day, and the temperature is a comfortable 22°C. From the city there is a stunning view of the nearly 6,000-metre-high volcano El Misti. It's active and sits tall, intimidating the city. I was lucky that there were good people in the hostel. For the most part they were decent people.

At 4am one morning I thought otherwise, however. I had just come back from a couple of days of hiking in the Colca canyon, one of the deepest canyons in the world at 3,500m. I had just climbed up the ladder into my top bunk in the dorm room when the beds started shaking. The area is known for its tremors and earthquakes. But the moaning and groaning sounds weren't consistent with an earthquake. An Argentine man and a German girl had found each other irresistible. The others in the room were either extremely heavy sleepers or just pretended to be asleep. I couldn't pretend. I wanted to sleep. I needed to sleep. I couldn't lie there listening to that. Extremely tired and now extremely annoyed, I climbed back down the ladder and turned the light on, standing over them with an unimpressed stare. I was still angry and tired when I saw the Argentine the next day. He didn't say hello.

Two weeks after Melgar against River I would get to see another game between two sides from Perú and Argentina going head to head in continental competition. Alianza Lima were hosting Club Atlético Independiente in the Copa Sudamericana.

I found a Peruvian who was willing to take me to the game. Diana was an Alianza season ticket holder and went to every home game. We were going to meet up early and grab some beers, but with protests in the central Plaza de Armas in Lima, we couldn't find each other in the relative chaos. By the time we had circumvented the crowds and police barriers, it was time to jump in a taxi to the ground.

The *Matute* was within walking distance had it not been in a *very* dodgy area. I had been to lots of dodgy areas to watch football games and felt more or less safe in a crowd of people with police flanking the streets (whatever people think of South American police, for me the sight helped). But this was different. Diana insisted we get a taxi right up to the entrance of the stadium because one street in particular was a street that 'even police didn't go down'. It was on this street that we would have to enter the ground.

Estadio Alejandro Villanueva, the ground's official name, is situated in the neighbourhood of La Victoria and holds about 34,000 fans. It's relatively new, built in the 1970s and, despite its surroundings, is probably the best club stadium Perú has to offer. Elton John must have thought the same, as he played a concert here in 1995, Diana said. It's a pity Watford haven't played a friendly against Alianza.

Independiente was a more attractive fixture. The format of the Copa Sudamericana in 2017 was the same as the old European Cup: a straight knockout from the first round to the final. And it was the first round in which Alianza and the Argentinian *Red Devils* met. In April they had drawn 0-0 in Avellaneda. Independiente edged a 1-0 win at the *Matute* on their way to winning the whole tournament. They beat Brazilians Flamengo in the final, and in the process added another international trophy to their collection, justifying their nickname 'the King of Cups' (*El Rey de Copas*).

The atmosphere was impressive. It was a tightly packed stadium with stands and terraces close to the pitch. Fences separated the terracing behind the goals from the pitch, but from the stands no barriers were in place. The *Comando Sur* unveiled a flag that covered the whole terrace before waving blue and white balloons and homemade ticker tape. The bags of ripped-up newspaper made it to our section and, once they had floated down from the night sky, the concrete steps were littered with squares of crudely torn confetti. I was glad I wouldn't be cleaning up after the game had finished.

Few Argentines had made the journey to Lima. The Independiente section looked like a slice of pizza – a narrow sliver crammed into the corner of the ground. Their red-and-white umbrellas (yes, it had been raining, but no, the umbrellas weren't for the rain) contrasted perfectly with the blue and white stripes of the home team. The umbrellas twirled incessantly and added to what had been an entertaining game but a disappointing result for the *Alianzistas*. After the game we finally had a chance to grab some beers and some food. We went back into the city centre to a football-themed pub and shared a table with a statue of Diego Armando Maradona. We talked football and Diana told me about Alianza's history. They were a hugely successful club with a full trophy cabinet and many legendary players. But it was a dark story that stood out, that of the 1987 Fokker F-27 air disaster. Forty-three people – of which 16 were players – died in the crash as the Alianza Lima squad were flying back from a league game in the jungle city of Pucallpa. Of the 44 people who boarded the plane, only the pilot, Edilberto Villar, survived. Villar would spend 11 hours trying to stay afloat in the choppy Pacific Ocean a few miles north of Lima before being rescued by a search-and-rescue team. Alianza's 'white tank' Alfredo Tomassini, a 23-year-old striker, had also survived the crash but, with two broken legs, couldn't stay afloat. His body was never recovered.

Nine years earlier in 1978, after the World Cup in Argentina, the Argentinian football magazine *El Gráfico* heralded the Peruvian midfield three – all playing for Alianza Lima – the best in world football. They had won the 1975 Copa América with Perú, and with Alianza the Peruvian title three out of the past four years (1975, 1977 and 1978). As a result of their success, all three players – Teófilo Cubillas, César Cueto and José Velásquez – were sold after the World Cup: two went to Colombia, one to the NASL in the US. Alianza Lima wouldn't win the title for another 19 years, despite coming close on several occasions.

The closest they came in the intervening years was in 1987/88. Led by the 1975 Copa América-winning manager Marcos Calderón, Alianza had started the campaign well with ten wins from their opening 17 games (five draws, two defeats). Their 18th game was against Deportivo Pucallpa on 8 December 1987.

Alianza were top of the table going into the December summer break after their 1-0 win in Pucallpa. The two points gained in the Amazon jungle maintained their good start. But the young team, nicknamed *los potrillos* (the foals), perished on their return to Lima. The average age of the 16 players who died that December was under 23. The oldest, 33-year-old goalkeeper José *Caico* Gonzáles Ganoza (uncle of Paolo Guerrero, another Alianza Lima legend), had been their first choice since he was 19, racking up over 500 games.

The youngest player in the squad was 18 years old. Luis Antonio Escobar had just turned 15 when he made his debut for Alianza, scoring twice (the first after five minutes) against reigning champions Sporting Cristal. Before his 16th birthday Escobar had scored his first goal in a Peruvian *superclásico* against Universitario de Deportes. That goal came in a 1-0 win in the debut of Perú's national team goalkeeper Ramón Quiroga. Escobar would score seven goals against Alianza's fiercest rivals, including two in a 5-1 win 'which sent the goalkeeper of the Peruvian World

Cup squad Ramón Quiroga into retirement'. By the age of 18, Escobar had played 144 games for Alianza, scoring 48 goals. In his last game against Pucallpa he wore the No. 19 on the back of his blue-and-white-striped kit – 19 was an age he wouldn't reach.

The cause of the plane crash is shrouded in doubt. The political and social situation of Perú in the 1980s was a turbulent one. The Shining Light (*Sendero Luminoso*) Marxist-Leninist revolutionaries had taken their guerrilla warfare from the Andean highlands to Lima, undertaking kidnappings, car bombings and assassinations. The government responded by giving the police and military special powers to detain anyone suspected of being a member of one of several left-wing parties. But these new powers were abused. Human rights abuses including rape and torture became commonplace, as did extrajudicial executions.

Corruption was rampant and the military had been accused of trafficking cocaine, something that would come to light in the 1990s when 170kg of cocaine was seized on a Peruvian Air Force plane headed for Russia. After the Fokker disaster, disturbing rumours circulated that the Alianza squad travelling back on the light aircraft chartered from the navy had seen drugs being transported. One theory is that a fight between players and armed officers on board the plane might have been what brought the plane down.

Once the plane had crashed into the ocean, only the navy were allowed to conduct search-and-rescue missions, despite Tomassini's family desperately wanting to hire a boat to help. Several bodies were never discovered, along with parts of the plane that disappeared. The players' families, as well as journalists, arrived at the naval base in the city to enquire about the pilot but were intimidated by shots fired into the air. The official investigation into the crash was never made public. Instead, the documents were illegally locked away in a safe in Florida in the US until 2006, when they were discovered by journalists.

And what of the sole survivor, the pilot? Lieutenant Edilberto Villar disappeared. He never testified; he never spoke to the press; he never spoke to the families of the 43 men who boarded his plane and who subsequently died. It has been claimed that he was given a new identity and relocated to the US.

And what of the club? There were five Alianza players who didn't travel to Pucallpa, either because of suspension or injury. They were joined by the three legendary midfielders from the 1970s who returned to lend a hand (Teófilo Cubillas coming out of retirement). Three other clubs in Lima – namely Sporting Cristal, Sport Boys and Deportivo Municipal – loaned Alianza players, as did the Chilean team Colo-Colo, who sent four players to the Peruvian capital.

Alianza Lima and Colo-Colo, subsequently, have maintained a footballing friendship since the 1987 tragedy. The Chilean club were especially moved by the accident as there had been two similar accidents in Chile over the preceding two decades. In 1961 the Chilean football team Club de Deportes Green Cross were decimated in an air disaster, followed a decade later by the Uruguayan rugby team who crashed in the Chilean Andes in 1972, about which the 1993 film *Alive* was made.

For the remaining 12 games, Alianza were spared away trips, playing four games in Lima's Estadio Nacional as the away team. The makeshift team did okay, picking up six wins and four draws in the run-in, finishing second behind

Sporting Cristal (to whom Alianza lost twice during the regular season). As it was, the top six teams went on to contest a mini-league, which Alianza Lima won. It wasn't a trophy, but it saw Alianza qualify for the league play-off final where they would meet rivals Universitario. The game ended 1-0 to *La U* and Alianza finished a promising yet ultimately tragic season empty-handed.

El clásico de los clásicos. Only three days after the Alianza-Independiente game, it was time for *el superclásico peruano*, the so-called 'derby of derbies' (in a Peruvian context). Getting a ticket wasn't difficult: a trip to the big supermarket close to where I was staying, showing ID, was all it took.

I had met a girl called Johanna, who said she was a Universitario de Deportes fan but she hadn't been to a game for years. I hadn't been in Lima long enough to meet a *fanático* who would take me to this game so Johanna would do. In the centre of Lima was a *cevichería* that had a dish called Ceviche 'U' vs 'Alianza'. It would be the perfect lunch before heading to the ground. Johanna turned up about 40 minutes late, by which time I was on my third Cusqueña beer.

Traffic in Lima is terrible at the best of times. It's a city where the metropolitan bus lanes – built to ease congestion and give commuters a smoother ride – are congested with metropolitan buses bursting at the seams. Standing on the platform, we could see our bus 50 metres down the bus lane. It wasn't moving. We got a taxi instead and arrived just as the players were coming out on to the pitch. The Estadio Monumental de La U is eight miles from the main square heading out of the city. The road is always busy.

When we finally got to the ground, we realised why it hadn't been difficult to get a ticket. Disappointingly, the ground was just over half full. Fans were packed into the home end behind one goal, a huge block of white without interruption from one corner flag to the other. In stark contrast, the terracing behind the other goal was totally empty, a block of motionless, sad grey concrete. Away fans were, of course, banned. Even in the main stands there were many empty seats.

El Monumental in Lima is a curious stadium. It sits on the very edge of town, separating the city border from a desert mountain range, which stretches east for mile after mile. Looming over the stadium are the first dusty hills, which begin the *cordillera*. Inside, the lower tier is a huge bowl consisting of rows of terracing and seats. The upper tier looks like apartment blocks: six levels of big, concrete balconies bearing down on the people below. It looks like two different structures merged into one. The magnitude and design of the thin upper tier makes it unique. It's comparable to La Bombonera's thin, east stand but taller, more intimidating and stretching around the whole stadium.

The rather dull grey terracing behind the goals is partially countered by the colourful seats in the two main stands. There is no colour scheme or design, just many different colours mixed in randomly as if the seats had been bought from a football stadium scrap lot, picking up a selection of colours from other clubs. Their kits are cream coloured – you couldn't have a stadium solely of cream seating, anyway. A nice detail, however, is the face of a former player mosaiced into the east stand. Had the ground been full, I thought, I never would have known of its existence. The face is that of Univeristario and Perú legend Lolo Fernández after whom *La U*'s former stadium was named.

With Lolo looking on, the game began. He had an excellent view of the penalty awarded to his team after three minutes. The Panamanian, Tejada, missed the spot kick but made up for it 60 seconds later to make it 1-0 to *La U.* Alianza equalised before half-time and won it in the second half with a stunning shot with the inside of the captain's left foot from 25 yards, which sailed into the goalkeeper's top-right corner. Unstoppable. I had already developed an affiliation for Alianza and had to suppress a little smile. As the final whistle blew, a Universitario player petulantly kicked out at an Alianza player and a huge brawl kicked off. A swarm of players, coaching staff, riot police and reporters all joined the melee, all jockeying for position – each one trying either to get stuck in, to hold people back, or to get the perfect photo for tomorrow's newspapers. The ebb and flow of the 60-plus people on the pitch was strangely beautiful – it reminded me of the starlings at the West Pier in Brighton, each and every creature incessantly trying to get into the middle of an undulating flock.

Regrettably, I didn't visit any of the other teams in the capital. Both Sporting Cristal and Sport Boys were accessible grounds. Instead, I spent the next couple of weeks eating myself around the city famed for its cuisine. Wandering around the city, visiting new neighbourhoods, it wasn't difficult to find a place to eat. Ceviche, leche de tigre, ají de gallina, lomo saltado, papa la huancaina, caldo de gallina. And then there were the fruits: guanábana, guava, chirimoya, lúcuma, pitahaya. Whole chocolate pods were sold in the supermarket and I bought one to try my hand at drying and roasting the bitter cacao beans covered in a white fleshy fruit. Clearly most of these foods weren't from the capital and it piqued my interest to explore the markets in other regions on my way north.

The next football match I would see was in the city of Huaraz, an eight-hour overnight bus ride from Lima. The town is spectacularly unattractive with its red-brick, shack-looking buildings and thick pollution from the many cars, taxis and buses roaming around. Its ugliness is made more pronounced by the stunning snow-tipped mountains surrounding the city.

I had plans on the day of Sport Rosario's Primera clash with Melgar. It was taking place in the Estadio Rosas Pampa across the road from my hostel, but my travels couldn't revolve around football. Or could they? With only 15 minutes left of the game, we were passing the ground and decided to have a look through the outer gates. At this point the stewards opened the doors. A dozen people had congregated for this moment and flooded into the ground to catch the last quarter of an hour. I wandered in to see another half-empty stadium decked out in the yellow and blue of the home team. Sport Rosario called themselves *El Canalla de los Andes*, a reference to the Argentinian team Rosario Central. Plagiarism is the greatest form of flattery, after all.

Top tier football wasn't common in Huaraz. Sport Rosario had won the Copa Perú in 2016, having started in the Liga distrital de Huaraz. Nine months later they had won the whole tournament and been granted a place in the top division for the following season. They did pretty well, qualifying for the 2018 Copa Sudamericana, but were knocked out in the first round by Cerro from Uruguay. By now they had lost their rich owner, who died in a car crash. In the 2018 Primera, they came 12th of 16 teams in that season's Apertura but rock bottom in the Clausura with 12 losses from 15 games. That was the end of Sport Rosario's short stint in the professional leagues of Perú.

The city of Huaraz had an excuse for being ugly. Perú and the whole Andean stretch of mountains from Colombia in the north to Chile in the south are predisposed to earthquakes. The worst Perú has suffered to date is the earthquake that struck on 31 May 1970. Measuring 7.9 on the Richter scale and striking a few miles off the Pacific coast, the whole country felt it. But it was an area bigger than Belgium and the Netherlands combined that was hit the worst – Áncash and the region's capital Huaraz in particular. Ninety-seven per cent of the city was flattened and 10,000 people died. Without much faith that they wouldn't have to rebuild the city again in the future, not much money was spent on the rebuild. (The financial hit of the huge earthquake on an already poor country meant there wasn't any money anyway.)

Further up the valley was a town called Yungay. During the 45 seconds of the earthquake, a section of the 6,750-metre mountain, Huascarán dislodged and surged towards the town at speeds of up to 500mph. It didn't take long to travel the ten miles to Yungay, and within a couple of minutes the town was under several million tonnes of ice, rock and mud from Perú's tallest mountain. Another 10,000 people died in Yungay. Only 300 survived. Of the survivors, many were children attending a circus performance at the municipal sports arena, which luckily didn't suffer any damage. As a result of the obliteration of the town, many of these children had to be given up for adoption. Many ended up moving to new families abroad.

Another handful of survivors were found at the cemetery situated on a hill tall enough to avoid the onrushing mountain debris. A statue of Jesus Christ is the centrepiece of the graveyard. With his arms spread out, his gaze looking out over the town, even he was powerless to stop the disaster. Having survived the initial avalanche and without anywhere to go, tourists and locals visiting relatives were forced to open graves to steal clothes from the dead to make it through the cold night.

Santo Domingo de Yungay was a colonial town founded by the Spanish in 1540. The site has never been dug up. The Peruvian government declared it a burial site. Walking over the town was strange. The guide led us over the grassy area with palm trees and nicely pruned flower beds, but we knew what was underfoot stuck for eternity. A new town – Nuevo Yungay – was built less than a mile north of the old location/burial site.

Overall, up to 80,000 people were killed by the earthquake, resulting avalanches and floods. It's Perú's most severe natural disaster, and every 31 May schools and other institutions practise their escape drills should another earthquake strike.

After Huaraz – and via the cities of Trujillo and Chiclayo – I arrived in Chachapoyas. It was a town that most backpackers on the gringo trail wouldn't come across, as the beach resort Máncora was more popular. But Chachapoyas turned out to be my favourite town to visit in the whole of South America.

The town itself was quiet. It had a nice square in the centre with colonial buildings around the streets lining the Plaza de Armas. People weren't rushing around, and the cars passed by at a calming pace. Although it was the capital of the region called Amazonas, the name was misleading: the temperature and climate were perfectly comfortable, around the 20°C mark. I had feared it would be rainforest humid and hot.

The civilisation who lived in this area withstood the Incan Empire for several generations. The word Chachapoya was used by the Incas about this indigenous tribe – what they referred to themselves as is lost in the annals of time. Protected in their hilltop fortress, Kuélap (one of several citadels similar to but predating Machu Picchu), the Chachapoya fought bravely until eventually falling and becoming part of the Incan world. Shortly after, the Spanish arrived, and by the mid-1800s the Chachapoya had all died off.

They were a curious race. Different to the rest of the indigenous tribes and peoples along the Andes *cordillera* stretching from Chile to Colombia, the Chachapoya were said to be tall, with lighter skin and fairer hair. When tribal leaders died, their bodies were placed inside a two-metre-tall sarcophagus called a *purumachu*. The *purumachu* had a human form with a decorative mask. It looked more like a bowling pin: body and head but no arms or legs. Inside the clay sarcophagus were the mummified remains of an important tribal figure. On the outside, the skull of an enemy was placed atop of the head of the coffin. The locals referred to the structures as 'the wise men'.

To make these sarcophagi even more intriguing, they were placed on a rock face up to 30 metres from the ground. Archaeologists believe that cliff balconies were etched into the cliff face and that the *purumachus* were built on the balconies rather than transferred up from ground level. Either way, it would involve hoisting the bodies of these warrior chiefs up a rock face and entombing them whilst dangling over the drop below. I was fascinated.

First, I visited Karajía, gawping up from the wooden platform below the six sarcophagi perched on a ledge above. There was something magical about these thousand-year-old figures that captivated me. I stayed there for a couple of hours in their company with very few tourists passing by. The next day I set off for San Jerónimo, a small town an hour from the town of Chachapoyas. I got off the bus at a small concrete bridge over the Utcubamba river. Waiting for me was a tuk-tuk driver. He wanted S/30 (about £7) for the 20-minute drive up the hill. I thought he was trying to take advantage of the gringo, but after hiking uphill for two hours I found out that was the price. It was extortionately expensive for the locals.

From the front room of the man charged with San Jerónimo tourism I bought my ticket to visit El Tigre. I needed a guide. Nobody was allowed to go without a guide, he told me. He phoned his niece, who arrived within ten minutes. Another two and a half hours of hiking and we arrived at El Tigre mountain, two humps of forested rock taking the form of a camel's back. It was here that another burial site was discovered in 2013. For a thousand years only a handful of locals knew about their existence.

But it was difficult to see the 14 sarcophagi above. Being a flat cliff wall, they were directly overhead but out of sight. To that end, a tree-house-looking structure stuck out from the cliff. A wooden ladder went out from the mountain to a watch tower from which you could view the eminent yet eerie figures. Below was a 100-metre drop into the so-called cloud forest.

Chachapoyas had been a pleasant surprise. I had wanted to visit Machu Picchu's older cousin, Kuélap, as well as Gocta, one of the world's tallest waterfalls. But arriving at the town I hadn't even heard of the sarcophagi at Karajía or El Tigre. I left Chachapoyas enchanted with the town, the locals and the legend of the Chachapoya people. I made a promise to myself to come back one day.

My last stop in Perú was the jungle city of Iquitos, the largest city in the world inaccessible by road. Only by boat or by plane could one get there, and for me the former appealed more. It wasn't something that could be booked. I would have to make the journey to the port at the jungle village Yurimaguas and find out which boat was leaving for the north towards Colombia and Brazil along the tributaries of the Amazon river.

There were small cargo ships heading north, which let travellers sleep on deck. It would take up to three days but there were faster cruisers that took only 15 hours. I lumped for the slow boat and the experience, but having hung my hammock from the metal girders on deck, I got the message that we wouldn't be leaving for another 24 hours. The captain was waiting for clearance. A handful of other tourists jumped ship and booked themselves on the cruiser, while I went to find beer.

The port was on the muddy banks of the Huallaga river. There was a frenzied chaos with lorries arriving and unloading, tuk-tuk taxis whizzing in tooting their horns and a lot of people milling about waiting in the heat. The little shops and restaurants facing the water's edge were ramshackle, to say the least, sitting ominously on thin wooden stilts, but at least they sold 600ml bottles of cold Pilsen. I asked for a bottle and sat on my own at a table, watching the mayhem, glad for some shade and relative peace. My solitude lasted for all of four minutes before I was invited to join three Peruvians at the next table. They were on business, wheeler-dealer types importing something or other, and looked as if they were used to having to wait at this port. I hadn't seen them arrive nor would I see them leave. Our encounter was stuck in time and the thought crossed my mind that maybe they had always been there, sitting at the plastic table looking out over the port. And always would be.

For a couple of hours we practised a Peruvian drinking ritual that was new to me. With one bottle of beer and one small glass between four people, the glass is filled three-quarters full. The bottle of beer is passed on to the next person while the glass stays with the first drinker. The rest of the group wait, chatting. The beer doesn't have to be drunk immediately, but you certainly wouldn't be popular if you kept the next person waiting too long. Around and around the bottle goes, always one step ahead of the glass, the bottle denoting whose turn it is next. It wasn't too dissimilar to drinking *yerba mate* in Argentina, but the preparation was simpler, and it was more intoxicating. Both ceremonies are social ones that bring a group of people together.

As it got dark, I went to find my hammock on deck. From about eight people, there was now only one other backpacker on the boat, a Frenchman who was driving through the Americas on his motorbike. He wasn't very talkative. I spent the night in my hammock on a stationary boat that would soon – hopefully – be transporting pigs, tourists and locals north. Added to the smell of the pigs, the ship parked next to ours was full of chickens: two tiers with thousands of them tightly packed together. The combination of the pigs and the chickens made for a foul smell and I was relieved when we finally set off and the smell was blown by the currents of air out into the river.

Forty-eight hours later we arrived at Iquitos. I had enjoyed the journey, although there was no onboard entertainment. One could read. One could look out into the thick foliage of trees and bushes on one side or the thick foliage of trees and bushes on the other side. Or one could try spotting the pink river dolphins in the brown muddy waters every time the boat stopped to let someone off at a little jungle village in the middle of nowhere. Alternatively, I could try to talk to the Gallic biker. There was more chance of striking up conversation with one of the pretty little dolphins. By the end of the trip I was ready for the next urban destination, middle-of-the-jungle urban.

There was a charity football match planned, and on my second day in the city I wandered over to the stadium to enquire about tickets. It took half an hour to walk from the centre to the 25,000-seater Estadio Max Augustín. I had no plans for the day and the stroll gave me a chance to explore the city. In truth there was little to see in this part of town. There was also very little information to be found about the game, just a handwritten note on an A4 piece of paper detailing the game. Without a ticket, I walked back to my hostel vowing to return the next day.

I made the same pilgrimage some 24 hours later, making sure I had lots of time to buy a ticket in case of a big crowd. The hosts were a team called J. Vargas Guerra, with Sport Boys, one of the big clubs from Lima, the visitors. I paid S/7 for the ticket (£2) and took one of the many empty seats. There was still an hour until kick-off, but the stadium was definitely not going to fill up. The sun was setting, and as it got darker it became clear that there was an issue with the floodlights. The officials were out in the semi-darkness warming up, assuming that the game would go ahead, but with less than half an hour to go until kick-off it seemed unlikely. Groups of players were pottering about on the pitch as if they had just arrived and were inspecting the pitch. A couple of the younger players found the PA equipment and began singing into the microphone to entertain themselves.

Spectators got out of their seats and began leaving the ground. I was about to get up to leave when a lady came up to me. She said she had been looking for me, but I didn't recognise her. She was giving me my money back. I hadn't even thought about bothering trying to get a refund, but was very thankful that she had made the effort. For every cynical local trying to rip off the visiting foreigners, there was an honest person balancing the scale.

Two weeks later it was time to leave Perú. From Iquitos, boats went west towards Ecuador or further north towards Colombia and Brazil. My travel funds were critically low, so I booked myself on a boat going north. I would have to skip Ecuador, for now. The fast boat service went from Iquitos to Santa Rosa, a tiny border town. In reality, it was barely a village, just a single street where the border bureaucrat sits. Before dawn I found my seat on the cruiser to see the logo on the seats: embossed on the headrest it said 'Fjord1', the name of a company operating ferries on the Norwegian west coast. This boat had been bought from Norway, but they had kept the seats.

The boat left at 5am, arriving 13 hours later. I was tired when we arrived so instead of stamping out of Perú at Santa Rosa I jumped straight on a five-minute motorised canoe taxi service over to Colombia, crossing the border without stamping in nor out. I found a hostel and had a few beers with the people I found waiting for me, leaving the paperwork for the next day. I was physically in Colombia but bureaucratically in Perú.

I had to get up early anyway. It was August and the Community Shield was being played. The Arsenal were facing Chelsea again, only a matter of weeks after their clash in the FA Cup Final. The game kicked off at 7.30am Colombian time. A red-haired Irish Man Utd fan was already sitting by the TV, waiting for the same game. Despite the contrast in our allegiances, we got on, talking about football and our travels.

After the last penalty in a penalty shoot-out won by Arsenal, Irish John was keen to get out and about. I told him I had to sort out my exit stamp and we got the canoe service over to Perú so that I could officially leave the country. I had to pay a fine for having overstayed my 90-day tourist visa. The fine was about £1 per day for overstaying. I was happy to pay the £30 for my extended stay. I had loved Perú.

Leaving the immigration office, we came up with a good plan: we could have a beer in Perú, Colombia and Brazil on the same day. I'd had my last beer at 1am so I had technically already had a Colombian beer, but John hadn't. It had to be done properly, anyway. We grabbed lunch at a restaurant overlooking the Amazon river, peering into Colombia on the other side, having our first beer of the day – Cusqueña, my preferred Peruvian lager. Back across the river, we walked into Brazil. It was a 30-minute walk or a five-minute tuk-tuk ride.

We didn't have to show our passports entering the Brazilian town of Tabatinga. We headed straight for a corner shop but soon found out that we had visited Brazil on a dry day. There were elections and alcohol wasn't being sold. I had experienced this in Argentina. On the day of elections *la veda* is in operation: a dry period. They don't want hangovers to get in the way of people voting.

We saw people drinking anyway and managed to find a little kiosk owner who would sell us beer. We would have preferred to have sat down somewhere but we finished the cheap Itaipava lager standing, then wandered back to Colombia where we finished the feat with an Águila beer. (Two years later I would repeat this gimmick on the tri-border of Argentina, Brazil and Paraguay.) From now on it would be Colombian beer. I was getting closer to my final destination, and not before time.

Bogotá: English referee scores winner against Millonarios

MY COLOMBIAN arrival came hastily. I had spent a lot more time in Perú than planned and had very little money left. I had to hop over Ecuador altogether in an attempt to get to Medellín to start working again. The money I had saved for over a year working hard in Buenos Aires had taken me five months to get through. Had I been less frivolous, I could have travelled further. But I had backpacker fatigue and was keen to settle down somewhere now. The plan was to spend a year in Medellín. But I had to get there first.

The Colombian border town of Leticia is nice enough but there isn't a lot to do in the town itself. Ernesto 'Che' Guevara famously stopped off here on his own travels in the early 1950s, coaching an amateur team with his childhood friend, Alberto Granado. Granado played as a striker, while Che, who had severe asthma, stood in goal. Writing to his mother, Che said, 'I saved a penalty which will stay in the annals of the history of Leticia.' This was shortly before the pair flew to Bogotá and met up with another Argentine, Alfredo di Stéfano. Like Che and Alberto, I had a flight to the Colombian capital to experience her football.

The same day I arrived in the Colombian capital from Leticia, I met up with an Austrian guy I had met twice before on my journey from Buenos Aires. We had stayed in the same hostel in Cochabamba in Bolivia before bumping into each other on the street in Cusco. We spent a lot of time together in Perú and, as we both happened to be in the same city again, we planned to get a Colombian beer in the evening. A couple of days later we met again, this time for a coffee.

Just as I sat down opposite Fabian in a café in the central Bogotá neighbourhood of La Candelaria, in walked an English girl I thought I recognised. Out of the corner of my eye I saw her. Twelve years earlier, we had lived together for two years at university, in a house of seven students. I hadn't seen nor spoken to her since that time. I convinced myself it wasn't her. She hadn't seen me and sat with her friends behind me. When she spoke, I knew it was her. I didn't turn around. To this day she is probably unaware of our paths having crossed. Another crazy encounter for the 'small world' chronicles. By definition, these encounters were rare, but they were happening more often.

Bumping into other backpackers you would meet along the journey wasn't unexpected, though. Both Fabian and I were travelling south to north along the gringo trail. Others were travelling in the opposite direction. There was next to no travelling east to west or west to east; the Pacific Ocean to the west and the Amazon jungle to the east made sure of that. Meeting the same travellers again and again along the journey was a given. Fabian and I were travelling at the same pace, much slower than the regular gap-year or sabbatical backpacker. We would later meet up in Medellín, too.

Fabian didn't like football, but Irish John was also travelling south to north. A new Premier League season was starting, and I dragged Irish John with me across town to hang out with Arsenal Colombia Supporters' Club. They were getting together to watch the Friday evening game – lunchtime kick-off in Colombian time – at an odd little bar in the neighbourhood of Chapinero. It wasn't so much a bar as a little newsagent that had a flatscreen TV on the wall and some plastic tables and chairs, promotional gifts from a Colombian beer manufacturer. A crowd of about 20 Colombian Arsenal fans had gathered to watch a 4-3 opening day win over Leicester City.

Being close to the city's biggest stadium, Irish John and I decided to make the short pilgrimage. El Campín is home to the two big clubs from the capital, Millonarios and Independiente Santa Fe. Santa Fe had a game here two days later and we wanted to get tickets. But unlike Premier League stadiums where the club shop is open every day, there was no activity on this Friday afternoon. We couldn't find a shop or ticket office, so we wandered back from whence we came, where we found the Bogotá Beer Company. With excellent craft beers, we stayed longer than we should have, and as Colombians were getting ready to go out, we stumbled back into the centre of town to the hostel to hit the sack.

The Lions versus the Tigers: Independiente Santa Fe versus Tigres. Back in Buenos Aires I had played football regularly with a Colombian guy called Oscar. We got on well and, knowing that I was now in his hometown, I sent him a message. Oscar put me in touch with his cousin, a Santa Fe season ticket holder. It was Leo who sorted Irish John and me out with our tickets for their next home match. All we had to do is meet them at the ground. We found the little bar where they wanted to meet us and conspicuously walked in past some hard-looking Colombian fans. We found a table in the corner and ordered a couple of bottles of Poker beer from the bar. In the hostel we had met two Dutch backpackers who had been mugged at this ground, so we were wary. It has never been a bad idea to be alert in a new South American football environment. But a few beers later, we felt at ease once again. We spent a long time trying to spot my friend's cousin, but it was another hour before they arrived.

Leo wasn't too keen on Poker, so the next round we ordered bottles of Club Colombia beers. We handed over the 17,000 Colombian pesos the ticket had cost – about £3.50. The beers were even cheaper, and after a few more we left for the stadium, getting into the ground after the game had kicked off. I wondered whether we weren't the only latecomers. The 36,000-seater stadium was less than half full.

Only 13,000 people had bothered to turn up for this league game. Uninspired, the players made about as much effort as the majority who had stayed at home, and Tigres took all three points, winning 1-0 in a game of little quality. Whilst Tigres were also from Bogotá, this game definitely wasn't a *clásico*. There was nothing to suggest so. Santa Fe were preparing for a Copa Sudamericana knockout game, having originally qualified for the 2017 Copa Libertadores. They had won the Finalización, the second half of the 2016 Colombian league season. But they were knocked out of the Libertadores group stages and subsequently went into the Sudamericana.

The Colombian league season is played over the course of a calendar year, from January to December, with a break in June and July. The first half of the season – the Apertura

– sees 20 teams play each other once, either home or away, but for their closest rivals whom they play twice (similar to Argentina's 30-team league format). After 20 games, the top eight teams are put into either two mini-leagues of four teams or a knockout play-off competition. Which of the two formats utilised varies, as the Colombian FA chops and changes on a whim. The winners of the two mini-leagues meet in a two-legged final, whereas if the play-off format is used, teams meet home and away in quarter-finals, semi-finals and a two-legged final. (Some seasons see a mini-league format used in the Apertura and a play-off format used in the Finalización.)

The Finalización sees the same format. If, for example, Santa Fe played away to Atlético Nacional in the Apertura, they would now host them in the Finalización. After 20 more games and the resulting mini-league series or play-offs, there are two league tables for the calendar year as a whole. One league table aggregates the total number of games played during the year, including mini-leagues and/ or play-offs, with points awarded for wins and draws in a knockout play-off. The result of this is that approximately half of the teams in the league finish the season having played 40 games: home and away versus 19 teams, plus two extra *clásicos*. (In 2018 each team only played two derby games instead of four, in an effort to reduce the length of the season because of the World Cup.) The other half of the teams in the league can have played anywhere between 40 and 52 games, depending on their success in the mini-leagues or play-offs.

Leo could see I was struggling to understand all of this. He suggested we order another round of Club Colombias and he would explain it again.

Take 2018 as an example: Deportivo Independiente Medellín (DIM) and Deportes Tolima topped the aggregated league table, both having played 48 games, ten games more than the bottom six teams. DIM had 86 points, one point ahead of Tolima, but Tolima and Junior (who won the Apertura and Finalización, respectively) were the teams who finished the season with silverware. Topping the aggregated table doesn't offer a trophy (although maybe it should). What DIM *did* win was qualification to next season's Copa Libertadores second qualifying round.

The second league table for the year is a relegation table with an average points total calculated over three seasons, common in other South American leagues. In 2018 the bottom two teams – Boyacá Chicó and Leones – averaged 1.068 and 0.949 points per game over 118 games and were subsequently relegated.

To understand the intricacies of the league system of any South American nation requires either a lot of studying and reviewing of old league tables, or a lot of time spent at games in the country to learn little by little. I had a year to talk Colombian football and try to understand all of this. But it was tricky to get my head around. In Europe, there is very little tinkering with the system. In countries like Colombia and Argentina, there seems to be little stopping FAs rearranging league structures and formats arbitrarily.

Interestingly, of the 36 players in the Santa Fe versus Tigres matchday squads, only two were not Colombian. Santa Fe brought an Argentine off the bench, whereas Tigres had an unused Mexican substitute. This was a far cry from the halcyon days of *El Dorado,* the rogue Colombian league of the early 1950s where at one point 287 of the 440 top-flight players were foreign imports. And there were some real superstars among them.

Prior to 1948, Colombian football had been amateur and without a national league. Adefútbol was the association pulling the strings and were FIFA affiliated, when along came a new association looking to commercialise and modernise Colombian football: División Mayor (abbreviated to Dimayor). Despite having played football since the first decade of the 20th century, Colombian football had developed much slower than other South American nations and, having seen professional Argentinian teams touring Colombia in the 1940s (namely Vélez Sarsfield and San Lorenzo), there was an appetite for professional football. Businessmen looking to capitalise on a new commercial opportunity were especially pushy. Dimayor managed to convince ten teams to join their league, some jumping ship from Adefútbol, others joining from amateur metropolitan or district leagues.

Due to start in early 1949, the new professional league was brought forward to August 1948 in an attempt to draw attention away from the ongoing political and social turmoil the country was experiencing. Only some five months earlier, the hugely popular presidential candidate Jorge Eliécer Gaitán – almost certain to win the elections a year later – was assassinated, shot on his way out of his office building on Carrera 7 in downtown Bogotá. What followed was severe rioting in the capital in which 5,000 people died over a matter of hours. Nicknamed *El Bogotazo*, the riots spread throughout the country and would lead to a ten-year civil war referred to simply as *La Violencia*. Estimates suggest that as many as 300,000 people were killed over the decade of *La Violencia* in attacks from paramilitary groups on either side of the political divide, mostly in rural Colombia.

As is so often the case, particularly in Latin America, football was seen as a way of deflecting people's attention from politics to sport. The inaugural Dimayor season of 1948 was a success in doing so. Independiente Santa Fe won the 1948 campaign, winning 12 of their 18 games. The first champions of Colombia played in red shirts with white sleeves, having copied Arsenal FC's famous kit. The club's founder, initial captain and, by the time of *El Dorado*, president, Luis Robledo, had studied at the University of Cambridge and became an Arsenal fan whilst living in England. Naturally, I had to pick up a Santa Fe shirt for my collection.

Having seen their Bogotá rivals win the league, Millonarios felt that they needed to strengthen their team ahead of the 1949 season. They looked to exploit the footballing turmoil in Argentina and Uruguay where players were on strike, fighting for a minimum wage and freedom of contract. Amid the conflict, the Argentinian 1948 season petered out with small crowds watching amateur and youth team players playing out the remaining games while legendary superstars were sitting at home.

One such player was Adolfo Pedernera, one of River Plate's legendary *La Maquina* team that dominated Argentinian football in the 1940s. By now, 31-year-old *El Maestro* Pedernera was at Huracán, having left the Argentinian *Los Millonarios* after nearly 300 games. But why would he go to a nascent Colombian league with no comparable history and only recently professionalised?

Dimayor were offering ridiculous signing-on fees and wages as they saved money on not paying transfer fees.

Adefútbol had complained to FIFA about the creation of a competing league and Dimayor were outlawed by the international football community, the result of which meant that their clubs didn't have to abide by FIFA rules when it came to buying players. What's more, they could offer the player exactly what they wanted in terms of a signing-on fee and salary. Pedernera wanted US$5,000 to sign with Millonarios and a salary of US$500, which the club's directors sanctioned. It was an awful lot of money back then. But Pedernera paid for himself. It's said that *El Maestro*'s unveiling at the next *Millos* game brought in so much money in gate receipts that it covered his astronomical signing-on fee. Other clubs jumped on the bandwagon and suddenly Colombia found itself with some of the world's best talent.

Millonarios had nine Argentines turning out in their blue kit. Cúcuta Deportivo went for Uruguayans and ended up with many of the 1950 World Cup-winning squad on their books. Brazilians were picked up by Junior and brought to the city of Barranquilla on the north coast. Deportivo Pereira in 'the coffee axis' and Boca Juniors de Cali both became mostly Paraguayan (on the pitch, at least). In fact, all members of the Paraguayan and Peruvian national team squads of the era now plied their trade in Colombia.

Deportivo Cali – who were challenging Millonarios in 1949 for the league title – had sent a small plane to Perú looking for new recruits. Landing in Cali, the plane had come back with 14 new players on board and the team lined up with a front five entirely made up of Peruvians. They came to be known as *El Rodillo Negro*, the 'black steamroller'. Imagine the sight in today's football: it's transfer deadline day and Sky Sports are outside the ground of a

Premier League team, awaiting news of a new signing or two and, as the countdown clock approaches zero, a shuttle bus arrives from the airport with 14 players dressed in random training kit from the clubs they have hastily been ripped away from. *That* would get people watching.

Who did Santa Fe go for? With an Anglophile president, they opted for British footballers. Charlie Mitten left Manchester United to cash in on one of the *El Dorado* contracts up for grabs. Mitten went from being an early Busby Babe (before the term was coined) to being 'the Bogotá Bandit'. United had been touring the US, and instead of returning with the squad to the UK, he left New York for Bogotá, having received an offer he couldn't refuse. He was joining Neil Franklin and George Mountford, who had already left First Division side Stoke City to try to resettle in Bogotá with *El Primer Campeón*. Scottish player Bobby Flavell from Hearts and the Irish player Billy Higgins from Everton joined city rivals *Millos*.

Another three Englishmen were due to join the *Millos* ranks, but their moves were soon blocked by Pedernera, who asked Millonarios directors whether they were a team of Argentines or Englishmen. He threatened to leave if the answer were the latter. The three new recruits spent a week in the Colombian capital before returning to the UK, and the Brits and Irish already there were further isolated and made to feel unwelcome by the rest of the Millonarios squad. They didn't last long in Colombia.

English referees, however, *were* welcome. The standard of refereeing in 1948 had been very poor and nothing had been put in place to improve local referees for the higher standard of football being played. A shortcut was to seek out experienced, foreign referees. Six English officials – as well as referees from other European nations – signed one-year contracts with the Dimayor league. One of these foreign imports would go down in Colombian football legend for scoring a goal that saw Millonarios robbed of the 1950 league title.

In July 1950, Englishman Tom Pounder was in charge of Millonarios' home game against Universidad Nacional de Bogotá when a late cross from Osito Solano hit Pounder's back and went past the *Millos* goalkeeper. The visitors held out to win 1-0. It might not have been the last game of the season, but the loss rocked the reigning champions and their form subsequently dipped. The dropped points allowed Deportes Caldas to pip them to the title. Making up for the disappointment of 1950, *Millos* went on to win the next three league titles.

El Dorado only lasted for a handful of years. Quite early into the adventure, with a lot of pressure from clubs around the world fed up at losing their best players for nothing, Dimayor agreed to end the pirate league. The Lima Pact was signed, signalling an end to the madness. However, a clause in the agreement allowed the league to keep the players they had already signed until 1954, when they could return to their original clubs or go elsewhere. Pedernera – after a successful spell as player-manager at Millonarios – went back to Huracán, albeit briefly. Alfredo Di Stéfano, however, was at the beginning of his career. *La Saeta Rubia* – 'the Blonde Arrow' – was destined for even bigger things across the Atlantic in Spain.

In 1952, at the age of 25, Di Stéfano had played against Real Madrid in the Spanish club's 50-year anniversary tournament. Real Madrid had initially invited the Swedish champions IFK Norrköping and River Plate from Buenos

Aires to their Bodas de Oro del Real Madrid (Bodas de Oro meaning golden wedding anniversary). Rumour has it that directors at Millonarios contacted Real Madrid to suggest that the Colombian champions replace River Plate, seeing as they considered themselves the best team in South America. If true, it was an ingenious way of securing a ticket to the show in order to show off the talent they had. They knew the *El Dorado* period was coming to an end and now would be the time to cash in on their players.

In March 1952, in preparation for the tournament, *Millos* played four exhibition games on a tour of Spain and Portugal (beating Porto, drawing against Valencia and Sevilla and losing to UD Las Palmas). Then came the big occasion. Di Stéfano shone in Madrid, scoring first against the Swedes in a 2-2 draw before scoring a brace in a 4-2 victory over the hosts the next day. Even before those three goals, the Argentine was described by Real Madrid president Santiago Bernabéu as 'smelling of good football' after the two took part in a radio debate about football on the eve of the friendly tournament. *Millos'* performances in Madrid led to the Spanish press giving them the nickname *El Ballet Azul* ('The Blue Ballet').

Bernabéu and Di Stéfano would meet again three months later in Venezuela in the first-ever Pequeña Copa del Mundo de Clubes ('Small World Cup of Clubs': predecessor to the Intercontinental Cup, which itself was succeeded in 2004 by the FIFA Club World Cup). Despite coming third in La Liga, it was Real Madrid who were invited to join Colombian champions Millonarios, Brazilians Botafogo and Venezuelan champions La Salle for the inaugural tournament, which Real Madrid won. The four teams met each other twice, with Real Madrid and Botafogo topping the table with eight points each (two victories apiece and four draws). Botafogo had a better goal difference but the deciding factor was goal average. A system that divided goals scored by goals conceded saw Real Madrid lift the inaugural trophy.

The Pequeña Copa del Mundo de Clubes – always held in Venezuela – ran from 1952 to 1957 and, after five years without a competition, again from 1963 to 1975. The first five tournaments – starting before the realisation of what's now the Champions League in 1955 – were seen as prestigious cups worth winning. After five years without the tournament and the foundation of the new Intercontinental Cup, the competition lost its appeal. Only the 1963 and 1965 editions of the second period are considered worthy of the name. The last winners of the competition in 1975 were an East Germany XI.

Di Stéfano had now faced Real Madrid a few times, but naturally *los blancos* weren't the only team interested in the Blonde Arrow of the Blue Ballet. Barcelona had also been scouting the Argentine and had already signed a deal with River Plate to take the player to Catalonia. Real Madrid then signed a deal with Millonarios. But who was it who owned the player? Clearly, the *El Dorado* situation muddied the waters, and the protracted transfer(s) reached an impasse. A mediator was brought in to resolve the dispute and an agreement was reached in which Di Stéfano would play one season for Real Madrid, thereafter one season for Barcelona, moving between the clubs each summer. Needless to say, this never happened. Unsubstantiated claims point to the then Spanish ruler, dictator Francisco Franco, getting involved by blackmailing certain members of the Barcelona board. Suddenly Martí Carreto, who had brokered the initial deal for the Catalonian club, resigned and Barcelona relinquished their interest in the player. A few weeks later the two clubs met in the league. Real Madrid beat their rivals 5-0 with two goals from Di Stéfano.

El Dorado was in its last season and many players had already left to return home from whence they came. With the adventure over, fickle fans stayed away, and many clubs struggled financially. Ahead of the 1954 season, four clubs had to pull out (some eventually folding, others having to merge to survive), with two new teams coming in. Club Atlético Nacional, from Colombia's second city of Medellín, won the league that season. Whilst other teams brought in foreign stars, Nacional – as the name suggests – had a policy of only playing Colombian-born players. Initially, this was to their disadvantage, with players such as Pedernera and Di Stéfano turning out for their rivals. But the other teams did little to heed the warning that these players would one day take their money and leave Colombia. Rather than encouraging these stars to pass on their knowledge to youth or reserve team players through coaching, the clubs were thinking about the now.

By 1957, Millonarios had finished bottom of the league – without relegation, the wooden spoon was enough shame for a team that achieved such heights only a handful of years previously. They had been forced to play youth players and so-called journeymen. As other teams struggled, Nacional's policy had worked in the medium term and they picked up their first league title in 1954. By now they had begun hiring foreign players. Their coach was an Argentine by the name of Fernando Paternoster, and four other Argentine players took the field in the green and white of the team from Antioquia.

Medellín in Antioquia would be my next stop. My five-month journey from Buenos Aires to the city where I wanted to settle for a year was at its end. It was time to get back to work.

The city of eternal spring. I was getting dizzy and borderline car sick. The journey from Bogotá to Medellín takes nine hours. Nine hours of driving up and over hills and round bends and more bends. Seemingly there were no straight stretches and my body was being constantly cajoled in different directions before I'd had a chance to get used to the last position that I found myself in. I was relieved when we arrived in the city and I could book myself into a hostel to relax. So tired was I from the winding, night bus ride that I wrote 'today will be a *right* off' in my travel notes. I slept a few hours on the hostel's sofa, oblivious to the bustle of other backpackers around me.

It had taken five months, but I had finally arrived in the city that I had heard so much about. My whole journey had been about reaching Medellín, the 'city of eternal spring'. With temperatures of between 25°C and 30°C all year round and a reputation for the prettiest girls in Colombia, the attraction of the city was clear to see. Within a couple of days of arriving in Medellín I had found a flat, started work, found a football team to play for, got tickets for the upcoming *clásico paisa* and met Austrian Fabian one last time for a few beers.

The football team I would play for was the inevitable gringo/Colombian mix of backpackers, long-term expats and some slightly unhinged locals. At a friendly match that served as a trial, I was told before the game that I was a cert for the team because I could kick the ball. It made me wonder what kind of players they had playing for them before. The guy who gave me the good news was a short Londoner with Pierluigi Collina hair, a player who turned out to be more unhinged than the Colombians put together.

James had found his place in the world. After games he would be more than happy to regale us with stories of his time as a part of Chelsea's 'firm'. Every week I would suggest sticking around for a few beers and a newcomer to the team would have to sit through the same stories. James had been attacked with a machete and had to flee the UK. Already having a cocaine problem, he chose Medellín. But he had managed to kick the habit and was teetotal, choosing rather to focus on his management of the motley crew of footballers he was involved in organising. The fact that every time he played he would get sent off meant that he had a lot of time on the sidelines to bark orders and get verbally stuck in to opposing players and referees alike.

We were taking part in an 11-a-side league in Envigado, a town to the south of Medellín, which has become enveloped by the metropolitan area. Our first game ended with two players getting sent off. James wasn't playing. He was, of course, suspended. Our goalkeeper – a Colombian model who had played semi-professionally in Argentina – had a bust-up with their striker and a small brawl ensued. This would become a trend: almost every match that took place at Cancha El Dorado would have at least one mass brawl. Too many men, too much testosterone, too few who had realised their full potential, for which the only remedy was to show you were *hard*. I can't say I wasn't caught up in it all. I was also frustrated at never having made it.

Watching on from the crowd was a man who looked like Carlos Valderrama. I stared intently at him each time I saw him, waiting for him to wink at me as if to say I was the only one who had noticed his presence. It wasn't him. He often sat on his own, unassumingly watching the relatively dire football on display. We were mostly ageing gringos and expats playing against young Colombian upstarts. We didn't win many games. For all the organisation and combativeness we had, they had the skills and speed. The games were fun to play in but probably terrible to watch from the vantage point of *El Pibe* Valderrama's doppelganger. But week after week there he was, sitting and looking on.

I also had a good vantage point from the upper tier of the Estadio Atanasio Girardot, Colombia's third-biggest stadium. It hadn't been Colombian football that brought me to Medellín, but it was an added bonus that two of the country's best and most historic teams were from the city. I was living a ten-minute walk from the stadium and wandered down to get a ticket one afternoon. It had been easier than expected. It was a big city derby between the top two teams from the 2017 Apertura, and two of three eventual challengers for the Clausura.

Outside the ticket office of the stadium, standing in the shade of some trees, were several touts selling tickets. But the game hadn't sold out. There was no need to risk getting a dodgy ticket when the booth had tickets to sell. The touts weren't charging much more for their tickets than the club were. I paid 35,000 Colombian pesos for my ticket (£7 in 2017). The touts wanted 40,000, an extra £1.50. The *barra brava* often demand tickets from the club for free, so selling them on for face value or close to face value would give them 100 per cent profit. Had it been a final, they definitely would have charged more. Despite being a *clásico*, tickets were readily available.

Two mates from football were coming along. After a few beers at my new flat, we wandered down early to the Estadio Atanasio Girardot. It's owned by the city council and is shared by Deportivo Independiente Medellín also referred to as Independiente Medellín, or Medellín, or – even simpler – DIM and Atlético Nacional (Nacional). It was DIM who were the home team for this game and their red-and-blue colours pervaded the majority of the stadium, but for the south stand. From corner to corner Nacional fans turned the whole section green and white. The smoke from the flares hovered above the territory given to each set of fans.

Flare smoke filled the air, as did the smell of weed. The two gases were joined by the sound of brass instruments deployed by the DIM fans. The same melodies from *canchas* in Buenos Aires were heard here in Colombia. The sounds – slightly muffled – were coming from the concourses below the north stand. I went down to have a look. It was a homogeneous demographic that had assembled: all young men between 18 and 30, all either with a DIM kit on or bare-chested and sweaty from jumping around. The smell of weed wasn't coming from one or two joints but rather from over 100 joints smoked by the 300 fans present. It was as common as a pint of beer in the concourses of a British or European ground. But no alcohol was being sold here.

The reception of the two teams was on par with many top games in Argentina. Football in Argentina would always be a measuring stick when it came to South American football. It seemed that the whole continent looked to Buenos Aires and Rosario, in particular, for their football culture. The songs were of similar content set to the same melody. And the teams would be welcomed on to the pitch with an explosion of singing, ticker tape and flares. At least there were away fans in Colombia and it was pretty much full to the figurative rafters of the roofless stadium.

The football was free-flowing, and the quality was higher than I had expected for a derby match. There was only one goal, but it was a classy one. The move was started and the goal scored by a classy one: Juan Fernando Quintero. *Juanfer* Quintero was from the area, having started out – as so many young players from the city do – at Envigado FC, before moving to Atlético Nacional for a season. After a few years in Europe – Italy, Portugal, France – Quintero found himself on loan at Nacional's rivals, DIM. He would score a goal every other game during his short loan spell at home in Medellín, and it was he who scored the only goal of this game.

Neat hair with highlights darkened by the rain, No. 10 on his back and a bright-yellow captain's armband around the red, left sleeve of his kit, *Juanfer* picked up the ball in the middle of the park and played a pass down the right wing to a marauding full-back, who cut the ball back. Quintero himself collected the ball on the edge of the box and finished past his future River Plate team-mate, Franco Armani, in Nacional's goal. It was a decent goal and, with the home team having scored and the roar experienced, I was content. I could leave and go home happy. I didn't. The remaining 73 minutes were of decent enough quality on the pitch and fantastic quality in the stands. It would be difficult to beat this at Colombian grounds, I thought, but coming up less than three months later was the return league fixture, Atlético Nacional *at home* to Deportivo Independiente Medellín.

In the intervening 11 weeks between the two *clásicos* I got to know the city, visiting its museums, parks, pubs and restaurants. I understood people's fascination with the place; it was definitely a nice city. But for some reason I didn't share the same love as most of the expats and travellers I had met. I had fallen in love with Buenos Aires, so it felt dishonest developing feelings for another city. Back in Argentina I had good mates and a good work-life-football balance, but at the same time I had to take the opportunity to travel. I wanted to explore the rest of the continent and to find out what the fuss about Medellín and Colombia was about.

The travelling itself had taken its toll. And I was missing friends in Buenos Aires with whom I could have a decent conversation. It can be hard to find deep conversations on the road. The backpacker small talk is fairly limited. Where do you come from? Where have you been? Where are you going? You find yourself repeating the same information every time you meet new people. And you meet new people every single day.

I was on 'the trip of a lifetime', travelling freely around South America, seeing some incredible sights and meeting great people. But I found myself getting impatient very easily. I was a bit older and had been in South America for years. I spoke the language. I looked down on other backpackers who were seemingly just ticking off well-known places, getting drunk and then moving on to the next location to tick off more places. Travelling had become too easy and there were too many of us doing the same activities and ticking off the same sights. The majority seemed to be sleepwalking through their backpacking trip. Little effort was required.

I was ready to settle down and get into a routine. In my new flat in Laureles, Medellín, I would wake up early to teach English online. I often started classes at 6am so that I could be finished for the day by midday. Every day I would go out for lunch. An Irish guy from football would join me and we would pay £2–3 for a two-course lunch. Much like Perú, restaurants were full at lunchtime, serving decent quality two- or three-course lunches, but at night those same restaurants were closed. In Buenos Aires it was the other way around: places were open between 8pm and midnight or later. My eating habits changed to having a big lunch and a small meal in the evening.

With work out of the way and the afternoons off, I was free to explore the city. If I wasn't playing football, I would have lots of time to get to know Medellín, grab some beers or lie in the hammock on the balcony reading. Watching the daily dramatic downpours from the hammock was therapeutic. At least until the rainwaters ran past the house. The little neighbourhood green was a popular dog-airing park. And a popular place for the neighbourhood dogs to do their business. As the tropical torrent washed over the green-and-brown grass, it would wash the contents down the street in front of our balcony and into a drain outside our front door. The waft of fresh faecal matter was off-putting, but it taught me a lot about the dog owners I shared a barrio with.

Medellín: Plata o plomo
and el narco-fútbol

INCONSIDERATE DOG owners aside, Medellín had a more nefarious reputation. The Spanish phrase synonymous with the city was *no des papaya*. 'Don't give papaya' had become a city motto, with T-shirts sold and cafés named bearing the advice. If you were to offer *papaya*, you would be giving a Colombian the opportunity to take advantage. Leaving your phone on the table or getting too drunk and stumbling home were examples of *dar papaya*. It felt more like a phrase putting the blame on the victim. Or maybe it was an honest self-reflection that Colombians didn't feel they could trust themselves. The recent past had not shown the country in the greatest light.

Pablo Emilio Escobar Gaviria was born on 1 December 1949. It was the second year of *La Violencia*, which had started with the assassination of presidential candidate Jorge Eliécer Gaitán. Escobar was born into an inherently violent country. But he would be responsible for untold violence himself until his death on 2 December 1993.

Everyone was talking about *Narcos*. I had started watching the TV series before moving to Colombia. But after a couple of episodes I heard about the original Colombian version, *El Patron del Mal*. It would be a good way to improve my Spanish and to familiarise myself with Colombia. I laboured through the poor acting and poor production of 30 episodes of the 75-episode series, but inevitably gave up. Well-made or otherwise, both series seemed to glorify the actions of a man most consider a terrorist. Yet others look upon him as a Colombian Robin Hood.

One of the latter was a Colombian girl I met in Buenos Aires. She was from a small town in Antioquia, not far from Medellín. Andrea was a typical *paisa* and excessively proud of her city and region. But she had lived in Argentina for five years without having returned home for a visit. Apart from her lingerie modelling and 48 tattoos, the thing that stood out was her story about Pablo Escobar. As a four-year-old, she had received cash directly from the hand of the drug kingpin. Her family lived in a small town in a somewhat rural area, not impoverished but far from well off, and the cash donation was welcomed. To Andrea, Escobar was a hero.

Escobar certainly had money to share with the poor. Through his Medellín cartel, he was responsible for an estimated 80 per cent of all the cocaine consumed in the US in the 1980s. It gave *El Patrón* a worth of US$25–US$50 *billion* at the peak of his cocaine smuggling operation. He was supposedly earning up to US$50 million *a day*. It was so much money that Escobar and his associates had to bury cash in the countryside just to get it out of the way. (When the Spanish arrived in modern-day Colombia, they began looking for a town made of gold, El Dorado. Maybe the real El Dorado for modern-day treasure hunters would be to find this pirate's hidden piles of cash.)

Some of Escobar's money was spent on Colombia's poorest, with Escobar – a huge football fan – building floodlit football pitches in slums. These were areas that produced, possibly in part thanks to the improved facilities, players who would go on to represent teams in the Colombian Primera División as well as the *la selección colombiana*: Alexis García, *Chicho* Serna, Leonel Álvarez and René *El Loco* Higuita.

Whitewashing their ill-gotten gains through football was one way of legitimising some of the money coming in. With turnstiles taking cash, it was easy to be creative with the attendance figures of any given match, and to this end Escobar and the Medellín cartel became involved in all three major clubs in the city: Deportivo Independiente Medellín, Atlético Nacional and Envigado FC. Cartels in other cities did the same, most notably Millonarios in Bogotá and América de Cali in Cali. *Narcoball* was born and the money that came flooding into the game brought in foreign players, just like during *El Dorado* of 1949–1954. More importantly, it meant that Colombian football could afford to keep its own stars from going abroad, whilst also making their teams more competitive in South America.

Escobar was an Independiente Medellín fan, but it was their rivals Atlético Nacional who would benefit the most from the cartel's involvement. Nacional became the first Colombian side to win the Copa Libertadores in 1989. They went one better than the two teams from Cali, who had both made it to the final but lost. Deportivo Cali lost the 1978 final to Boca Juniors, whilst América de Cali lost three in a row: 1985 to Argentinos Juniors; 1986 to River Plate; and 1987 to Peñarol, in which they had won the first game, led the second, before losing the third and decisive match.

Atlético Nacional boasted many homegrown talents and a legendary former player turned manager, Francisco *Pacho* Maturana (also Colombia manager at the time). But they started the 1989 final poorly, losing the first leg 2-0 against Olimpia in Paraguay. Forced to play in Bogotá for their *home* leg, Nacional won 2-0, taking the final into a penalty shoot-out. It was a dramatic shoot-out in which 18 penalties were taken. Both Andrés Escobar and René Higuita scored, but another four were missed by Nacional. Olimpia missed five of their nine penalties and – by hook or by crook – Colombia had the best team in South America.

Off the pitch (and on it, at times) 1989 was another bloody year on the streets of Colombia. Five years after the assassination of the 37-year-old Minister of Justice, Rodrigo Lara Bonilla, by the Medellín cartel, presidential candidate Luis Carlos Galán – hoping to win the upcoming election on an anti-cartel platform – was shot dead campaigning in Soacha just outside the Bogotá city limits. Galán's successor, César Gaviria (no relation, of course, to Pablo Emilio Escobar Gaviria), was targeted next. He was due to board the Avianca Flight 203 from Bogotá to Cali but was stopped by an American DEA agent at the boarding gate. Shortly after take-off, and flying over the same town where Galán had met his end, a bomb was set off, killing 107 people on board and a further three on the ground hit by falling debris. After a lucky escape, César Gaviria went on to win the 1990 presidential election.

Whilst the new president of Colombia wasn't corruptible, most politicians in the country were. Similarly, referees could expect to have to deal with the cartels. They would be given the choice: *plata o plomo*, silver or lead, cash or a bullet. Referees were bribed, intimidated and even killed.

Two Argentine football officials have in subsequent years told stories of their involvement in Nacional's successful 1989 Copa Libertadores campaign. The experiences, independent of one another, involved games played on Colombian soil: the semi-final second leg between Nacional and the Uruguayan team Danubio, and the second leg of the final between Nacional and Paraguayans Olimpia.

Carlos Espósito, Juan Bava and Abel Gnecco were selected to officiate the game against Danubio. Having been picked up from the airport by a Colombian referee acting as attaché, they were given a tour of Medellín. But it wasn't a normal tour. The Colombian, Octavio Sierra Mesa, was making a point of highlighting all the spots where football officials had previously been murdered. 'Don't leave the hotel tonight, I would hate for something bad to happen,' Mesa said, dropping them off at Hotel Dann in the centre of the city. It could have been genuine concern for his colleagues, but it wasn't interpreted that way by the visiting Argentines.

At 1am, three masked men with machine guns entered their shared hotel suite. A fourth man, wearing black, handed the officials cash. 'Here is $50,000 each. Atlético Nacional must win. Did you hear that clearly?' Shellshocked, the Argentines discussed what to do. 'We are in God's hands,' said Gnecco. The two-metre-tall Bava, who would be running the line the following day, replied: 'Listen, *flaco*, do what you want. But if after ten minutes the home team are not winning 2-0, I'm going to throw my flag *a la mierda*, go on to the pitch and head the ball into the net, do you understand? I have kids to raise.'

Nacional won 6-0 after having drawn the first leg 0-0. There were some odd goals: one from 40 metres, others the result of unusual defensive errors by a decent side. Either way, Nacional had qualified for the final of the Copa Libertadores. The second leg of the final – due to be played in Medellín – was moved to Bogotá because the Atanasio Girardot stadium was deemed too small. That was the official explanation, at least.

Three new Argentines – Juan Carlos Loustau, Jorge Romero and Francisco Lamolina – arrived in Bogotá for the final. They would also meet a man dressed in black. 'Colombia cannot lose more finals,' he said, putting a briefcase under the table where they ate dinner the night before the game. Popular opinion says that the officials had a flawless game in El Campín that night. Nacional won 2-0 and the game went to penalties.

Penalty shoot-outs are dramatic at the best of times, but none more so than for the Argentines watching, standing alongside the players. For every penalty taken, their lives hung in the balance. Eighteen times the pendulum swung. Olimpia missed five penalties: it's not unthinkable that the Paraguayans hadn't been intimidated, much like Danubio seemingly had been in the previous round. Regardless of the circumstances, Nacional lifted the Copa Libertadores trophy and were champions of the continent.

The referee, Loustau, wasn't in the clear yet. Arriving back at the hotel by taxi, he was met by two cars and four machine-gun-carrying henchmen who drove him to the edge of the city. There they left him, deserted. Terrified and unsure of what was to follow, he ran to a nearby house and was told where he could get a taxi back into Bogotá. He found his linesmen, who by now were panicking. Romero and Lamolina got Loustau into a hot bath and gave him sedatives to calm him down.

Only a few months later, in November 1989, Álvaro Ortega Madero would take charge of a league game between América de Cali and Escobar's Independiente Medellín (not Atlético Nacional, as is often wrongly cited). According to some, referee Ortega was favourable to América. Whether he had accepted bribes or simply succumbed to pressure from the Cali cartel is impossible to know. But with América leading 3-2 in the final minute, Ortega disallowed Carlos Castro's overhead kick. It would have been the equaliser for DIM. The Medellín cartel were incensed. Three weeks later the two teams met again, this time in Medellín, and this time Ortega was running the line. A colleague was desperately trying to get the Colombian FA to change his appointment as linesman for this game, to no avail. After a 0-0 draw, Ortega was shot outside a restaurant in downtown Medellín for having robbed DIM of a crucial point in Cali three weeks earlier.

The fallout of the killing of a referee led to the Colombian championship being cancelled for the 1989 season. It was the first and only time that no champion had been crowned. Atlético Nacional, having won the Copa Libertadores on 31 May 1989, were allowed back into the competition for the 1990 campaign as champions. No other Colombian teams qualified for continental competitions due to the cancellation of the league campaign.

Much like in the 1940s and 1950s, football was a source of pride for Colombians during a violent time. *El Dorado* had been seen as a way of deflecting people's attention away from *La Violencia*. *Narcobol* would very much do the same. Football was escapism. It allowed Colombians to pretend the country was successful, when really it was living a new nightmare. When reality was a nightmare, they could close their eyes and dream. The footballing dreams continued.

Not only did Colombia have Nacional winning the biggest competition in South America, but their national team had qualified for Italia 1990. It would be their first World Cup since their only other appearance in Chile in 1962. Colombian football's success had spread to the national team. Within a short space of time they were considered one of the best in the world.

But thanks to a mistake by goalkeeper *El Loco* Higuita – losing the ball to 38-year-old Roger Milla some 35 yards from his goal – Colombia were knocked out in the last 16 by Cameroon in Naples. The game had ended 0-0 after 90 minutes. Having just conceded to go 1-0 behind in the 106th minute, Higuita received a hoofed clearance and tried to dribble past Milla, as was his wont. Higuita had done it many times before but got caught out on the biggest stage. Colombia pulled one back but lost 2-1 after extra time. Despite the loss, Colombian football was on the rise.

Between 31 July 1992 and their first World Cup 1994 game on 18 June 1994, *la selección colombiana* lost only once in 34 games (over 90 or 120 minutes). However, of these 34 games only 12 were meaningful: six games at Copa América 1993 in Ecuador (losing on penalties to eventual champions Argentina in the semi-final), and six USA 1994 qualifiers (Colombia topped their qualifying group, winning four and drawing two). Of the 22 friendlies, nine were drawn. Draws against Paraguay (twice), Venezuela (twice), a Central American XI and a 1-0 pre-World Cup friendly loss to Bolivia put the run into some context, without discrediting it altogether. After all, you can only beat who's put in front of you.

Colombia were undoubtedly a force to be reckoned with. The undeniable highlight of the run was the 5-0 demolition of Argentina in El Monumental. The victory in Buenos Aires saw the Colombians receive a standing ovation from the Argentines in attendance. It was 3 September 1993 and both teams had to win the final game of the four-team qualifying group. Argentina started aggressively, but it was Colombia who took the lead, scoring just before and after half-time. Argentina, having to attack to score three, were picked off on the counter by a brilliant Colombia side boasting a golden generation, including Carlos *El Pibe* Valderrama, Freddy Rincón and Faustino Asprilla, amongst others.

Argentina were the newly crowned Copa América champions and had reached the 1990 World Cup Final, yet they had been humiliated in their own national stadium. As a result, Pelé famously tipped Colombia to win the 1994 World Cup.

Pablo Escobar wouldn't live to watch the World Cup in the US. In December 1993, *El Patrón* was dead. He had been on the run with one bodyguard, but even when pursued, Escobar would listen to Colombia's qualifiers on a transistor radio hiding in a ditch.

He was fleeing from the Colombian police and army for 18 months after walking out of his *La Catedral* prison. Escobar and other cartel leaders had campaigned for a decade against extradition to the US on drug-trafficking charges. 'We would rather have a grave in Colombia than a jail cell in the US,' is what they would proclaim. In 1991 Escobar handed himself over to the authorities on the condition that he wouldn't be extradited and that he could build his own prison where he was guarded by officers loyal to him. *La Catedral* was more of a fortress to keep enemies out than a prison to keep *El Señor* locked away.

Also referred to as 'Hotel Escobar' or 'Club Medellín', the prison had a football pitch, which was used on several occasions to host matches played by some of the world's best footballers. Players were smuggled into the prison grounds in cars, with towels over their heads to avoid recognition by the journalists camped outside the gates. However, on one occasion, René Higuita stopped to talk to the press, and with that the goalkeeper famed for escaping his penalty area had let the cat out of the bag as to what Escobar was up to in his prison.

The most high-profile visitor to *La Catedral* was Diego Maradona. *El Diez* claimed not to have known who the cocaine baron was when he visited in 1991. He didn't read newspapers or watch the news, he said. At the time, Maradona was serving a 15-month ban from football, having tested positive for cocaine use.

Invited to play a lucrative football match at the behest of Escobar, Maradona was taken to the prison gates. 'What the fuck is going on? Am I being arrested?!' Maradona said, retelling the story nearly 25 years later. Describing the facilities at the prison as on par with those only his future employers, the Sheikhs in Dubai, could afford, Diego said: 'We played the game, and everyone enjoyed themselves. Later that evening, we had a party with the best girls I have ever seen in my life. And it was in a prison! I couldn't believe it. The next morning, he paid me and said goodbye.'

A 24-year-old Higuita watched Colombia's 5-0 win in Buenos Aires from a Bogotá prison cell. His brazen visit to *La Catedral* gave the authorities the opportunity to bring the goalkeeper in for questioning. In an attempt to get Higuita to frame Escobar, they intimidated him and threatened him with a charge of being involved in a kidnapping. The charge eventually stuck. He served seven months in a Colombian prison and missed the 1994 World Cup due to a lack of fitness.

Escobar was gunned down by police on a rooftop in December 1993. The resulting power vacuum led to even more violence and even more lawlessness, with cartels warring across the country. His downfall was depicted in two paintings by fellow *paisa* Fernando Botero, famous for exaggerating his objects' size by inflating them in a style known as *Boterismo*.

Going to the US with an inflated expectation and with the volatile situation at home, Colombia lost their opening two matches of the group stage and were already knocked out when they won their third match 2-0 against Switzerland. The pressure on the players was intense. Not only were cartels betting on the games, they were also deciding who would play. They demanded that certain players had to play to showcase them on the world stage. Lucrative international transfers represented another business opportunity. Other players were not to be picked to play and the punishment for disobeying these orders would be death. Threats were made directly to the players. They simply had to perform. Chillingly, a message appeared on the TV screens in the players' hotel rooms. It was 1994; the cartel weren't hacking the hotel's system from abroad. The message made two things clear: first, they had to win; second, the players now knew how close the cartel were to them, even on foreign soil in the US.

Having lost their first game and with the pressure at boiling point, an unfortunate own goal by Andrés Escobar in the second game versus the hosts USA condemned Colombia to an early exit. Escobar – again, no relation to his namesake Pablo – was reportedly on his way to AC Milan after the World Cup, but within ten days of his own goal, and only a few days after his return to Colombia, he had been shot dead outside a nightclub in Medellín's bar district, El Poblado.

Escobar was called 'the gentleman of football' and was apparently uneasy with the invitations to play at *El Patrón*'s ranch and later at *La Catedral*. He was a model professional from a middle-class family who captained both Atlético Nacional and the Colombian national team from a young age. He was a part of the Nacional team who won the 1989 Copa Libertadores, taking the first penalty in the shoot-out, having just turned 22.

Aged 27, he was trying to forget the Colombian nightmare at USA 1994. On the flight home, Escobar had pleaded with infamous party animal Faustino Asprilla not to go out on the town. But, ignoring his own advice, Escobar went out for a few drinks with friends. He wanted to show his face, to own his mistake and take responsibility for the national team's poor showing at the World Cup. But his night ended with taunts about his own goal. He was at Parque Lleras. It was 3am. Not knowing who it was who was mocking him, he confronted them in the car park. Six shots rang out. With every shot of the gun that killed Escobar the footballer, the shooter shouted *GOL, GOL, GOL*. Some 120,000 people attended his funeral during a week of national mourning.

Escobar had run into the Gallón Henao brothers, violent drug dealers and associates of Fidel Castaño, the leader of *Los Pepes* (Los Perseguidos por Pablo Escobar, 'those persecuted by Escobar'). *Los Pepes* was an organisation of criminals threatened and marginalised by the main drug lord. It was *Los Pepes*, working with the Colombian army, who brought down Pablo. Now the bodyguard of two *Los Pepes* members had killed Andrés with six bullets.

The bodyguard escaped punishment when the brothers said that it had been their driver who had delivered the fatal shots. Humberto Muñoz was sentenced to 45 years in prison but released after only 11. The brothers were sentenced to 15 months' house arrest for trying to cover up the murder. The house arrest wasn't respected. In a corrupt country and with their status elevated and more power gained, the brothers were free to continue their drug-trafficking operations.

This was my new home. I had heard the stories, read articles and watched series and documentaries about all of this before, but only walking around the same streets did the fragments of the puzzle begin to piece together. Trying to get to know my new city, I went around the tourist spots and wandered around different parts of town. Pablo Escobar's house is now a museum, which I thought I should check out.

The house wasn't easy to find. Inadvertently linking 'the two Escobars', I started off in the heart of El Poblado at the square Parque Lleras, close to where Andrés was killed. It looked easy enough to find Pablo's house according to the map, but a series of winding roads up the hills led me astray. I walked for over an hour past many tall, red-brick apartment blocks but I must have passed the museum. I had to regain my composure. After taking a break from the sun and heat in an air-conditioned shopping centre, I found the house I was looking for.

There was a driveway leading up to the big, white, metal gate, which was closed. There was a little intercom system, which a dark, sinister voice answered. Rather than a friendly tour guide keen to show visitors around, this sounded more like a henchman's voice. It wasn't the most welcoming museum I had been to. They were charging a ridiculous amount for entry – a steep price in a steep, hilly area of the town – so I turned around and went home. I had, at least, got to know a new neighbourhood.

By now I had decided that I wasn't going to stay in Medellín. It wasn't for me. It wasn't Buenos Aires. It was unfair to compare a new city with a place where I had lived for over three years, where I adored the locals and where I had good mates. Argentines seemed more genuine in the way they engaged with each other than other peoples on the continent. I found them to be charming in a way I didn't find elsewhere in South America.

Teaching English online one day, the topic came up. A Brazilian asked me what I thought of Brazilians compared to Argentines. I had to carefully consider how best to answer. He jumped in before I could articulate my opinions. He reasoned that, with so many authors, poets, musicians and philosophers, Argentines were the intellectuals of South America. In his words, Brazilians were more about the party – dancing and drinking. It made me think. Brazilians and Colombians were similar in this regard. Maybe it could be attributed to the climate. There is a clear cultural split between the northern half and the southern half of the continent. It's too simplistic but this Brazilian student's question had put words to my experience.

Medellín was a nice city. I definitely saw the attraction of year-round spring/summer temperatures, of a city with a handful of football clubs to visit. But it was also an odd city. It attracted the *wrong* people with its reputation for cocaine tourism and young girls. Creepy old men from western countries could be seen dating a young, plastic princess, and obnoxious expats or travellers would bore you to death with stories of coke and prostitutes.

Luckily for me, teaching English online meant that I didn't have to stay in one place. I had got to know Medellín better than most visitors, but now I wanted to see more of Colombia. Being relatively cheap, Colombia allowed me to have a work-life balance weighted heavily towards the living end of the scales. I could squeeze a week's work into a couple of days. And sacrificing a week by sitting in front of my laptop would allow me to travel for the remaining three weeks of the month. It was time I would need, as I had a girl from Argentina visiting in February and my mum visiting in March. Both wanted to see different parts of the country.

Pasto, Popayán, San Agustín, Cartagena, Santa Marta, Manizales, Pereira, Salento, Filandia, Montenegro and Colombia's Caribbean island, San Andrés, were all visited in a few weeks of backpacking. Cali and the Pacific Coast was the last destination I wanted to explore. Conveniently the *clásico Vallecaucano* was on, the second of three Colombian derbies I had hoped to catch.

Cali: Garabato's curse

AFTER AN intensive week of online English classes, I was ready for three weeks in Santiago de Cali. I left my small, rented room overlooking the bars of La Candelaria neighbourhood of Bogotá and travelled 300 miles and 12 hours south-west to Cali. Colombia's third city was the final place I wanted to visit, having seen a lot of the country over the past few months. First things first, however: I had to get hold of a ticket for the upcoming derby match.

Whilst the game would only take up 90 minutes of the three weeks, it was worth planning around. I would have lots of time to hike into Ponce, a little town in the hills outside the city, or visit the Pacific coast, with a bumpy boat ride from Buenaventura out to Juanchaco, a little fishermen's village on what is a wild western coast of Colombia. And I had lots of time to get tickets for the big game.

From the hipster neighbourhood of San Antonio, it took about an hour to walk to the shopping centre where tickets were being sold. The walk took me past the city's stadium, so I popped by to see if there was anything there, but alas, nothing. It would have been better to sell the tickets here, I thought. But no. At the shopping mall I found the little counter selling tickets and bought four. I knew my

Argentine mate, Maxi, who was also in Cali, would like to go, and an American called Ocean was keen, even though he had never watched a 'soccer' match before. At quite short notice, the game was moved from 5pm on Sunday to 8pm on Saturday. Ocean had plans; he was prioritising a salsa event over the football. Whatever the timing, someone would want the tickets.

Both the Argentine Maxi and the American Ocean were interesting characters. I had met Maxi in Bolivia and we hit it off immediately, talking about football over a *matecito*. He was travelling with his French girlfriend, but when I caught up with him in Cali, he was travelling solo again. I never asked what had happened, but I wasn't surprised – they spent a lot of time arguing in Bolivia. Maxi – tall, lean, with curious, wide-open blue eyes – kept vagabonding around South America after the last time I saw him. He *walked* from Colombia through Ecuador to Perú, stopping wherever he wanted and walking when it was time to leave. For most backpackers, taking the long-distance buses from city to city was considered slumming it. I met other travellers who spent two years or more cycling or riding a motorbike throughout the Americas. But Maxi was walking.

Ocean was a different kind of intriguing. Fittingly, the first time we met I found him lounging in the swimming pool of a hostel in Leticia. From San Francisco, Ocean was in his early 40s, with Fabrizio Ravanelli hair – not grey but white – and had a deep, seductive voice that, when I arrived, was telling an enchanted crowd that had gathered around the pool of his writing exploits working as a journalist in South America. He had mostly written about his experiences with *ayahuasca* and other types of jungle psychedelics and had two books in the making. He had a very nomadic lifestyle, arriving in cities he already knew well without any specific plans, just taking each day as it came, looking for adventure or inspiration. He would be shacked up with a girl after the first night and in a relationship for the next few months. It was Ocean who put me in touch with a cocaine-selling lawyer from whom I rented my room in Bogotá. And it was Ocean who gave me all the advice I needed with tips of great places to visit off the beaten track in Colombia. I felt bad because the only thing I could offer him in return were football stories and a bottle of Club Colombia every other round.

And while Ocean was getting ready for his salsa evening, I was heading to meet Maxi for some beers. He was working at a hostel close to the ground and we sat on the balcony with some bottles of Poker before heading to the *clásico*. Little did we know that we would be breathalysed before entering the Estadio Olímpico Pascual Guerrero. We hadn't had a lot to drink, but my heart skipped a beat when I saw the security measures. Despite having had a couple of beers, I got in without any problems. Maybe the limit was set at ten beers?

Just as I had started to relax, Maxi was stopped by one of the armed Colombian police officers manning the gates. It wasn't for failing the breathalyser, but rather for his tattoos. Despite his Argentinian accent, a River Plate tattoo on his forearm and his 'Mascherano 14' shirt from the 2006 World Cup, the policeman was concerned that he might be a Deportivo Cali fan. No away fans had been invited to this derby clash played under a huge *Fútbol En Paz* ('Football in Peace') banner. Had Maxi been a fan of the banned opposition, he would surely have a tattoo to prove it. After carefully inspecting Maxi's lean, muscly arms, the police officer asked him to lift his shirt to show his midriff. Even as a veteran of Argentinian football, Maxi had never experienced this level of security before but took it in his stride. And off we strode to our seats in the main stand on the halfway line.

Built in the 1930s, the stadium had been home to all three of the city's professional teams – América de Cali, Deportivo Cali and Boca Juniors de Cali. In 2000, Deportivo built their own ground, Estadio Deportivo Cali, a few miles out of the city limits. Deportivo were formed in 1912 and therefore can claim the nickname *El Decano*, translating to 'the dean' or 'principal'. It's a badge of honour across the continent signalling a club's claim as the original club of a city, region or country. In Uruguay, for example, both of the two big clubs – Peñarol and Nacional – claim to be *El Decano*, despite the fact that Albion Football Club existed 22 years before Peñarol, and a decade before Nacional.

Another of Deportivo Cali's nicknames is *el desaparecido verdiblanco*, 'the disappeared green-whites' or 'the missing green-whites'. With the financial pressures of the conclusion of *El Dorado* in 1954, Deportivo went bankrupt and finished second-bottom and then bottom of the Colombian league in 1955 and 1956, respectively. Out of business, they were unaffiliated from Dimayor and missed the next three seasons, coming back in 1959. The equivalent of a relegation in modern-day footballing terms, they bounced back much stronger, having restructured, and went on to have the best decade of their existence between 1965 and 1974, winning five league titles. In 1978 they lost to the original Boca Juniors (of Argentina) in the final of the Copa Libertadores.

América de Cali first played in 1918, but it wasn't until 1927 that they formally created a football club under the same name. América was the name chosen to celebrate the centenary of Colombian independence. They would go on to become one of Colombia's biggest teams, but it took them some time to get going. Part of the reason for this was the 'curse of *Garabato*'.

One of América's founders and players in 1927 was 15-year-old Benjamín Urrea, nicknamed *Garabato* (scribble) for his mazy dribbles. As a club director in 1948, he argued against the professionalisation of Colombian football and particularly that of América de Cali. Clashing with his fellow directors, Urrea was thrown out of the club. Having given so much of his life to América, he was so offended by his expulsion and the club's decision to join Dimayor that he cursed the club. In the face of opposition, *Garabato* left the meeting, exclaiming, 'Make América professional, do whatever you want with América, but by God, América will never be champions.'

Under the *Garabato* curse, América suffered for the next 31 years. After only a few years of professionalism, they – like many others in early 1950s Colombian football – were suffering financially. They had to miss the 1953 season, returning in 1954 but finishing second-bottom in 1957 and bottom in 1958 and 1959. They fared much better in the 1960s, coming second and third, but never quite managing to win their first-ever title.

In 1979, *Garabato* was interviewed by the *El Colombiano* newspaper. He admitted to having cursed his own team, the team for which he had played from the age of 15 and who he continued to support. Urrea told the journalist: 'When they threw me out, having served the club for so many years, I went to a canteen called El Hoyo and, amongst ladies of the night, I started drinking. I grabbed a bottle of aguardiente, and with each sip I cursed the players and the directors of América (one by one). The curse landed on the team [rather than the individuals] because the club never became champions.'

Shortly after this interview, *Garabato* was contacted by the club and a mass was performed at the Pascual Guerrero stadium, lifting the curse with Urrea's consent. Titles would soon follow, but other developments were concurrently taking place at América that aided the forthcoming success.

The same year as the ceremony at their ground, the club hired Gabriel Ochoa Uribe, a six-time winner of the championship as manager (five with Millonarios and once with Santa Fe). Deeply religious, Uribe was uncomfortable with América's club badge: a red devil carrying a trident. The badge crest was changed and América were ready to enter their most successful period as a club. After 15 years of watching city rivals Deportivo Cali competing at the top, América took on the mantle, immediately winning the 1979 league title. Deportivo came second in 1976, 1977, 1978 and 1980. Cali now had two big teams.

América took their badge and nickname from Los Diablos Rojos, a Colombian basketball team. In 1931 América visited Barranquilla and were invited to attend a local basketball match. The whole squad in attendance were said to be so taken aback by the red kits that they decided to change the club's colours there and then. Up until 1931 the club had been wearing white and light blue stripes and had been referred to as *El Racing* of Colombia, inspired by having read about Racing Club de Avellaneda in a copy of *El Gráfico*. América de Cali went from being the

Colombian Racing to being the Colombian Independiente. (The Argentinian Independiente also went from white and blue to red.)

The lifting of the *Garabato* curse, the removal of the devil from the badge and the new manager were all factors that undeniably assisted América de Cali's rise. The final ingredient, however, would be cocaine. The Cali cartel, like their contemporaries in Medellín and elsewhere, began using the club to cover up their devilish operations, investing their illicit cash in an attempt to whitewash and legitimise their gains. It would also win the hearts and minds of the people of Cali. Their involvement provided enough impetus for América to win five consecutive titles between 1982 and 1986.

The manager, Uribe, said that he had laughed when the media talked about América being cursed. But he wasn't laughing after their third consecutive loss in a Copa Libertadores final. In 1985, América lost to Argentinos Juniors over three games, the following year to River Plate, after losing both legs of the final (1-2 at home, 0-1 away). The most crushing of the three final defeats was the last. In 1987, Uribe's América met Óscar Washington Tabárez's Peñarol over what would again be three games. On 21 October 1987, América de Cali won the first leg 2-0 in the Estadio Olímpico Pascual Guerrero in front of 65,000 spectators. In the return match at Estadio Centenario in Montevideo a week later, América were 1-0 up before losing 2-1 to an 87th-minute winner for the Uruguayans. A draw would have been enough. In today's game with aggregated scores, a 2-1 loss to Peñarol would have been enough to see América win 3-2 over two ties. But the format was different: a third game was scheduled as a tiebreaker, *el desempate*.

Should the tiebreaker end in a draw, the scores would then be aggregated, and the Colombians would be champions, but only after extra time.

The third game finished 0-0 after 90 minutes, and with 120 minutes on the clock, Peñarol scored to win the decisive game and the 1987 Copa Libertadores. América were eight seconds from winning that elusive title, and after the game Uribe finally admitted that maybe the club was cursed after all. 'I only believe in God, but what happened to us in those Copa Libertadores finals cannot be explained.'

In the 1990s the devil was back on the shirts. Antony de Ávila – a striker who had been given his debut by Uribe in the league-winning season of 1982, aged 19 – was another member of that generation who had an issue with wearing *el diablo* on his chest. Also a devout Christian, when the devil returned to América's kits after Uribe's departure in 1990, de Ávila would put tape over the logo on his shirt and shorts, encouraging other players to do the same. So religious was the diminutive striker – less than 1.60m in height and nicknamed 'The Smurf' – that he would travel to away games with a sword so that he could perform a ritual exorcism on hotel beds, not knowing who had previously slept there.

In de Ávila's last season for América (but for a return in 2009 for one season at the age of 47), *Los Escarlatas* ('The Scarlets', to avoid calling them by their other, less holy nickname) again reached the final of the Copa Libertadores in 1996. Once again, they lost. With tape over the devil, de Ávila scored a goal from the goal line, curling the ball behind the River Plate goalkeeper who had come out of his six-yard box. With a 1-0 lead from the Estadio Pascual Guerrero, América went to Buenos Aires and lost 2-0 to two goals from a 20-year-old Hernán Crespo. A 20-year-old Marcelo Gallardo would replace Crespo for the last five minutes of that final.

It went from bad to worse for América with more strife after the lost 1996 final. As a result of the Cali cartel's involvement with the club, América were put on the Clinton List (or Specially Designated Nationals list) by the US Treasury Department. With Pablo Escobar dead, Cali cartel's leader, Miguel Rodríguez Orejuela, now ran an estimated 90 per cent of the world's cocaine operations. The arrests of the Orejuela brothers in 1995 (both extradited to the US in the mid-2000s) and their ties to América de Cali meant that the club's accounts were frozen. The financial hit was significant and in 2009 the club were relegated. Four years later they were taken off the Clinton List, returning to Colombia's top flight in 2017 after five years in the second tier. The devil came back for a final time, the idea that he was responsible for their financial and sporting calamities refuted. After all, 'neither before, nor now, has the devil on the badge played football [for América]'.

It wasn't just América de Cali who suffered bad luck. In 2002 Deportivo Cali lost two players to a lightning strike at their training ground. Hernán *Carepa* Gaviria (32) and Giovanni Córdoba (24) were killed by the freak event. In pictures, *Carepa's* body can be seen lying next to where the lightning hit, the green grass scorched. Córdoba survived the initial strike but had five heart attacks and died a few days later in hospital. Seven years later, Córdoba's younger brother and former Deportivo Cali player Hernán – aged 19 – would die in a car crash along with a fellow Atlético Huila player, Mario Beltrán. Tragedy was everywhere, it seemed.

Colombia and Colombian football had seen a lot of tragedy. Both had seen good and evil. The ban on away fans for this *clásico* was a necessary evil, although it turned out that simply checking for tattoos of the opposing team wasn't the foolproof system they maybe thought it was. Several times throughout the game a commotion could be seen somewhere in the stadium where a Deportivo Cali fan had managed to get into the ground but not quite managed to keep his or her mouth shut. Whether it was a little squeal of excitement at a *verdiblanco* chance or a full-on scream of indignation at something or other happening on the pitch, little fights were breaking out and these brave – and slightly daft – away fans were escorted from the ground. 'Better the devil you know' maybe, but I'm not sure I would have braved the feat.

América raced into a 2-0 lead, scoring in the 1st and 14th minutes, both coming after good build-up play. Deportivo Cali got a consolation goal late on, but América held out. The stadium was about three-quarters full, one end essentially empty, its upper tier sporadically dotted with red home shirts. Our seats were in the main stand, but during half-time Maxi and I made the decision to go behind the goal América would be attacking in the second half, the end where their fans were making noise. The two early goals had freed the home fans from any nerves they might have had. Luckily for us, it was easy to make our way across to join them.

Both Maxi and I were happier amongst the contingent behind the one goal, although this wasn't a peaceful place to be. América got the nickname 'the Red Devils' in part because of an early style of play that was frenetic, the players restless and irreverent, looking possessed when chasing the ball. The crowd behind the goal where Maxi and I now found ourselves were restless and irreverent, cocaine being taken in the stands and fights breaking out, seemingly amongst the home fans. There were only home fans in the ground, unless they had discovered an away fan who had managed to sneak in. Yes, there are people stupid enough to try this. The fact that América were winning put us at ease. We certainly weren't going to get involved in any turf wars that might be taking place in the stands.

Only ten days earlier I had seen América de Cali playing in Bogotá in a game they lost 3-1 to Millonarios. It was one of the big non-geographical derbies in Colombia and another *clásico* to cross off. Based on the number of titles won by certain teams, there is a ranking of the biggest (non-geographical) derbies. Nacional versus Millonarios is the biggest of these derbies, closely followed by Nacional versus América. The last of the triangular most-titles-won series sees Millonarios against América de Cali.

My mum was now visiting Colombia. It was her first of three trips to South America in the same year: three weeks in Colombia, three weeks in Perú, and towards the end of 2018 three weeks in Argentina with my brother. As she got off the plane at Bogotá's El Dorado airport, I mentioned that there was a big game on whilst she was visiting the Colombian capital. As ever, she was keen to catch a game. Growing up in north London, *la vieja* had regularly gone to see Barnet FC and Arsenal games, until she moved to Norway in 1970. She had already ticked off the Maracaná stadium in 2015 and would finally visit La Bombonera later in 2018.

In between the two most iconic grounds in South America, we visited El Campín in Bogotá. With my mum in tow, I hailed a taxi. We had already had two bad experiences taking public transport in the city, although on neither occasion was the service to blame. On both occasions it was late at night.

On the first, we were sitting at the back of a TransMilenio bus when two Colombians got on. The friends took up two of the five seats along the back row in which we were already sitting. They seemed relatively normal, two young men heading into town ready for a night out. But not long after having got on, one of the two took out a small plastic bottle with a thick yellow substance in the bottom. I had seen this before. They both began to breath in the fumes radiating from the chemical at the bottom of the bottle. My mum was unaware of what was happening, so she was surprised when I suggested we should move closer to the front of the bus.

The second time, we had just got off the same bus service and were walking back to La Candelaria neighbourhood in the centre of the city. A small, clearly drugged-up kid in his late teens came up behind us asking for money. I said no, but the kid was insistent, buoyed by the lack of people in the square and the easy gringo targets in front of him. His low-sunk, dark eyelids and menacing look suggested he wasn't *asking* for money. It was nearly midnight. He was persistent and kept following us until I told him to get lost. In situations like these – being pestered by an insistent down-and-out or drug addict – being aggressive towards them was the only thing that worked. Some tried being nice and apologetic, showing sympathy, and often ended up getting into trouble. I was sympathetic to their situation, but this was about self-preservation. Without anything to threaten us with, this chancer eventually wandered off in a different direction.

My mum had been apprehensive about visiting Colombia, which has a very violent recent history and a less violent but still uncomfortable current situation. I experienced nothing during the months I spent in Colombia, nor had I in any other part of South America, although I did have a few close encounters like this one.

Playing guide again in Rio a few years earlier, my mum and I were on another bus, going from Zona Sul through the city's centre. It was midday and the bus was essentially empty, but for four locals and the two tourists. We were in traffic entering the centre and, looking out of the window, I saw four young lads wandering aimlessly, out of place in the hustle and bustle of a Thursday morning. I thought nothing of it until two minutes later they jumped on to the bus through the back windows. I had witnessed this before in Rio but only ever from the street looking on. I half expected the bus driver or the conductor sitting at the driver's side to say something, but they kept their eyes on the traffic in front, turning a blind eye to the kids. The atmosphere on the bus changed rapidly. All of a sudden, the thick, hot air stood deadly still. Two of the four people on the bus hastily got off as if they hadn't been paying attention and suddenly realised that they were at their stop. Or was something more sinister underway?

My mum was looking out of the window, completely oblivious to the situation. She has an annoying habit of reading all the signs she sees, and she was butchering the Portuguese names, listing the names of the shops, newsagents and restaurants we were driving past. I was cringing at the sounds coming from my right but more concerned about what was happening to my left. One of the four kids had moved from the back to sit next to us, across the narrow aisle. He was sitting next to the window. I slid my phone between the seat cushions to hide it while contemplating what to do. We still had a long way to go to our destination. If the last two passengers were to get off the bus, we would be sitting ducks once we left the city centre. We would be on our own with no help from the driver or conductor to rely on. But if we got up to make a move, they might pounce.

The second option was the better and I told my mum that we were getting off, nudging her uneasily and nodding my head towards the door. I grabbed my phone from between the seats. As I was waiting for the back doors of the bus to open, my heart was pounding. The doors opened excruciatingly slowly, and I pushed my mum off. I led her straight into the first shop, the open door directly in front of us. It was a florist's. 'Is this where we were going?' she said. I was trembling. I held my right hand out in front of her to show her and explained what had happened. She hadn't noticed and was disappointed that we wouldn't be visiting the marketplace we had been aiming to visit.

With the three bus experiences fresh in my memory, we ordered a taxi to get us to El Campín. We met up with an Anglophile Colombian Arsenal fan and his girlfriend, who supported *Millos*, for a beer before the game. The heavens had opened, as they so often did in Bogotá (and Colombia in general) and we were grateful for the plastic poncho seller passing by us as we were sheltering under the roof of the little café opposite the ground. We bought a couple of bottles of Águila beer. While I was chatting to Nelson, my mum – dressed in a blue plastic rain poncho with her pink camera dangling off her right wrist – was off talking to the police horses mounted by bemused and grumpy police officers on the lookout for trouble in one of the country's fiercest derbies.

As it was, recently promoted América's star had fallen somewhat and it was an easy win for *Millos*, leading 3-0 and threatening a humiliation. América got a consolation and the game ended 3-1 in front of some 30,000 fans. The Red Devils' consolation was put past the 20-year-old Venezuelan goalkeeper, Wuilker Fariñez, who had just signed for Millonarios, playing only his fifth game after having joined from Caracas. So much had been said about this promising young goalkeeper that I was excited to see him play live, despite the fact that he had very little to do in this particular game. Fariñez had been part of the Venezuela team that made it to the U20 World Cup Final in 2017, which *la vinotinto* (red wine, as they are nicknamed after the colour of their shirts) lost 1-0 to England. I felt as if I was scouting this young goalkeeper for my own club as we had been in desperate need of a quality number one since Jens Lehmann left.

After my mum had left Colombia with thousands of photos, countless souvenirs and a handful of stories about the glue-sniffing, TransMilenio-riding locals, I had time to catch two more games before leaving the country myself. First up was Santa Fe's 1-0 loss to eventual champions River Plate in the 2018 Copa Libertadores. River Plate had the Colombian *Juanfer* Quintero pulling the strings from midfield. It had only been six months since I had seen *Juanfer* scoring the winner in the Medellín derby. The defeat was Santa Fe's only loss in the group stages, but they also only registered one win, drawing the other four. River Plate and Flamengo went through Group D, with Santa Fe going into the Copa Sudamericana.

My seat was in the main stand amongst the home fans, but I was there really to see River Plate. Once more, I was loath to turn down the chance to see an Argentinian team abroad. I had seen River play in Arequipa almost a year before, but managed to get an away ticket that day. I had seen Independiente play in Lima, but I was in amongst the Alianza fans. Speaking Spanish, my accent was Argentinian, so I had to be a bit careful when going to games involving teams from Buenos Aires. I had to keep my mouth tightly sealed as the Santa Fe fans were slagging off the Argentines with typical stereotypes. I wasn't a River Plate fan, nor an Argentine, but I was offended by the slurs. Replying would have been daft and I bit my tongue. It was a good thing I didn't have any tattoos showing my allegiance for any Argentinian club.

Three days later it was the last city derby on my list and the last big game I had wanted to catch whilst in Colombia. I had seen two in the second city, Medellín, and the Cali derby, too, in the country's third city. Now for the capital. Santa Fe were again the hosts and again I was in with the red and yellow of the home crowd, having bought a ticket to go on my own. A section behind one of the goals was reserved for a few thousand away fans wearing blue. Santa Fe versus Millonarios.

The same ground, the same hosts and the same scoreline as on the Thursday night. This time, however, it was Santa Fe who would have the bragging rights. Wuilker Fariñez lived up to the hype and kept *Millos* in the game against an aggressive and in-form Santa Fe team. The scoreline could have and should have been 3-0 or 4-0 to the home side before they managed to get two players sent off.

It's another footballing cliché, and one that I hate but use myself: the claim that a team *could have* or *should have* been winning by two/three/four goals just because they have created a few mediocre-to-decent chances. It's a cliché I wince at when I hear it on the radio, TV or a podcast. If every shot on goal – whatever the distance, angle or concentration of other players – was a goal, why have goalkeepers?

The answer was provided by Wuilker Fariñez. With the score at 1-0 thanks to the acrobatic shot-stopping of Fariñez, Millonarios had a chance to snatch an undeserved draw against the nine remaining city rivals. And they got a huge chance towards the end of the match, the back-post header put wide. A draw would have seen *Millos* reach the end-of-season mini-league (a play-off series contested by the top eight teams in the league). Alas, it wasn't to be. *Millos* weren't able to defend the title they had won at the end of 2017 by beating Santa Fe in a two-legged final.

The 1-0 win was sweet revenge for the home team, who showed their distaste for their neighbours by ripping off the fingers of the promotional paper hands left on the seats – paper hands in the style of the foam hands seen in US sports – leaving only the middle finger to taunt the opposition. It had been a feisty game played under floodlights in a fully packed Estadio El Campín and a good way to end nine months in Colombia. I had two women waiting for me in Perú and a one-way VivaAir flight booked from Bogotá to Lima.

Lima calling

THE PLAN to stay a year in Medellín didn't work out. I had been lucky to travel around for a few months, working little and seeing a lot of an interesting country. Nine months earlier I had met a girl in Lima and our relationship had grown stronger over the months, despite living in different countries. We wanted to give our relationship a real go and I went to Lima to move in with her and her two boys, aged four and seven.

Most of the girls I had met and got to know during six years in South America had children. The Argentine, the Colombian, the Bolivian and now the Peruvian. I got a reputation for dating mothers. Passing 30 years of age – I tried explaining – the chances of meeting someone with kids is higher, but the goading continued. The fact that Olga had *two* children reinforced the joke. There are many different reasons why girls in South America have children at a young age, but a lack of education and communication on the birds and the bees ranks high on the list across a region ruled by the Church.

I flew from Bogotá to Lima. Initially I only had six months, partly because of the tourist visa I was on, but also because I had committed to being in Buenos Aires at the end of October. A good mate from school who was visiting Argentina, a plan set in stone long before the idea to move to Lima came up.

Soon after I moved in with Olga and her two sons, we received our first visitor from abroad: my own mother. Three months after our three weeks together in Colombia, *la vieja* was back. Her birthday was coming up in June – in the middle of the World Cup in Russia – and I had promised to take her to Machu Picchu. The Inca citadel is the most popular and most visited attraction in the whole of South America. I hadn't realised it when I suggested her visit to Perú, but I would be sacrificing a lot of the World Cup. Perú's first World Cup since 1982.

The build-up to the World Cup was feverish for the locals. Flags, banners, kits and Panini football stickers took over Perú's capital, Lima. The staff at the little restaurant where I ate lunch every day wore the famous white shirt with a red sash, and the tablecloths were identical, with decorations and bunting inside and out. The terrible buses of Lima had some form of decorations, too, although often half-arsed – they were more concerned with cramming as many locals into their vans as possible. The bigger buses were often packed. Worse were the little vans, only slightly bigger than an estate or people-carrier – up to 30 people would be squeezed into these. There wasn't much room for decorations.

Olga's two boys were completely taken by the tournament. I envied them experiencing their first World Cup. I made it clear to them how lucky they were that Perú would be a part of it. Previous generations hadn't been so lucky. The Norwegian half of me knew what it was like to be excluded from the party tournament after tournament.

The stickers and sticker album helped them get into it; within a couple of months the two young boys learned the names of all the Peruvian and England players, as well as many others. They also learned about 32 different countries and recognised the flags of countries they hadn't even heard of a few weeks prior.

Looking to exchange stickers, we would go to the central plaza in Miraflores. The seven-year-old would have to negotiate with teenagers and grown-ups to complete his album. The Panini phenomenon really took off in Perú that year and the square was mostly middle-aged male and female collectors, with a few kids dotted amongst them. There were some unscrupulous adults tricking children into parting ways with a sticker they needed. I grew to dislike some elements of Peruvian culture during my next few months there. Adults shamelessly ripping off children for football stickers was one of those aspects.

Perú was eight hours behind Russia. It brought back memories of the 2002 World Cup in Japan and South Korea. I was 17 years old, going to sixth-form, college and games started before classes. The earliest games for Peruvians would begin at 8am, with the second game at 11am and the third at 2pm. The kick-off times inevitably clashed with our sightseeing, whilst many Peruvians would be at work or school. Lucky for everyone concerned then that *Los Incas* first game was on the first Saturday of the tournament.

Mum and I had booked a flight to Cusco for that Saturday. We had watched Argentina's 1-1 with Iceland at home before leaving for the airport. Our only hope to catch the Perú game was to find a bar or restaurant at the Jorge Chávez International Airport for the 11am kick-off. When we arrived, however, the only screen showing the game was that of a credit card company who had a little stand in the check-in area. There must have been about 70 people crammed around the small TV screen to watch the game. The two salespeople dressed from head to toe in the red colours of the credit card company stood idly to the side, knowing that they wouldn't be selling anything for the next 90 minutes. Even the police dog handlers found a good vantage point from which to watch Perú's first game at a World Cup for 36 years.

La Blanquirroja had been ranked as the tenth-best team in the world only a year earlier, up 80 places from their footballing nadir 11 years earlier when they were ranked 91st. It had been a good turnaround. They took a decent squad to Russia, consisting of some dynamic, energetic young players and the experienced heads of Jefferson Farfán and Paolo Guerrero, aged 33 and 34 respectively. Guerrero was their talisman and was very lucky to be playing at the World Cup. He had failed a drug test and had been banned for the tournament, but on appeal it was suspended, allowing him to play.

With Guerrero on the bench, Perú started well against Denmark, winning a penalty on the stroke of half-time. A 1-0 half-time lead would have been deserved but Christian Cueva sent his penalty miles over the crossbar. The Danes scored in the second half to win 1-0. It was a result that was unfair on Perú, who went on to create and spurn a handful of chances. 'It could have been 3-2', as the cliché would suggest.

At half-time we had to rush off through security to departures, missing the rest of the game. Most airports had bars and TVs for football, but it didn't surprise me much that Lima's didn't. Catching only half the game would begin an unfortunate pattern. We caught the second half of Perú's 1-0 defeat to France, having just arrived in Aguas Calientes (now known as Machu Picchu Pueblo). We got off the train and rushed to the nearest restaurant for a cold Cusqueña beer and another 45 minutes of Peruvian World Cup football. It was another 1-0 defeat for *Los Incas*, when a draw probably would have been a fair result. Instead of sitting on four points after two group games, Perú had none and were already eliminated from the World Cup.

After the Perú-France game we had enough time to check into our hotel and find a pub for the next game: Argentina versus Croatia. The next day we would be getting up early to visit Machu Picchu on my mother's 68th birthday, so I reasoned that we should take it easy, having spent the day travelling. It hadn't really been so taxing to get to the village, which sits at the foot of the Machu Picchu mountain, but I wanted to watch Argentina. My mum was happy to get some good food and have a few beers in front of the football.

22 June: We watched the last 20 minutes of Brazil versus Costa Rica from the restaurant at the archaeological site of Machu Picchu. It was 0-0 and there were many tense-looking Brazilian visitors biting their fingers. They had also planned poorly and were missing the game, or maybe they had underestimated Costa Rica. Brazil scored two injury-time goals and won 2-0. Brazil had always been admired and were probably a lot of people's second team on the international stage, but there was something about this version of Brazil, Neymar Junior's Brazil. Neymar quickly became the pantomime villain of the tournament with pathetic, toddler-like histrionics. I wanted his team – and the petulant little spoiled man-child – to drop points to Costa Rica, and I got the impression most of the others having a break from hiking around Machu Picchu did, too. It was disappointing when Coutinho scored in the 91st minute, with Neymar himself adding another in the 97th minute.

23 June: We left Aguas Calientes for Ollantaytambo and arrived before Germany played Sweden. I settled into the sofa at our hostel to see Toni Kroos' 95th-minute wonder strike. Ollantaytambo is a popular tourist town in the Urubamba Valley, also known as the Sacred Valley of the Incas. It was the scene of a battle between the Incas and the Spanish in the mid-1500s. The Incas – led by Manco Inca Yupanqui, father of Túpac Amaru – won the battle with 30,000 Inca warriors, but when Spanish reinforcements arrived in the former Inca capital, Cusco, they left Ollantaytambo for Vilcabamba, where they established the Neo-Inca State, which lasted for the next 35 years until Túpac's execution. Along with its history, it was a stunningly charming little village, and we didn't mind missing Belgium versus Tunisia to potter around the small, cobbled streets.

24 June: We wanted to continue our sightseeing of Ollantaytambo and the Sacred Valley but first things first: we had to watch England's 6-1 thrashing of Panama at 8am. With the game out of the way we could wander around town, visiting another Incan archaeological site, the Pinkuylluna. I was impressed with all the hiking up and down hills and in and out of these Incan masterpieces that my mum could handle, especially when you consider the altitude and mum's lungs, veterans of the cigarette. By early afternoon, however, we were both tired and it was time for a sit-down with some Peruvian cuisine, a Cusqueña and Poland against Colombia.

26 June: We had moved on along the Sacred Valley and were in Pisaq, an hour from Ollantaytambo, along the Urubamba river. The town has a reputation for spirituality, with many visitors seeking yoga, meditation and hallucinogenic experiences from so-called plant medicine. I was only there for the Cusqueña and the football. Argentina were facing Nigeria in a final Group D game. I wasn't the only Argentina fan in the little, hippy café we found ourselves in. The whole place exploded when Marcus Rojo scored late against Nigeria to send Argentina through to the knockout stages.

The hippy café was run by a middle-aged Englishman who had lived in the Sacred Valley for several years. A year earlier, on my solo travels, I had been sitting on the same café's balcony overlooking Pisaq's botanic gardens. I was having a beer with an Argentine backpacker who had a fascinating story about ayahuasca, a brew made from hallucinogenic plants, which has been used as a spiritual medicine by indigenous peoples throughout the continent for centuries. Ayahuasca and other plant-psychedelics have become a huge part of the tourism industry, and like everyone else, I was intrigued.

Throughout my five months of travelling through Bolivia, Perú and Colombia the year before, I had come across more and more people telling their stories of ayahuasca. For every genuine experience had, someone had a story of a bogus ceremony. Fake shamans were preying on the cash-rich but time-poor visitors and taking advantage. Tourists flew into the region to pay several hundred dollars to drink a tea they really had no idea about: no idea about the intended use, the history, the risks and the setting. I met one American girl who had flown to Cusco specifically to take ayahuasca. She only had a week of holidays, so it had to be quick, she had no time to waste. After her session, she came back to the hostel to tell us that she had been violently sick and been to the toilet several times but had had no real psychedelic effects. But at least she can say she has done it.

The ayahuasca process is rather more complicated. To get something out of the experience, a two- to three-week detox of city life, mobile phone screens, pollution, red meat, alcohol and even sex is recommended in order to prepare your body for a ceremony. Even then, the first sitting will simply purge your body physically. Each session after that will provide deeper psychedelic trips and more psyche-cleansing will take place. Even paying money for what should be a spiritual ritual is looked down upon by the real shamans and indigenous people to whom the culture belongs.

Sitting on the balcony with a cold Cusqueña, I was chatting to a fast-talking Argentine. Just when I thought I had mastered the language, I got a jolt by someone thinking I would understand them if they spoke as they would with their mates back home. It was a compliment to my Spanish, but it made me realise I hadn't mastered the language yet. What I did understand of the story was that he'd had a very positive experience of ayahuasca in Brazil. He told me that he was sitting on the kerb in Rio crying, overwhelmed by the emotion of having lost a brother and a sister in separate accidents a short time prior to going travelling. Someone saw his despair and went to check on him and, after an hour of talking, invited him to join him and his friends for some food. The group of friends were planning an ayahuasca session and invited the Argentine along. 'You see, ayahuasca will find you,' he told me. Many travellers look desperately to find these psychedelic experiences and invariably many get ripped off or have a disappointing experience. From that moment on, I stopped looking into the possibilities and decided to wait for the experience to find me.

27 June: For now, with the psychedelics put off for the foreseeable future, I was back on the coca leaves, cramming them into my cheek for yet more hiking through Inca ruins. Sitting on the hill overlooking the town, the Pisaq ruins are impressive. It was a tough climb for my mum, who was game, as ever. Sporty old girl, I thought. And she was doing it all without coca leaves, having refused to use them due to their use in the production of cocaine. For being such a sporty travel companion, the very least she deserved was a cold Cusqueña and some football. In fact, we hadn't sought out the Brazil-Serbia game, but it happened to be on in the cheap, local restaurant where we plonked ourselves down after another day of activity at altitude to watch another irritating Neymar performance.

28 June: We had been on the road for 12 days now and it was time to fly back to Lima. Arriving at the small airport in Cusco, however, we found out that our flight had been cancelled due to high winds in the mountains. The queue for information and a refund was already huge, as were the queues leading to other airlines, all of which seemed to be flying. Our airline – the low-cost disaster that was VivaColombia, later VivaAir – had a bad reputation for cancelling flights willy-nilly and providing little to no help to stranded travellers. We bought another flight online, but we now had five hours to kill at the Alejandro Velasco Astete International Airport. Luckily for us, the waiting areas in the airport were kitted out with televisions and we got to watch the whole of the meaningless England-Belgium group game.

3 July: Another England game, but a lot more meaningful than the loss to Belgium. Mum and I were now back in Lima, reunited with Olga and the boys. There was a cheap, no-frills Peruvian restaurant around the corner from where the boys went to school. The neighbourhood was dusty and needed a lick of paint, but the school at least was modern. England versus Colombia kicked off at 9pm Moscow time, 1pm in Lima, and the boys left school around 2pm. Perfect! We got to watch the first half with a cold Cusqueña and some food. The boys had worn their new England kits to school, and I was convinced they would be enthused by the knockout stages of the World Cup. I was excited to see them enjoying football. And what could be more enticing than a penalty shoot-out? We tucked into our starter soup and plates of chicharron, aji de gallina and tallarines con huancaina – all for £2 – and nervously enjoyed the last-16 match.

England went through and their travelling around Russia would continue. Our travelling in Perú wasn't finished, either. We had two options: stay in Lima with Olga and the boys to see more parts of the city, or travel four hours south to Ica and Nazca. There was no football on now; we were in that brutal period between quarter-finals and semi-finals where all of a sudden there are no games. Up until now, we had at least had the option to switch the telly on and see a game if we had time to kill. It had served as a good excuse to find somewhere for a cold Cusqueña. But the fact there was no football to be missed swayed the decision; we would head south.

'Will I need my passport?' asked my mum, shortly before we left the house. 'What for? We're only jumping on a bus and travelling a few hours; we will be nowhere near the border.' She left hers at home, but as mine was already in my backpack, I ended up taking it. It was 7am when we were due to board the bus, but as we arrived to the front of the queue, I had a nagging feeling that we were going to have to show our passports. Fuck! I had been travelling for months in Perú and had always shown my passport, but figured it was for the ID. My mum had ID, but not her passport. I managed to convince the lady to let us on to the bus, but she warned me that we might not be able to board a bus coming back.

Our first stop was the desert oasis at Huacachina – an incredibly touristic spot on a little lake surrounded by sand dunes stretching towards the Pacific coast. I could see the appeal of the place, but it had gone from charming little gem to tourist trap with aggressive salespeople, tacky bars and restaurants and high prices. This is what we gringos do: flood these attractive little places and turn them into greedy, soulless monsters.

The next day we visited Nazca, an awful little town that had also been possessed by the tourism devil. The reason for the town's popularity were the Nazca lines, geoglyphs – or drawings – etched into the desert sand by tribes inhabiting the area 2000 years ago. Some geoglyphs are over a kilometre long, and the best way to see them is to jump into a small plane and cruise over them. The dog, the condor, the fish, the spider and the most famous of them all, the hummingbird, were all visible, although we had to put up with the loud noise of the propeller.

We would have been able to put up with the noise had they flown us back to Lima because getting a bus back proved to be tricky. I had hoped to be able to convince them to let us on – it had worked in Lima – but the bus operators of Nazca were a miserably stubborn lot. We tried all the companies, walking up and down the town's main street, but to no avail. With Mum's flight back to London the next day, we only had one option: go to the police station to report the passport lost or stolen.

We spent an hour in the police officer's office. He had loads of time and seemed pleased to have someone to talk to. It turns out this Peruvian copper was a big fan of the Norwegian pop group A-Ha. Who wasn't?! After an hour of music, football and travelling talk, we left the police station with a permit to travel and the policeman's phone number. He lived in Lima and wanted to meet up for a beer to talk about football. I never did ring him; I thought he might find out about the little white lie.

10 July: The end of Wendy's second of three trips to the continent had come to an end. With her safely back in the UK, I could watch the World Cup semi-finals after the boys had finished school. Again wearing their England shirts with pride, the two boys came out of school and we ate lunch at a *cevichería* in Barranco. They didn't quite grasp the enormity of the occasion. They had just seen England lose in the semi-final of a World Cup. Regardless of people's expectations for the tournament, I expected them to be more downbeat. England's loss to Croatia wasn't their Euro 1996 moment.

15 July: The World Cup Final. France versus Croatia. Olga and I went to an Irish bar, one I had got to know well over the past two months as I played football with one of the owners. Molly's Pub was exactly what Buenos Aires had lacked: a pub that showed all sports at all hours of the day – just ask and they put it on. For Olga, it was her first taste of an English (or 'Irish') breakfast. For me, it wasn't my first taste of Cusqueña, my second love in the country famed for cuisine. Another country famed for its cuisine would be taking on England's conquerors and it turned out to be an entertaining game. Most finals are dour occasions, with two teams afraid of putting a foot wrong. For Olga and me, it was a chance to let our hair down after a few busy weeks.

Travelling with your mum has its upsides and downsides. More than anything, it was nice to see her, having spent a few years abroad and only coming home twice in the six years I had spent in South America. And, because *la vieja* was unwilling to live every aspect of the backpackers' lifestyle, the quality of accommodation and restaurants invariably increased. Whilst very sporty and generally easy-going, a six-bed dorm room was not something my nearly 70-year-old mother was keen on experiencing. I was happy to act as a guide, revisiting places I had already been to, but also having the chance to go to new parts of the country, so far unseen.

International cricket aspirations. Perú's national team were due a send-off before the World Cup and I had wanted to visit the Estadio Nacional in Lima. They were playing Scotland in a friendly and sold out in a flash. After the World Cup, however, another Lima *clásico* was on the cards and it would be played at the national stadium. The game between Universitario de Deportes and Alianza Lima gave me a new opportunity to tick off another ground in the capital.

La U were again the home side. I would have happily gone to the game alone, but I thought it would be a good opportunity for the boys to go to their first game. Olga was an Alianza Lima fan, but no away fans were allowed to attend. We had to make it clear to the boys that they

With Los Pibes de Soldati. Enjoying the build-up to River Plate versus Boca Juniors in the 2014 Copa Sudamericana semi-final at El Monumental.

El Monumental. The monumental Estadio Antonio Vespucio Liberti is the home of Club Atlético River Plate and the Argentinian national team.

El fantasma de la B. The so-called 'Ghost of the B' at La Bombonera for Boca Juniors versus River Plate in 2015. This was very probably the same drone that paid a visit to El Monumental six months earlier.

World Cup qualifying: Argentina versus Brazil at El Monumental.

Club Deportivo Palestino caused controversy when the club changed the No. 1 on their kits to represent the outline of Palestine pre-1948.

Santiago de Chile. Gate 8 at the Estadio Nacional de Santiago has been left untouched since the horrors witnessed by the stadium at the start of the General Augusto Pinochet military dictatorship in 1973.

My local team. Fourth tier Club Atlético Excursionistas' ground El Coliseo del Bajo Belgrano. Our amateur team played regularly here.

La Paz. Bolivia's Estadio Hernando Siles is the world's highest national team stadium at 3,600 metres. There are only a handful of grounds at a higher altitude.

Bolivia 2-0 Argentina, March 2017 at Estadio Hernando Siles. Lionel Messi had made the trip but been handed a suspension by CONMEBOL whilst on the flight to La Paz.

El Monumental de 'La U'. Universitario de Deportes' stadium on the outskirts of Lima, Perú.

Chachapoyas, Perú. The enchanting sarcophagi at El Tigre mountain.

Bogotá, Colombia. El Campín – officially Estadio Nemesio Camacho – is home to both Independiente Santa Fe and Millonarios.

Medellín, Colombia. Deportivo Independiente Medellín 1-0 Atlético Nacional at Estadio Atanasio Girardot.

The second of two clásicos paisas: Atlético Nacional 0-0 Independiente Deportivo Medellín.

In Patagonia. Perito Moreno glacier, 30 miles from the Patagonian town El Calafate.

Stunning view of Mount Fitz Roy from the road leading to El Chaltén in southern Patagonia.

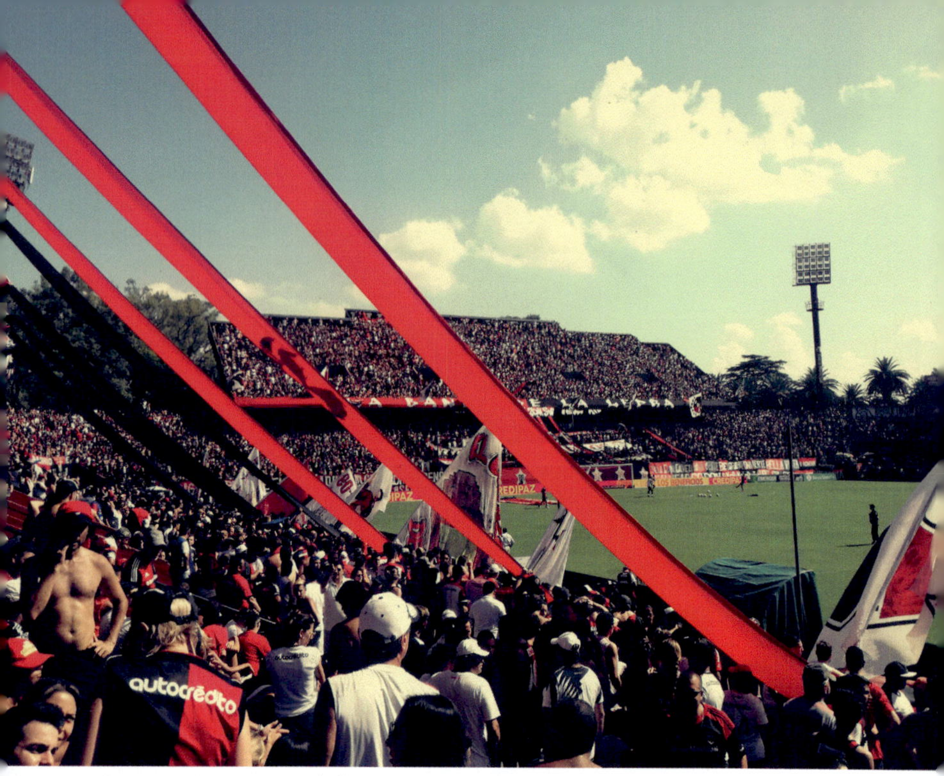

Rosario, Argentina. El clásico rosarino: Newell's Old Boys 0-0 Rosario Central at Estadio Marcelo Bielsa.

Morón, Buenos Aires. Seventeen-year-old Mariano Guaraz was the 200th person to die as a result of violence at an Argentinian football match. His mural at Estadio Nuevo Francisco Urbano ensures that he will not be forgotten.

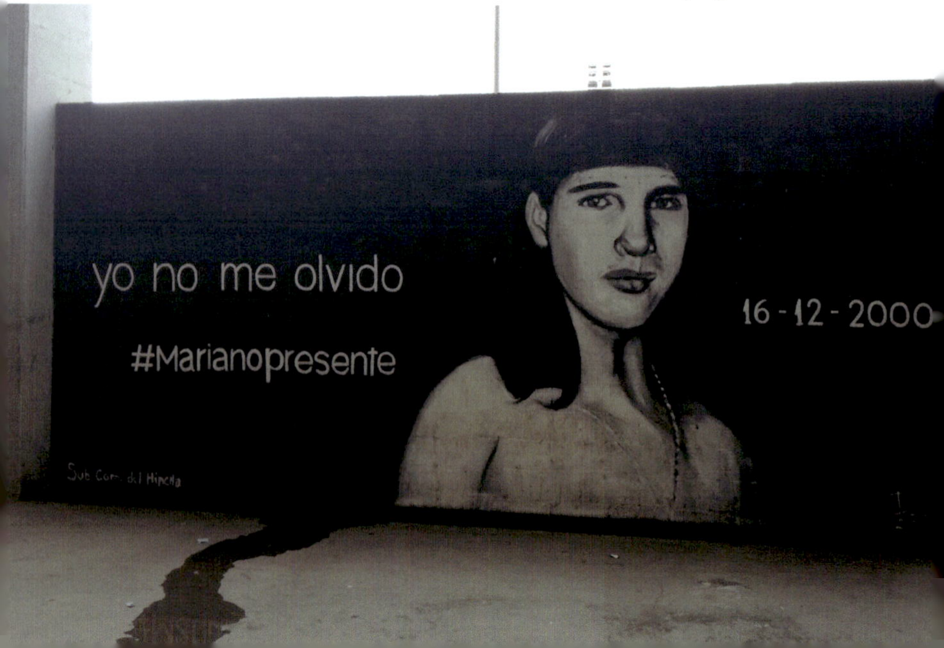

yo no me olvido

#Marianopresente

16 - 12 - 2000

couldn't celebrate if Alianza scored. We practised the non-celebration before leaving home.

When we arrived at the ground the policemen were again breathalysing fans. Much like in Cali only a few months earlier, I hadn't even considered the prospect of dry games. I had ordered a cold Cusqueña with my lunch, and with my other half's blessing another Cusqueña whilst waiting for the boys to finish their lunch. Were they slow eaters or was I especially thirsty? The police officer, seeing that I was accompanying my girlfriend and her two young children, realised that this fair-haired gringo probably wasn't a part of the *barra brava* and let me through. For a brief moment I feared we would all be turned away. I had met a lot of officious officials in South America; I was lucky that this one was reasonable.

We were sitting high up in the upper tier of the Estadio Nacional de Lima for a typical derby game. The tense game finished 1-1. It didn't compare for entertainment with the first *La U*-Alianza game, but I was happy to have been to the three major grounds in Lima. And to have seen Alianza Lima play in all three was a nice thread that tied the three games together. When it came to seeing other teams at other grounds – Sporting Cristal, Sports Boys and Deportivo Municipal – I was a bit lazy, using family life and work as an excuse. One needs to save some for a return visit, though, right?

When it came to playing football, however, I made the time. Passing through Lima the year before, I had met some British expats living there. We were watching an Arsenal game at an English pub in the gringo neighbourhood of Miraflores and they invited me to play. A year later and having moved to the city, I got in touch with them again.

I went along to train with the Kiteflyers. At first it seemed that the Kiteflyers was an unremarkable pub side for expats living abroad, but, as I was to learn, they had more heritage than most other such teams. They had been going for a couple of decades, with both football and cricket teams. And they often played games at the Lima Cricket and Football Club in San Isidro, a private country club with over 150 years of sporting history.

Lima Cricket and Football Club was the first football team founded in the Americas in 1859 (and, going further back, the first cricket team, too). In 1912 they won the first Peruvian football championship, coming runners-up in 1913 and winning it again in 1914. They stopped competing in the league in 1916 in order to 'focus on other sports'. A century later they now compete in the Copa Perú, along with the 22,000 other amateur teams in the country.

I made my debut for the Kiteflyers at Lima Cricket and Football ground, playing against the Tartan Army, visiting Lima for the Perú-Scotland friendly. Playing at one of the oldest football grounds in all of the Americas for a football nerd like me was not insignificant. Even though I was essentially playing for a pub side in a friendly against still-drunk-from-last-night Scots, I enjoyed the run around. I even got a goal so as to be able to say I had scored on the hallowed turf where the first-ever Peruvian league game took place. During my five months in Lima, I enjoyed my time with the Kiteflyers, playing once a week and enjoying the social side at Molly's. The expat community is always one you can rely on when you find yourself in a big city in Latin America.

More importantly, it opened the door to arguably my greatest sporting achievement – on paper at least. Sitting in the beer garden of the Irish pub at the Lima Cricket and

Football Club, my new team-mates would relate stories of their international cricket careers. Many of them had turned out for the Perú national cricket team. In Argentina, I had also met a few Brits who had represented the Argentinian national cricket team. I was envious – I also wanted to say that I had played a sport at an international level. Any sport.

I hadn't played cricket since school, and even then never showed any particular promise. Seventeen years later I didn't want to be that newbie who wants to play despite being awful compared to the rest. I had met several such people on the football pitches in Buenos Aires – almost exclusively from the US. They wanted to play, but had no conception of the disparity in level between those who had been playing a sport for decades and those who had been playing for a few months. These were people who could barely kick a soccer ball, whose run-up involved a hop, skip and a jump. Any contact was invariably followed by a whooping sound. 'This is suuuper fun.'

I didn't want to be *that* person. Nevertheless, the Inca cricketing gods wouldn't let me back out and my international cricket cap was forced upon me in auspicious circumstances. A friendly tournament had been organised between Argentina, Perú and Chile in Buenos Aires.

My six months in Lima had come to an end and I had said my goodbyes to the Kiteflyers, Lima Cricket and Football Club and Perú and gone back to Argentina, leaving Olga and the boys for a few months. Shortly after returning to Buenos Aires, I received a message saying that some of the Molly's pub regulars would be in town, that we should grab some beers. Of course I was keen.

But a couple of days before the international friendly cricket tournament, I got another message. Was I keen on playing cricket for the Peruvian national cricket team? This was my calling. For official International Cricket Council games, players only needed three years of residency in the country to qualify. Had it been Argentina, I would have qualified to play (but the call-up wasn't forthcoming). When it came to international friendlies, anyone could play. And I was that *anyone*.

I was a little bit nervous when the day came around. It was autumn in Buenos Aires, a little on the nippy side with rain in the air. We got on the hired double-decker coach to take us out of town to an old country club, which had probably been used by some of the first British settlers well over a century earlier. Out on the field, I bowled a couple of practice overs and they weren't too bad. It was suggested that I might get an over in the game itself. I started building myself up to the eventuality, half of me wanting to do it, the other hesitant.

I had already drafted a text message to one of my best mates from school who had moved to Australia on a cricket scholarship. Ben was a promising bowler and captain of our county's youth team. And I couldn't wait to rub it in his face that after two decades of his striving to reach a decent level of the game, I had taken a shortcut and surpassed him. (Receiving the message on the other side of the world, Ben laughed and congratulated me. I got the impression he wasn't taking the achievement as seriously as he should.)

Needless to say, we lost our first match against Argentina. I didn't know any of the Brits amongst the Argentina contingent. In fact, it looked as if they were all Argentines, although I suspect the majority came from Anglo-Argentine families, of which there were many. My over never came, but I fielded competently on the damp grass. I was the eleventh and final batsman and, as the tail end was quickly depleting, my heart skipped a beat as I was asked to put my pads on. I had no box and wasn't too keen to borrow one, so I left that decision hanging until the final minute. I would have liked to have faced some balls on what would probably be my only international cricket cap, but rain intervened. With only four overs left and already beaten, we threw in the towel and headed for the bar.

With a litre of cold Quilmes in my hand, I was presented with a Perú cricket cap – an actual, physical *baseball* cap with the Perú cricket badge. It was a thing of beauty. There weren't, however, enough caps to go round so I made sure it was given to someone more deserving: a young Peruvian who would play again for his national team. For me, a picture would suffice. I would need evidence when telling my grandchildren about having played cricket on the international stage for the 53rd-ranked nation.

In Patagonia

I PICKED up Bruce Chatwin's 1977 book *In Patagonia* for a third time. By 2019 I had spent more than five years in South America, with nearly four of those in Argentina, yet I hadn't made it further south than Bariloche. The town was halfway along the western spine of the country, nearly equidistant from the northern to the southern borders of Argentina. There were another 1,200 miles of open land to the self-titled 'southernmost city of Ushuaia'.

Scores of expats and backpackers had shared their experiences of travelling south. Before leaving the continent for good, I had to embark on the expedition myself. And the timing was perfect. Argentina had never been cheaper, for the gringo at least. A devaluation of the Argentine peso in mid-2018 meant the European prices became South American prices. Argentina had always been dear, much more so than Bolivia, Perú and Colombia, where the cost of living was significantly lower. While it was good for those who earned foreign currency, it was terrible for the locals, whose spending power on their own holidays abroad halved.

I was torn. It was difficult to take pleasure in the juxtaposition: much lower prices for me = good; local friends' travel budgets halved overnight = bad. Argentines love to travel, and the devaluation severely affected my friends' possibilities of backpacking throughout their own continent. I had been lucky enough to travel extensively outside of Argentina and could now travel twice as far or long around Patagonia on the money saved up in my bank account. Argentines would barely be able to travel for half of what they had previously dreamed of. On the flipside of the quandary, and being selfish, I had lived in the country for three and a half years paying over the odds for everything, so I had to look at this as a little bonus to be enjoyed before moving back to Europe.

Patagonia is a huge region spanning two countries – the southern halves of both Chile and Argentina. It's a vast expanse of essentially nothing and nobody. Dotted between the nothingness and nobodies are mountains, lakes, fjords, glaciers, deserts, islands, the last vestiges of indigenous tribes, flora and fauna and stories galore reigning supreme. There was a lot to see for a region of nothing.

But nobody went to Patagonia for the weather. Ushuaia at the southern tip of the continent has an average year-round temperature of about 6°C (despite the fact it's the main city of the archipelago named Tierra del Fuego, 'the Land of Fire'). The region is also infamous for its brutal wind. The fabled winds are said to make man go insane. This might explain why only two million people inhabit a region 1.5 times the size of the UK.

In 1519 Portuguese explorer Ferdinand Magellan – working for Spain's King Charles I – set off westwards headed for the East Indies (specifically Indonesia and the Philippines). Magellan and his fleet of five ships were struggling against the wild winds and decided to settle down for the winter. They made landfall on the southernmost tip of the Americas and immediately encountered the locals. The Tehuelche tribesmen they came across soared above them – they were giants compared to the small Europeans. The average male height in Europe at the time was 1.65m (5ft 5in) but these indigenous people were more than double this, with the male average of the natives over two metres. Reports claim that the tallest natives reached four metres of height.

Magellan named the giants Patagones. His Italian chronicler, Antonio Pigafetta, probably would have noted this down in his native tongue as Patagoni. Two theories exist as to the name. *Pata* means foot in Spanish and, referencing the footprints the crew had seen before encountering the tribespeople, *Patagon* could be interpreted to mean 'big feet'. More probably, Magellan was naming the tribesmen after a giant called Pathoagón from the Spanish novel *Primaleón*, published in 1512, shortly before the voyage. Whatever the reason, the conclusion was the same: the strange people they came across were huge.

With giants roaming the area mostly naked, despite the cold, Patagonia was a mystical place. Chatwin wrote about the giants living alongside a race of short people (the Yoshil, last sighted in 1928), about unicorns, as well as other fauna now extinct. Charles Darwin passed through on the *Beagle* in 1832–33 and his observations in Patagonia were key in forming his theories of evolution and natural selection. The region had so much intrigue and I couldn't wait to get on the road and experience the final frontier of my own time in South America.

Olga was joining me. We hadn't seen each other for a couple of months, and she had time off for the summer holidays. She had never been to Argentina. After a week of sightseeing in the capital and celebrating New Year's

Eve with some friends – a rooftop barbeque and beers in 35°C heat in the middle of summer – we jumped on a long-distance bus taking us south along the east coast, passing the beach towns of Pinamar, Mar del Plata, Miramar and any other amalgamation of letters and the prefix or suffix *mar* (sea). These seaside towns are where hundreds of thousands of *porteños* (Buenos Aires residents) flee to in order to avoid the scorching summer temperatures of the capital.

Of the next 34 nights of travelling, we would spend 32 in the tent, with two nights spent at a young couple's house in Bariloche, who were kind to put us up. Between us we were sharing one sleeping bag, Olga having left hers in Lima. Temperatures would at times be as low as 5°C at night but we couldn't squeeze into the same bag. We would have to use it as a duvet. But it wasn't too cold, yet.

Our first destination was the town of Puerto Madryn. For 20 hours we sat looking out of the coach window, initially seeing cityscapes, which were soon replaced by towns of single-storey buildings. And then hour after hour of semi-arid fields, fenced in to mark the land of a rich *estancia* owner. As the light changed, the scenery didn't, not until it was pitch-black outside, anyway.

Our double-decked, long-distance coach cruised along in the silence of the open, flat and straight highway. Thunderstorms are very common at this time of year, with the oppressive heat building up until the pressure explodes. They were fun to watch from the safety of a home, but it was something else to be sitting on the top deck watching a storm unfold many dozens of miles in the distance. The eerie thing about it was the silence. We were so far away from the storm that we couldn't hear the rumbling or the thunder crashing down.

The storm served as a diversion. The supposed entertainment provided on the buses in South America was torture. With one DVD system for the whole bus, there is no choice and no volume control. Those decisions fell to the middle-aged male conductor onboard. Inevitably, a dubbed Hollywood action film was selected with the sound of explosions, gunfire, shouting and tyres screeching on full volume. BOOOM, BRAP BRAP BRAP, EEEEEEEARGGGGCHH!!! Film after film after film, mile after mile after mile. Forget about reading a book or listening to a podcast.

Ears ringing, we got to Puerto Madryn, where we found the Argentinian equivalent of the British AA (Automobile Association). The ACA (Automóvil Club Argentino) ran a campsite. Fully loaded with a big full-to-the-brim backpack each and a smaller bag on our bellies, we walked from the bus station a couple of miles along the beach to find the site where we could pitch our tent. The walk took about an hour, enough time for me to listen to the second half of Arsenal versus Blackpool in the FA Cup third round. It was the first Saturday of the year after all.

After setting up the tent, we walked a couple of miles back along the beach into town to enquire about whale watching and anything else the town had to offer. But the whale-watching season had finished only a couple of weeks before, and anyway, boat trips out into the Golfo Nuevo weren't within our meagre budgets. We were travelling on AR$1,000 a day (about £24 or £1 per hour) shared between the two of us. We had to choose our activities and plan well. We walked back along the beach and spent the rest of the day playing Yahtzee in the sandy campsite, planning what to do next.

Without the oceanic boat trip, and having pottered around the central streets of the town, we felt we had seen enough of Puerto Madryn and wanted to move on to the next town. We packed up our backpacks and walked an hour back along the beach to the bus station. An hour's bus ride south took us to Trelew, a town founded by Welshman Lewis Jones (*tref* meaning town in Welsh, therefore 'Lewistown'). But, without much to see or do here either, we decided to continue another 20 minutes by bus to another Welsh town, that of Gaiman. We were a little pushed for time if we wanted to see both the Argentinian and Chilean Patagonia.

The next day I was on my way back to Trelew. We couldn't buy our next bus tickets in Gaiman, so another 20-minute bus ride and I had the tickets in my hand. We were off to Rio Gallegos in a couple of days, but not before we'd had afternoon tea in a Welsh tea house. It was like stepping back in time – or stepping 7,540 miles back to the Welsh valleys – with English and Welsh language books on the bookshelf, teapot with knitted cozy, the house's best china, and a cake stand full of delights. Olga, with much less of a sweet tooth than me, let me gorge myself on the cream-filled scones and other treats. We were surrounded by tea towels from across Wales, proudly hanging alongside Welsh love spoons. We stayed for two hours at Casa de Té Plas y Coed, enjoying the environment, snacks and wi-fi.

Throughout the province of Chubut there are several Welsh towns, from the eastern Atlantic coast, to the west bordering the Andes mountains. The Argentinian flag with a red dragon in the centre can be seen hoisted across the region. Talking about the Y Wladfa settlement in Argentina, Chatwin wrote: 'Their leaders had combed the earth for a stretch of open countryside uninhabited by Englishmen,' and 153 Welsh immigrants had made the trip across the Atlantic in 1865. It's said that some of the inhabitants of these towns speak Welsh even 150 years later. But we didn't stick around long enough to find out; we were back on the road again and a 16-hour bus ride from Trelew to Rio Gallegos.

The first few days of our trip had mostly been about getting as far south as possible as quickly as possible, by spending as little as possible. The plan had been working well so far. We had stopped off at a few places and seen several towns before reaching the last city before the Chilean border and Tierra del Fuego. We weren't planning to stay long in Rio Gallegos, a city that left a lot to be desired in terms of, well, everything.

One day would be enough to get an impression of the town, then we could set off for Ushuaia. But as our budget didn't stretch to the bus tickets for the ten-hour journey, we got our thumbs ready to try our hand at hitchhiking. On a shoestring budget, hitchhiking could save us money, which could be spent on more exciting exploits – like whale watching, had there been any whales to watch. At least we got to see Wales.

But Rio Gallegos presented several different challenges, setting the standard for our next couple of weeks in Patagonia. First, we misplaced our passports. Our campsite was a good 40-minute walk from the centre of town, where we had found an Italian restaurant with reasonable, if not a little leathery, pizzas, and cold Quilmes beer. We wandered around the town and to the Atlantic Ocean, where we could look out over to the Falkland Islands – we had to pretend to see it. There were 400 miles of open sea to the disputed islands. Las Malvinas wasn't at the forefront of our minds once we thought we had lost our passports. 'They must be in the restaurant,' Olga said when we got back to the campsite.

'To lose a passport was the least of one's worries. To lose a notebook was a catastrophe,' wrote Chatwin. Well, I had my notes backed up on a cloud, so that wasn't an issue. My devastation would have come at losing the pictures taken on the little notebook-sized mega computer I had in my pocket. Try explaining that to Chatwin. Luckily for us, the passports were easily recovered, looked after by the kind restaurant staff. It was a good thing we had left a tip. The 40-minute walk across town and then back again took us twice through council estate-looking areas in the middle of the town, areas crumbling and decrepit, seemingly forgotten about by the authorities in Buenos Aires. It wasn't the Patagonia we were expecting.

We had another dilemma. Hitchhiking to Ushuaia would take us across the border between Argentina and Chile. To get to the southernmost city in the world, one has to cross into Chile before crossing back into Argentina. On the trip I was carrying a little present I had been given in Buenos Aires. At the house where I was renting a room, the landlady's daughter had gone away on holiday and needed someone to water the three marijuana plants in the baking Buenos Aires summer sun. Before leaving on my own trip, I was given a lot of weed as a thank you for looking after her plants. I had only ever eaten the stuff on holiday in Amsterdam before moving to Argentina, but in Buenos Aires it was everywhere. Just walking down the street you would smell the plant growing on a balcony overhead.

Weed – like so many other things – represented a grey area in Argentinian law. Everyone smoked weed openly – sitting on a bar's roof terrace, every fifth person would be smoking a joint. Nearly everything seemed to be grey in Argentina, with only a few examples of white space on one end of the scale (breathing) and black on the other (murder). It did seem to leave a lot open to the whims of kind or not-so-kind officials.

Marijuana was technically illegal and trying to cross the international border would be frowned upon. The sniffer dogs weren't so good at the nuances. But Patagonia felt like the perfect place to enjoy my present, enjoying the wilderness, surrounded by lakes, mountains, trees and fresh air. At one with nature. The thought of crossing the Chilean border hadn't dawned on me, not until we decided to try our hand at hitchhiking to Ushuaia. I found a plastic bag, wrapped up the three big joints I had left and hid the lot in the campsite where we were staying. I could retrieve it later if we were to come back this way. Coming back from Ushuaia there was a big chance we would have to come back to Rio Gallegos anyway.

We spent a whole day trying to hitch a ride southwards. We got up at 5am and began packing up the tent as quietly as possible, leaving at 6am for the edge of town, where we hoped to catch a ride. We wrapped up warm under several layers in summer temperatures of around 5°C early in the morning. Soon after arriving, we were joined in the bitterly biting wind by other chancers and started to panic that they were going to pinch our lifts. I pictured an empty seven-seater or one of those fancy Mercedes Sprinter vans converted into a camper stopping to pick us up. The hope that just that vehicle was right around the corner kept me going for the next six hours. But the long, straight road leading south stayed mostly empty, but for the Patagonian wind that drives man insane.

The next day we tried again, gluttons for more punishment. We lasted only a few hours when, at midday, we decided to trek back to the bus station and head north towards El Calafate instead. I had enough time to run back to the campsite to pick up my little presents. Giving up on Ushuaia, we were finally on our way again.

El Calafate is a town in the same province as Rio Gallegos, namely Santa Cruz, but nearly 200 miles west towards the Andes *cordillera* on the shores of Lago Argentino. By going west, the landscape changes from coastal pampas to mountains, glaciers and glacial lakes. The town is extremely popular amongst visitors for its proximity to the vast glacier, Perito Moreno. The glacier's 19 miles of length makes it one of the biggest of the 48 glaciers in the region, and at over 70 metres above the water (another 170 metres below) it's a spectacular place to visit. In the sunlight, the glacier wall emits a vividly intense light blue colour, with the bright white of the snow on top and the radiant emerald-turquoise of the lake making a stunning confluence of colours.

We visited the glacier on our first full day, choosing to leave the large campsite by the river early enough to try hitchhiking the 50 miles out of the town. The glacier sits where the end of the long Lago Argentino meets the Southern Patagonian Ice Field, the world's third-largest reserve of fresh water. The ice field is an immense area of snow and ice sitting atop the mountain range and whose glaciers slowly move down towards more hospitable areas.

The Perito Moreno glacier moves forward during spring and summer, yet recedes during autumn and winter. It's in a constant state of flux. Every now and again, the glacier reaches land, splitting the lake in two and forming a dam on one side. The water levels on either side of the glacier can differ by up to 50 metres and the pressure builds up to such an extent that the tip of the glacier ruptures in an impressive explosion. Impressive if seen from afar – dozens of people have been killed by flying blocks of ice since the 1960s.

Our own drama would soon unfold. Our next stop, after a few days in Calafate, was El Chaltén, another 120 miles north. Again, we hoped our thumbs would help us catch a ride and this time we got lucky. Within an hour, a man in his late 20s, who had been in Calafate to pick up hamburger buns for his (north) American burger joint, gave us a lift. Crístian was originally from Buenos Aires and wasn't particularly talkative, but for the three-hour journey I kept trying. I would have liked nothing more than to have a snooze in the car, but I felt that I had to make the effort seeing as he had been so kind as to pick us up. Olga had already fallen asleep. I kept thinking he would ask me to shut up at any minute. I had never met such a reserved Argentine before, especially not a reserved *porteño*, albeit a *porteño* 1,500 miles from home.

The ride from Calafate to El Chaltén is an unforgettable journey, particularly the last 60-mile stretch along Ruta 23. Turning left off Ruta 40 (which runs the length of Argentina, along the Andes on the western border), a straight, single-laned highway took us in the direction of Fitz Roy mountain, the peak for which the area is famed. For one whole hour the 3,500m Fitz Roy looms ahead, at no point moving as the ride takes you directly towards it in a straight line. Gradually the mountain gets bigger and bigger, looming over the car more and more for every mile.

And finally we had arrived. A brief, cold shake of Crístian's hand and we were on our way. He had recommended heading straight up into the mountains. Heeding this advice, we set off from the village's main street up to Laguna Capri, an hour-and-a-half's steep hike. For five days we camped at the laguna, only returning to civilisation for provisions. We weren't alone; it was a popular place to camp. The lake, under the auspices of Fitz Roy, was ice cold, filled with newly melted glacial waters. It was the only place to refresh but having a dip was pleasant enough after a gruelling hike.

But El Chaltén was a trap. It was the middle of January, the hottest month both in terms of temperature (maximum of 18°C) but also popularity. The long-distance buses out of the area were booked up for the next five days. We had already spent five days here by the time we went to buy our bus tickets, and we didn't want to stay another five days. We were forced to try our hand at hitchhiking again, but the next leg of the journey would be at least 600 miles northwards towards the Patagonian lake district. There were only a handful of towns along the route, and not very interesting ones at that. The wind was blowing hard and the rain hammering down, so before we could take up a hitchhiking position, we would have to wait it out at the warm, bustling bus terminal on the edge of the village.

The bus terminal was always busy. Spanish, Hebrew, French words hung in the air. It was a place of refuge from the hellish wind and driving rain. And it was also the only place where wi-fi could be found in the whole village. Even a phone signal wasn't easy to get. But the best thing of all, when killing time, was that the little café had football on the TV and cold beer in the fridge. The Arsenal 2 Chelsea 0, sponsored by Quilmes.

The one supermarket in El Chaltén wasn't cheap. We couldn't stay much longer in the village, but with bad weather hampering our escape attempts, we jumped on a shuttle bus back to El Calafate, from whence we had come some six days previously. At least there we would have slightly better weather, slightly cheaper prices and much better connection, essential for finding bus tickets and other information. But bus tickets north were sold out here, too. We afforded ourselves a lazy day at a campsite before trying again.

The next day came, as is so often the case. Today was the day we were finally going to get our ride north. Four lifts later and we were back in El Chaltén. We felt powerless, as if some supernatural force were dragging us back there. The project began at 7am on the edge of El Calafate. Three hours later a sweet lady picked us up in her pickup truck. She was heading to the airport so dropped us off where the road out of the town veers off to the left. We were ten miles from Calafate and seemingly in the middle of nowhere in the unforgiving midday sun. It took another 30 minutes before we were picked up by another local, Antonio, who worked on a refinery site down the road.

I told him that I was an English teacher. Embarrassed, Antonio told us that he had never learned the 'colonial language'. Did it have anything to do with the Falklands War? *Sí, claro*. But now, in order to travel freely, he admitted that he would have to learn it. We were chatting away about so many things – football, travel, the area – that he forgot to drop us off at the turn-off for Ruta 40. We ended up more than ten miles past where we had wanted to go, in a different middle of nowhere.

A huge petrol tanker heading for El Calafate picked us up shortly after. It took him 30 metres just to stop once he had slammed the brakes. We had to rush after him before he changed his mind. It had taken three rides and a couple of hours, but we were finally at Ruta 40 with our thumbs out ready to head north. Standing out in the open vastness of Patagonia is when one realises what the region is: a lot of nothing. Arid, semi-desert for mile after mile. Getting closer to the Andes, one is treated to magnificent mountain peaks, glaciers and lakes, but the rest is tumbleweed, sand and wind.

Another couple of hours had passed when a man stopped: he was going to El Chaltén. 'We have just come from there,' we replied. 'I can take you 30 miles and leave you at the intersection of Ruta 23.' It sounded like a plan. We would at least be moving in the right direction. We told him how we had struggled to leave the area with the buses fully booked. 'An alternative,' he said, 'is to head to O'Higgins in Chile.' Okay, we're listening. 'You can walk from El Chaltén to the Chilean border, from there a boat takes you to the town of O'Higgins and you can travel up the Chilean side of Patagonia.'

We didn't have any set plans, we just wanted to continue our trip. He dropped us off outside Crístian's hamburger place and we set off for a fork in the road at the end of the village to continue towards the border. It was over 25 miles to the border, so yet again we were dependent on a ride. As we stood on the roadside waiting for a ride, the wind was so strong that it nearly lifted me off my feet. I was using a lot of energy leaning into the wind. The sand being blown in our faces was a secondary concern. We put our backpacks on the ground, crouching down. We were grateful when Alex, a girl from Leeds, picked us up in her Argentine boyfriend's car. The roads were dusty and rocky, but Alex drove as if she were on the M62. Scenic yes, comfortable no.

Alex was driving to a hotel 25 miles from El Chaltén, where she worked as a yoga teacher, and was happy to drop us off at Lago del Desierto, a long strip of water pointing towards Chile. We could either hike the eight miles along the lake or take a boat ride. It had already been a long day, which had started with an alarm before 6am. It was now nearly 7pm and we had to hike across the side of the long Lake of the Desert to the Argentinian border post. Three hours of hiking later we had made it halfway. We could continue tomorrow. We pitched our tent at a *mirador* looking out over the lake and over to the impressive mountains facing us on the other side. We could see glaciers almost hanging off the mountains and wanting to dive into the lake. The night was quiet, and we hadn't seen anyone since Alex said her goodbyes three hours earlier. It was the perfect place to camp.

Or so we thought. It was 24 January, my 34th birthday, and we were awoken at 4am by the howls of a Patagonian storm. The same wind that had nearly blown us over the previous afternoon was now playing aggressively with our tent, squishing and squashing the vulnerable little structure. It felt as if we were in an accordion, the hands of the wind stretching and compressing the tent, while tango dancers melancholically pranced about outside. But this wasn't a sombre dance, it was an aggressive attack. We had done something to offend the spirits of the mountains. This is why we had been lured back to El Chaltén.

It had been a calm evening when we pitched our tent. Whether or not the storm started gradually we will never know, as we were asleep. But it felt as if a button had been pressed and the storm had hit us full blast with *that* wind and *those* raindrops. It was dark outside. Not pitch-black, as I could see the dark mountains looking unsympathetically over at us as I peered through the tent's door.

I was scared and I felt the need to say it aloud to Olga. I had never said those words aloud to anyone before. But now I was really scared, and I needed to tell her.

We sat up in the tent. I was holding the two tent poles criss-crossing above our heads in my left hand, trying to give them a little bit more stability as they were being shoved and dragged from one side to another. I was looking at Olga. What were we going to do? We couldn't leave the tent. We would get drenched trying to pack up and leave now. How would we put the tent away in a storm? What were the chances of the tent – with us in it – being picked up by the wind and hurled into the lake 50 metres below? While I was pondering these seemingly life-or-death questions, Olga suddenly needed the toilet. She was desperate. 'You can't go outside in this,' I said. But when nature calls.

I was worried she wouldn't come back, that the mountain ghouls would consume her. Extremely wet and with a smile on her face, she came back in again. Whatever the situation, she always saw the funny side. Was she enjoying this? I was relieved to see her, but I wasn't enjoying it. The storm wasn't letting up and we were faced with the same dilemma. Surely the only option was to wait it out.

That's when the violent wind ripped a tent peg out of the ground and the top, waterproof sheet of the tent flew off. Water started pouring in through the air vent on the inner cover. I had to rush outside to grab the cover before it was taken away by the wind and before the other tent pegs went with the first. For an hour we continued like this: I had my left arm out of the tent door holding the one loose peg, fighting against a Patagonian storm;, and my right hand was holding the tent poles over our heads. Olga nipped off to the loo again, the excitement too much for her.

But the game was up. The sun wasn't going to show its face any time soon and everything we had was soaked through. There was only one thing to do, start walking. Walking and wet was much better than sitting still and wet. We couldn't get all of our wet belongings into the backpack. Luckily, I had some black plastic bin liners with me with which I could carry the wet and now extremely heavy sleeping bag.

Pro backpacking tip: bring plastic bags. A roll of the big rubbish bags – bin liners – will do. You can use them to keep your backpack dry should you get stuck in a rainstorm. Had I been smart, I would have kept a spare set of clothes tucked away in a bin liner in my backpack in case *everything* got wet. I would at least have a change of clothes.

But the evening before had been so peaceful. Patagonia can be brutal. For all its splendour, its weather can be unrelenting. It's a savage place where dinosaurs must have found it tough to survive (they did eventually succumb, of course). We had survived, for now. The chances of any real danger, the perilous type of danger, probably weren't more than 2/10, maybe at times 3/10. But 3/10 was terrifying enough.

We set off with our wet backpacks, carrying a wet tent and a bin liner stuffed with one wet sleeping bag. It wasn't even 6am. By 9am we had reached the end of the lake and the weather had eased. Walking through the forest on the eastern side of Lago del Desierto we saw fallen tree branches thicker than my thighs, victims of the storm. Maybe it was a good thing we hadn't camped in the forest. We would have been protected from the wind but not from the branches. Regardless of where we pitched our tent, we would have had a problem. I threw the last joint of Buenos Aires weed away into a bush, a sacrifice to the mountain gods. We would need their help. From the Argentinian border post at the end of the lake we had another 12 miles of hiking to do before reaching Chile. And we would have to get to a hostel by nightfall. We couldn't sleep in a wet sleeping bag in a wet tent surrounded by wet clothes with temperatures around 5–10°C.

The sun was coming out intermittently, so we spread all of our belongings out on the grass at Punta Norte. I went in to talk to the border guard who would stamp us out of the country. I told him our story. His face didn't change. He didn't want to hear the story. He didn't care. 'What do you recommend?' I asked. Meh. He mumbled something unintelligible.

We couldn't continue. Once we had hiked across 12 miles of no-man's land between Argentina and Chile, there was no guarantee that boats to O'Higgins would be going. They didn't sail every day and there would be a risk of us arriving at the port and having to wait a night or two on another lake's edge. Just over 12 hours earlier we had passed up the boat ride across Lago del Desierto to save some cash. But now we were sitting waiting for that same boat to take us back to where we had started. We were heading back to El Chaltén, yet again.

For a third time we entered the village of El Chaltén. It would be the last time. Enough was enough. We bought a ticket to leave for El Calafate (also for a third time). We would rather wait out the five days there. We had seven hours to wait for the shuttle bus, enough time to regroup, dry more clothes and charge phones. I went to the café to ask for hot water for my thermos. I was going to enjoy some warm yerba mate. That's when the mountain gods finally smiled upon us.

Walking back from the café with hot water in my thermos and the mate gourd in my hand, silver bombilla straw hovering around my lips, I caught the eye of a blonde-haired, blue-eyed man in his early 20s. He had the same thermos and was drinking mate. We gave each other a nod of approval. I thought nothing of it and went to find Olga.

About half an hour later the same mate-drinking man came up to talk to us. Calixto was from Tucuman in the north and travelling with his friend, Negro. They were two handsome young men, their eyes gleamed with adventure and they had mischievous but friendly smiles. Where we were headed, they asked. They had two spare seats in their car and were travelling north. 'When?!' I squealed, with delight. 'As soon as the petrol station has petrol.'

An hour later, we packed up the car and went to sit in a queue of cars leading to the petrol station. We were almost free, finally being taken away out of this village. But then the attendant at the petrol station signalled that there would be no petrol today. Come back tomorrow. We found a campsite in the main street and had a warm shower. We would try again in the morning. Negro and Calixto picked us up at the bus station at 8am but it wasn't before 3pm that we finally managed to fill up the car and leave. Arsenal were playing Manchester United in the FA Cup at 4pm Argentinian time, so I suggested waiting but …

Our chauffeurs *tucumanos* drove through the night without stopping. At 4.30am we jumped out at Esquel and waved them on their way. We had been dropped off right next to a campsite and within half an hour we were asleep, just as the sun was rising in Esquel.

We were relieved to have left southern Patagonia and to have arrived at something resembling normal civilisation. Our clothes were still wet and the tent still damp, so we laid everything out to dry in the hotter sun. We would be heading into the Parque Nacional Los Alerces, where the tent would be needed. The scenery had changed significantly. Mountains and glaciers were still present, but less dominant. The area was much greener, and the forests were thicker and a darker shade of green. The air seemed fresher and the wind had stopped.

Along the Ruta 71 of the Parque Nacional Los Alerces was a hop-on, hop-off bus service. The bus left the town of Esquel heading towards Trevelin, another Welsh town on the other side of the country from Gaiman and Trelew. We wouldn't visit Trevelin as the bus swung up towards the north.

Exiting the park a few days later, the bus stopped at Cholila, a small town of just over 2,000 people in the national park. Cholila, meaning 'land of strawberries' in a local indigenous tongue, is most famous for a cabin used by immigrants who fled to this part of the world in the early 1900s. The immigrants were members of the second Wild Bunch, a group of train robbers from the (north) American Old West.

Butch Cassidy, the Sundance Kid and Etta Place arrived in 1901 and settled near Cholila. In 1905 a group of English-speaking robbers attacked a bank in Rio Gallegos (600 miles south-east), fleeing back into the Patagonia steppes with a large sum of money. The heist stirred the local police forces and, with the law on their tails, the Americans sold their Cholila ranch and went on the run once again. Cassidy and the Sundance Kid are believed to have died three years later in Bolivia. Etta Place had returned to the US the year before, tired of life in Patagonia.

Alas, we had to pass through Cholila. Had we had more time and more energy, we would have hiked the two and a half miles to their cabin and back in the baking sun. But we were running out of time and were keen to continue on to El Bolsón, a small hippy town close to Bariloche. By now, I was retracing steps previously taken. I had already visited both El Bolsón and Bariloche before and had enjoyed both towns.

Bariloche is another favourite haunt of the gringo-trail backpacker. The town is the biggest throughout Patagonia and serves as a gateway in all directions, including west over the Andes into Chile. On a more local scale, it served as a gateway to the lakes to the north and the circuit of the seven lakes.

Samuel was a Korean-American we had met in town watching Arsenal lose to Manchester City. He was renting a car to drive the loop from Bariloche to San Martín de los Andes and back, and he invited us to join him for the 24-hour trip. The views of the lakes in the Patagonian lake district were fantastic. On the first leg of the journey, the western side of the loop, the road was smooth, and the scenery consisted of deep blue lakes flanked by dark green forests. This contrasted with the return leg, an arid desert and canyon landscape with slow, bumpy roads.

By now Samuel was panicking; he had a bus to catch and he was eager to get moving. The last two hours of the trip were tense as we hit traffic entering Bariloche. I took over the driving and returned the rental car after we had dropped Samuel off at the bus station. We were also heading for the bus station two days later, returning to Buenos Aires. This time we booked our bus in advance. Olga had a flight to Lima to catch, and I was off to the city of Rosario for a *clásico* I didn't want to miss.

Rosario: Lepers versus Scoundrels

THE VERY first ground I visited in Argentina was that of the Estadio Marcelo Bielsa in Rosario. On my first trip to Argentina in 2009 I travelled the four hours between Buenos Aires and Rosario. I didn't know who Marcelo Bielsa was. I didn't know anything about the two Rosario teams nor of their rivalry. But living in Argentina I was told that this *clásico* was – maybe – bigger even than the *superclásico* between Boca Juniors and River Plate.

Rosario is the third-largest city in Argentina, with a population of 1.2 million, behind the capital and the city of Córdoba. Unlike Buenos Aires, which is home to dozens of football teams across the top four divisions, Rosario has just two major clubs. The big five clubs have their *rosarino* fans, but the city is essentially split down the middle: locals are either a black-and-red 'leper' or a yellow-and-blue 'scoundrel'.

The nicknames can be traced back to the 1920s and a charity game organised to raise money for sufferers of leprosy. The city's two major teams were invited to play. While Newell's accepted the invitation, Rosario Central turned it down. The press and rival fans villainised Rosario Central for not taking part in the charity match and the nickname *Las Canallas* – roughly translated to scoundrels, bastards or rascals – stuck. As with all muck thrown at football fans, the nickname has been appropriated by Central fans who today proudly call themselves *Canallas*. Newell's Old Boys were henceforth known as *La Lepra* for their good deed.

The game went ahead without Rosario Central, although another Central took their place: Central Córdoba. It can get very confusing with the names – Central Córdoba are not from the city of Córdoba, but rather from Rosario. And they are not to be confused with their namesakes Central Córdoba from the town of Santiago del Estero (who in recent years have been doing very well and have reached the top tier, punching above their weight). Apropos of names, football enthusiasts tend to be curious as to why Newell's Old Boys have an English name. I certainly was. Isaac Newell was an English teacher from Kent who founded the Colegio Comercial Anglo Argentino in the city in 1884, the same year the first football arrived in the country. Newell became one of the pioneers of Argentinian football. Nearly two decades later, his son Claudio founded the club Newell's Old Boys using the school's colours as the club's colours.

Whilst Newell's Estadio Marcelo Bielsa was the first I ticked off in Argentina, it would also be one of the last I would visit. In Bolivia two years earlier I had met Lucio, a Rosario Central fan. We became good friends, spending days in a Sucre hostel garden drinking yerba mate and talking about football. He was having a tough time of it in Bolivia: he was missing his family and mates and was unsure how much longer he could bear being away from home. Argentines are extremely home-loving. As long as we spoke about football, however, he would be beaming from ear to ear, lively and animated. Since meeting him, I had promised to visit him in Rosario and, as my time in Argentina was coming to an end, I jumped on a coach headed north-west to the province of Santa Fe.

It was Lucio who had explained to me what the rivalry really meant for the city of Rosario. With a true sense of Argentinian melodrama, Lucio's group of mates had split in two when at school. They just couldn't get along. Around the age of 13–14 the footballing rivalry – and how it impacted their interactions – all got too much and the only solution was to divide down the middle: *lepras* to the left, *canallas* to the right. Lucio also told me the Fontanarrosa story of the legendary derby game of 1971.

Roberto *El Negro* Fontanarrosa was a writer and cartoonist from the city – a *rosarino* – and a huge Central fan. His story, entitled *19 December 1971*, is set at the time of the semi-final between Newell's Old Boys and Rosario Central played at El Monumental in Buenos Aires. It was a semi-final to decide who would play San Lorenzo – who had won their semi-final, beating Independiente on penalties – in the final of the league championship. The format at the time saw two groups contesting in a league format, playing each other only once, with the top two from each group playing a play-off. Independiente, winners of Zone A, met San Lorenzo, runners-up in Zone B, whilst Zone A's second-placed team, Newell's, met Zone B winners Central. Had Newell's got one more point in Zone A they would have been kept apart from Central and maybe the two would have met in the final, which – fate would have it – was to be played at Newell's stadium.

Up until 1971 no team from 'the provinces' had ever won the Argentinian championship. Teams from the capital had had a monopoly on the league title, but that was about to change in December 1971. Rosario Central's 2-1 victory over San Lorenzo in the final, however, is less important than the semi against Newell's. It was the first time the two teams had met in a knockout, winner-takes-all game. The importance of the match, as well as *how* it was won, has led to it becoming a massive part of the city's folklore. Fontanarrosa's story only adds to the legend.

19 de diciembre de 1971 is supposedly fictional. That doesn't stop people from believing that it actually happened. Football romantics love when the frontier between football fact and football fiction is indistinguishable. It's in this space that folklore is created. This is no more true than for the South American *futbolero*. When Lucio told me the story, he added that it wasn't clear whether or not it was true. That it could have happened, is not in doubt because of the Argentines' love for football and for their superstition.

Fontanarrosa's story tells of a kidnapping. The protagonists decide to abduct a man, the father of one of the friends. Against his own will and against his doctor's orders, the dad is taken 180 miles by car to El Monumental to watch the semi-final against Newell's. *El viejo* had never seen Central lose to Newell's, but he was getting older and had a weak heart, his doctor had advised him to stay away from the big games and take it easy. He had retired to the countryside to live a quieter life. But with the reputation of being Central's good luck charm – their *cábala* – the *viejo* was forced to make the journey to the capital.

His presence in the stadium worked. Central won 1-0 with a diving header – *una palomita* – from Aldo Pedro Poy. Fontanarrosa's story ends with the father suffering a heart attack at the final whistle, having seen his team beat the enemy and reach the league play-off final.

> 'The happiness in the face of this old man, brother, the craze of euphoria! This was the happiest day of his life. By far, BY FAR the happiest day because I promise that the joy he had at the moment was something unbelievable. And when I saw him fall, hitting the ground as if he'd been struck by lightning, the poor bloke, I thought: "What does it matter!" What else would he want than to die like this? This is how to die for us Canalla. To stay alive, what for? To live two or three more crappy years, as he had been living, inside a closet, humiliated by his wife and the whole family. Better to die like this, brother! He died jumping, happy, hugging the lads, outdoors, with the joy of having broken the arsehole of the lepers for the rest of eternity! That's how to die, to the point that I envy him, brother, I swear I envy him! Because if one could choose a way to die, I'd choose this, brother! I'd choose this!'

A note on Argentinian Spanish, so-called *argento*: 'to break the arsehole of somebody' (romper el orto de alguien) means to beat an opponent convincingly or to win a hugely important game. Central had broken Newell's arsehole with the 1-0 semi-final win in the capital.

The theme of cardiac arrests and heart attacks during football in Argentina is a recurring one. When Boca Juniors and River Plate played out their infamous 2018 Copa Libertadores Final, a radio station decided to transmit the game in as calm a manner as possible so that people who suffer from heart problems could listen without getting too worked up. AM550 Colonia, supported by the Argentinian Society of Cardiology (and a bottled sparkling water brand) ensured that the whole transmission would be almost monotone, without dramatising the most exciting – or dangerous – passages of play in order to keep heart rates low.

Another famous character in contemporary Argentinian football folklore is that of a middle-aged man, Santiago *El Tano* Pasman. *El Tano* (a nickname for Italians) was secretly filmed by his children watching his dear River Plate losing the first leg of a relegation play-off. In the video, filmed from behind Pasman's favourite armchair in a spare bedroom, a man is watching a small, old TV, flickering. Pasman was sitting right in front of the screen screaming and swearing, each time with more creativity and more furiously. Screaming at River's coach through the television screen, *El Tano* shouts: 'JJ López, your mum's ****, you put on the Boca shirt,' referring to one of 93 players who have played for both Boca and River Plate. JJ López's team lost the first leg and were relegated after a 1-1 home draw in the second, by which time the video had gone viral (before 'going viral' was even in the common nomenclature).

During the 2014 Copa Sudamericana semi-final second leg, while I was sitting below *Los Borrachos del Tablón* at El Monumental, *El Tano* was having a stroke at home. Ahead of the game, he'd had a check-up and was given the all-clear to watch the game, taking some pills to calm him down. He had survived his club's relegation to La B and three years later a stroke, and has gone on to become an authority on the pressures of watching his team's trials and tribulations. He is often interviewed ahead of big games, for example ahead of his team's 2018 Copa Libertadores Final against Boca.

Unlike *Tano*, the protagonist's father in Fontanarrosa's story may have passed but the goalscorer, Aldo Pedro Poy, has gone on to relive his *palomita* every 19 December for the last 49 years. HOY SOY POY they say in one half of Rosario: 'today I am Poy'. (As always, it sounds a lot better in Spanish.) In 2021 it will be the 50th anniversary of the goal and a special way of marking the day should be expected. In Jonathan Wilson's excellent book, *Angels with Dirty Faces*, about the history of Argentinian football, Chapter 31 'The Little Pigeon' has an interview with Poy where he says that every re-enactment of the diving header has hit the back of the net, so far. He dreads to think what would happen – with Central, with himself, with the universe – if he were to miss. Such is the superstition of Argentinian football. Born in 1945, there will come a time when he can no longer launch himself at an invitingly floated cross (or thrown ball) any longer.

The 1:21-minute long video Lucio showed me of this re-enactment was with Ernesto Guerava, the son of Rosario's most famous son, Ernesto *Che* Guevara. Standing on a dry pitch somewhere in the city, Ernesto junior softly throws the ball to Poy who hurls himself towards it. The *Canalla* legend's header goes past the stand-in goalkeeper and Poy is embraced by Guevara and mobbed by the crowd encroaching into the area in the subsequent celebrations.

After four weeks in Patagonia, I was off to Rosario. I was ready to return to the cities for a bit of summer warmth and football. El Coloso del Parque – as the ground was known prior to its renaming after Bielsa – sits in a big park in the heart of the city. It's the perfect place to enjoy a few beers before a game and, when hunger strikes, the streets are lined with grills serving barbecued meat. I bought myself a choripán and washed it down with beer.

It was a steaming 35°C in the city and nearly every male in the stadium had their top off. Beside me, a bald man in his 50s was showing off his Perón and Evita portrait tattoos. A 0-0 was on the cards and the game delivered the disappointingly predictable result. Even though I would have loved to have heard the roar of the home fans, towards the end of the game I was secretly willing on Central every time they attacked. I wanted to see a goal. Besides, I was staying at Lucio's after the game.

Avoiding defeat was the most important thing. Much like my own mother when Arsenal play Tottenham (because of split allegiances amongst her two sons), most mothers in Rosario would have been hoping for a draw in the Rosario derby. The risk of killings after a *clásico rosarino* win for either side is significantly higher as fans take to the streets in celebration. The city's iconic Monument of the Flag is where fans of the winning team flock, but celebrations happen all over the city, with victorious fans antagonising rival supporters.

I had tried getting tickets for the Rosario derby before. Shortly after the World Cup in Brazil, I travelled to Rosario with Gisela to meet her family for the first time. I had told her I wanted to go to a Newell's versus Central game, so we chose the derby weekend at the end of 2014 to make the trip. The game was being played at Central's ground, El Gigante de Arroyito ('The Giant of the Little Stream'), right on the banks of the river Paraná. Gisela would have been able to get me a ticket had it been a home game for Newell's, she said, but getting a ticket amongst Central fans would be difficult.

Bless her, she asked a lot of friends from her hometown but to no avail. A big *asado* on the Saturday night, meeting her parents, twin brothers and two sisters, tested my Spanish with those terribly awkward 'shhh, he's going to speak' moments when I ventured to open my mouth.

In an attempt to connect with Gisela's dad, who was stoking the embers of the *parrilla* in their small garden, I asked him about the following day's game. I knew I could connect with him about football, regardless of my lack of Español. The football conversation flowed, as did the beer – one-litre bottles of Stella Artois regularly grabbed from the fridge. The next day was a stark contrast. Without a ticket, I watched the derby with the family in their front room. In silence. There wasn't much to get excited about for Newell's – Central won 2-0 and there was no more talk of football. There was no more talk.

To break the spell of silence and sourness, we took Gisela's parents' car for a spin. We drove to the phallic Monument of the Flag tower where *las canallas* had assembled in great numbers. With the light-blue-and-white flag of Argentina flying 70 metres above their heads, yellow-and-blue flags were being waved at street level, with flares being set off and ecstatic fans bouncing, doing the fanning-of-the-face celebration. We parked up and walked down to watch them, envious of the fact that they had won the right to celebrate on this occasion.

In other parts of the city, however, people were being killed. Two people died that weekend. First, we read about a 39-year-old man who was shot from a car window by an enraged Newell's fan as a group of Central fans celebrated in the street. The other victim was a 22-year-old *canalla* who had been stabbed, although in the charity Salvemos

Al Fútbol's ('Let's Save Football') register of football-related deaths it seems he was stabbed by another Central fan. Both died in hospital.

Rosario has become an incredibly violent city due to drug-trafficking gangs, more so than any other Argentinian town or city. When football games are played, deaths often occur. Such is the intensity of having a city so engrossed by football with other tensions rumbling in the background. But it's also about the intensity of the rivalry. Buenos Aires, for all its love of the game, has many teams and while Boca-River are playing, the rest of the city is getting on with its own things. Or maybe watching the game as a neutral. Football is definitely intense there, but nothing like Rosario, where the focus ahead of and after a derby game is unrivalled.

Back to 2019 and back at Lucio's house, my host was telling me about Central's 'friendship' with a team called Chacarita Juniors. Chacarita was the neighbourhood next to Colegiales where I lived for a lot of my time in Buenos Aires and I would often walk the ten minutes down there for something to eat or to catch a bus. *Chaca's* ground is outside the city limits, some 15 minutes by train.

Chacarita Juniors were on my list of places to visit. A lot of locals had told me that San Martín, where the ground was, was a bit sketchy. Lucio told me that he had always wanted to go to see them play because of the friendship. Clubs having friendships is a foreign concept to most British fans but it's more common in South America or on the European continent, particularly Italy. Naturally, like many friendships, these *amistades* might not last the distance. There are many examples of short-lived relationships that have broken down due to small fallings-out. But not Central and *Chaca*: theirs is a 60-year-strong bond.

A month after the Rosario derby and back in Buenos Aires, an Irish friend and I finally went to see Deportivo Morón. It had been on the list since becoming aware of the team six years earlier. It was on the list primarily for the name. A 30-minute train ride out of the centre of Buenos Aires and a 20-minute walk across Morón town. It was a bit like taking a train from London to Crawley, from the tall buildings and hustle and bustle of the big city, arriving to a smaller, somewhat simpler town.

The match wasn't an especially big occasion. Morón were hosting a team called Brown Adrogué. The ground was far from full. We took our seats at the back of the concrete stand. Within a few minutes, curious Morón fans were coming to have a chat, welcoming us and asking for pictures with the gringos. It obviously wasn't usual to have foreign visitors. Both Killian and I now spoke the language fluently and with an Argentinian accent. Locals always found it amusing to hear a foreigner speak their Spanish and the novelty of our visit was doubled.

By the end of the match – a 1-0 home defeat, yet another game without having heard the home crowd cheer a goal – we had made new friends ourselves. The next time we came, they promised, we would have an *asado* with *muchas birras*. Their next home game was against their most-hated rivals, Nuevo Chicago. A few days later I got a text saying that a radio station in the town of Morón wanted to interview the Norwegian who had been at a game, but the phone call never came.

I was disappointed to miss their derby match with Nuevo Chicago. Obviously, not for the football. I wanted to visit my new friends and talk about Morón's old friends. Club Deportivo Morón and Club Atlético Tigre have been amigos since a game in 1975. The matchday started like any other. Two groups of *barra brava*, who had hated each other for years, met before the game to trade blows. It was an extremely violent clash, even for a country going through incidents of extreme violence and domestic terrorism on a weekly basis in the build-up to the military coup and subsequent 'dirty war'. With the pre-match battle over, fans promised to resume matters after the second division game at Morón's ground, the Estadio Francisco Urbano.

But the two *barras* wouldn't fight each other after the match. The match was abandoned. At the end of the first half, a drunken policeman took out his gun and shot a football rolling past him along the ground. The Tigre fans closest to the policeman couldn't believe their eyes and began mocking him. The officer couldn't take the abuse. He shot several times into the crowd, by chance hitting one of the most important members of their *barra*, El Negro Zamora. El Negro survived but spent the next few months in hospital.

Tigre fans' laughter turned to rage. Incensed, they tried getting at the policeman. In solidarity, the home fans joined in the fight with the police. A riot ensued and the game was suspended. Both sets of supporters left the stadium together to find the policeman, who had been taken into custody by his colleagues. Morón and Tigre fans boarded each other's buses and headed to the local police station where they suspected the police officer to be. The riot continued outside the police station with shots fired from both sides.

From that day on, the two clubs were forever linked. 'Tigre y Morón, un sólo corazón,' they sing: 'Tigre and Morón, one heart' (it rhymes in Spanish). The relationship was tested early on. Only two years after the incident that forged the friendship, Tigre beat Morón to send the latter to the third tier of Argentinian football. But the bonds were too strong for that to have an impact. When we visited the Estadio Nuevo Francisco Urbano, not only did we see people wearing Tigre shirts in the home end, but we also saw Morón fans with Tigre tattoos. As football friendships go, it's one of the strongest. Had I known from the first day of arriving in Argentina about Tigre-Morón, I would have pencilled one of their meetings in.

Only a matter of weeks after Deportivo Morón versus Brown Adrogué, I was chatting to a tattoo artist in the town of Haedo. I was telling him about going to the ground. His face became solemn, a downcast look spread from his eyebrows to his mouth. Juan used to go regularly to see his local team Morón with his amigos. But he hasn't been to the ground since 6 December 2000. That was the day his best friend lost his life, shot three times by the police. Mariano Guaraz – at the age of 17 – was the 200th victim of violence in Argentinian football. There is a mural in his honour as you enter the stand behind the goal at Estadio Nuevo Francisco Urbano. I had taken a picture of it at the game without knowing the story, but it was clear that the mural's object had passed away. How he had died, it didn't say. I showed him the picture I had taken of his friend. The smell of weed in his studio and the loud punk music all of a sudden were completely out of sync with the atmosphere. He changed the subject, he wanted to know about the burning of Norwegian *stav* churches by Norwegian black metal enthusiasts.

Buenos Aires: 'Half plus one'

'EVERYONE IS a Boca Juniors fan, just that some are late to realise it and others never find out.' When it came to *not* choosing a team in Argentina, I did grow fond of the team in blue and gold from the southern neighbourhood of La Boca. It's a popular choice and an easy choice. In Argentina, as well as the rest of South America, a lot of Boca shirts can be seen amongst locals, expats and backpackers alike. I was hesitant to be one of those visitors who immediately picks one of Boca or River, simply because they are the two that I vaguely knew something about. One of the biggest expat/ backpacker clichés is the gringo, backpacker or holiday visitor in their new Boca shirt. (Or if their trip starts in the north of the continent, a Colombia shirt.) Nowhere near as many people latch on to River Plate in the same way, despite the fact that their kits are almost just as iconic. In terms of the two, however, Boca Juniors have slightly more iconic kits, a slightly more iconic ground and have had slightly higher-profile players when compared to River Plate. *Gallinas* will argue against this to the death, naturally. Besides, River have won more trophies.

I ended up seeing Boca Juniors play 12 times in Argentina and once in London. It wasn't an impressive statistic, necessarily, nor was it by design. Boca's participation at the Emirates Cup in 2011 was unexpected yet glorious. Previously only first, second and third-tier European teams – from Juventus and Real Madrid to Lyon and Hamburg, for example – had participated. The 2011 version saw Boca Juniors and Thierry Henry's New York Red Bulls invited, along with Paris Saint-Germain and hosts Arsenal. Arsenal versus Boca Juniors came before I had even decided to move to Argentina. I had seen Boca Juniors versus Arsenal de Sarandí in 2009 and looked upon the Emirates Cup game as the second leg. Little did I know I would make another nine trips to La Bombonera during 2014 and 2018, as well as seeing them as the away team at Huracán and, of course, River Plate.

When it came to River, I found tickets harder to come by. I knew just as many *gallinas* as *bosteros*, but however well I got on with River fans they were less willing to invite me to the ground. Boca fans seemed warmer, more open, more welcoming. This may well explain their popularity across the whole of South America and, moreover, with immigrants to Buenos Aires from other Latin American countries. Another element is that Boca have the reputation for being the team of the working class.

River Plate fans will tell you that because they are more popular than Boca, tickets are harder to come by. They do have a bigger stadium. Boca's slogan – *La mitad más uno* ('Half [of the population] plus one') – boasts that they are the bigger of the two. It's a classic toing-and-froing with no definitive winner.

My third and final – for now – *superclásico* came in May 2015. Boca Juniors hosted River Plate at La Bombonera in the Primera División. A Honduran friend of mine –

again, another acquaintance from the five-a-side football pitches of Buenos Aires – had two tickets available for the derby. A Scottish colleague of mine, who had been a Celtic season ticket holder before moving to Argentina, was keen to find out what all the fuss was about. Caroline had been to umpteen Old Firm games and wanted to compare the derby-day experience.

But I had an inauspicious start to the Sunday. I had to get AR$2,500 out to pay for the ticket and had stupidly left it to the last minute. Little did I know that every cashpoint machine in the city would be empty. With Friday being a *feriado* – the Argentinian equivalent of a Bank Holiday, i.e. a day off – for *el día del trabajador*, it was a long weekend. Anticipating that the ATMs would be empty by Sunday evening, the locals had already withdrawn the cash needed for the long weekend. It took me years to adapt to having to deal with cash and the planning involved. Our journey from the northern neighbourhood of Palermo through the city to La Boca involved stopping by at least ten different banks before finally finding two that could give me two halves of the cash I needed. I was a relieved man.

It was a tense derby match, which seemed to be heading for a 0-0 draw. But two late goals in the 84th and 87th minutes, by Cristian Pavón and Pablo Pérez respectively, saw 85 minutes' worth of pent-up nerves and emotional energy transformed into a roar of derby-day delight. The three points were deposited in the bank and contributed to the Boca Juniors' winning of the 2015 league title.

Eleven days later the two teams met again in the second leg of the last 16 of the Copa Libertadores. In between the 2-0 league win for Boca, River had won the first leg of the Libertadores tie 1-0 with a late penalty.

The return fixture was the last of three meetings in less than two weeks.

And it was another game I had hoped to get a ticket for. It proved impossible. It was a Thursday evening game, and I should have been working until 9pm. The game kicked off at 9pm. Had I got a ticket I could have got someone to cover my classes, but in the end I was under the weather, phoned in ill for work and resigned myself to watching the game at home. The first half was easily forgettable. The second half would never be played and, for that very reason, will live long in the collective memory for all the wrong reasons.

I was watching in disbelief from my sofa. I wasn't feeling great, and I had been sleeping most of the day. But seeing what was unfolding in front of me made me perk up a little bit, not because of the glory of the incident – it certainly wasn't anything Boca Juniors would be proud of – but because of the awful audacity of it. These diabolical incidences – which don't involve death or serious injury – *are* entertaining. While no one would condone or try to defend some of the things football fans do, some actions become legendary despite the negative nature of whatever the action might have been.

This *superclásico* provided one such example. In South America, grounds tend to have separate tunnels for each team, often coming from underground. To protect the players, inflatable tunnels are deployed. One benefit is that the fans can't see them coming, although often the TV cameras pointing down the tunnel or the movement of people at the exit of the tunnel give it away. As the River Plate players were coming back up the stairs from their changing room and through their inflatable tunnel, a Boca Juniors fan – pressing himself up against the fencing that separated *La Doce* from the pitch – had managed to squeeze his arms through, cut a hole in the plastic and spray pepper spray at the opposition as they returned for the second half.

TV images showed five River Plate players in the centre circle frantically rubbing their eyes. Team-mates surrounded them, as did the rest of the club's entourage. It didn't take long for the media to find out what had happened. My Spanish was good enough to understand what was being said. Somewhat ironically, 45 minutes passed before it was decided that the second half couldn't go ahead. For the River Plate players affected, it must have been hell and possibly a real concern that their eyesight might be affected long term, not knowing exactly what had been sprayed at them. Police pepper spray, a homemade irritant or acid? It was impossible there and then to know. Once it had been deemed safe for them to leave the pitch – which took another two hours – they were carted off to hospital. Unsurprisingly, CONMEBOL awarded the game to River Plate. The 3-0 walkover gave *los millonarios* a 4-0 aggregate victory. River went on to win the whole tournament, one of the many trophies won after returning from having been relegated and under former player Marcelo Gallardo's tutelage.

All games that weekend were postponed. Whilst the lack of safety at La Bombonera was clearly an issue, that wasn't the reason. Unrelated to events in the Libertadores, a player in the Argentinian fourth division had tragically lost his life after colliding with a brick wall. Emanuel Ortega, 21 years old, was chasing a ball heading for a throw-in, running at a 90-degree angle towards the sideline. He twisted his body to wrap his foot around the ball to keep it in play, but in doing so fell backwards and smashed the back of his head against the concrete wall where the pitch ends and the terracing starts. Ortega was rushed to hospital but passed away ten days later. Argentinian football suspended all games.

Under these circumstances, there was extra time for reflection and debate. There was extra time for River fans to rub in the shame of what had happened. Boca fans had for the past few years enjoyed a twist they had imposed on River's name: replacing the V in River with a B. The two sounds in Spanish are almost indistinguishable and one often has to specify which letter is needed if spelling something out: is it a 'long b or a short b?' they will ask. With the second division in Argentina called B Nacional – informally La B – the new spelling of RiBer was simple but effective. River Plate graffiti all over the city was altered, a simple red letter B drawn over the V, with tens of thousands subsequently offended.

After the infamous incident at La Bombonera in their knockout Copa Libertadores game, River fans had their own twist on the same slight by changing the B of Boca to a V for *vergüenza*, meaning disgrace or indignity. My Boca-supporting students weren't keen to talk about the game the next day. I had been eager to bring it up, not to antagonise but to find out how football fans felt about it. I was still high on adrenaline. I had never seen anything like it before and I wanted to talk about it for days. But Boca fans were unwilling. They simply said it was an embarrassment and a symptom of Argentinian football and even society on a grander scale. I felt bad insisting on the topic and soon gave up, my students for once happier to be reviewing English grammar and the third conditional sentence structure over talking about football. 'Complete the sentence: 'Had I been a River Plate player at La Bombonera last night, I would have _____.'

Three years later the two would meet in the final of the Copa Libertadores in 2018 in what some billed as the biggest football match of all time. With that pressure, it wasn't unthinkable that something similar would happen. And fate did indeed repeat itself. Rather than a last-16 game, this time it was the final. Rather than River Plate being the victims, they were now the aggressors, albeit in slightly different circumstances.

The first leg of the 2018 final was played at La Bombonera. A Scottish friend and I had made our way down to La Boca. We made it despite our bus being commandeered by a group of hardy Boca fans. We were coming from Colegiales on the other side of town – River country, although a lot of richer Boca fans lived there, too. Our bus was pretty much empty the whole journey towards the south of the city. It was a Saturday morning and several hours until kick-off. As the 168 bus chugged along Avenida Corrientes, a huge group of Boca fans came out into the road to forcibly stop our bus. The bus driver didn't open the doors and a few of the frustrated fans – worried that they would have to walk the last six miles to their final first leg against their arch-rivals – were getting worked up. A calmer *bostero* went to the bus driver's window and had a relatively civilised conversation for all of five minutes while his pals blocked the road. The driver gave in and opened the doors. I think he realised he didn't have much choice; the fans weren't budging.

From being on an empty bus, we were suddenly squeezed in amongst an already drunk group of hardcore Boca fans from a town called Merlo, an hour outside of the city. The fans explained to us that their bus had broken down and the big group had waited patiently for a bus to stop, but all the city buses had just driven past them. Relieved to be back on the road and excited about the first leg of the final, a few of the fans began to chant Boca songs. They were quickly told to shut up: 'The bus driver has been so kind as to let us on, don't let us down now, *boludo*.' Gregor and I were sitting in the back row with the naughty boys. One of them kept trying to start up some songs again, but the rest behaved.

Their *trago locos* had worked well so far. We were offered a sip of their Fanta and wine in an adapted two-litre Coca-Cola bottle. By cutting the top off the bottle, they make a large vessel from which a so-called 'crazy cocktail' can be shared. We – respectfully – declined the offer. They also suggested that we could hang out with them for this first leg of the final. They had planned to rush the gates. This was a common practice and one I had seen in the flesh at La Bombonera before.

Ahead of a game against Tigre when they could win the first 30-team, 30-game league season, together with my mate Bruno – who I had met outside La Bombonera 18 months previously – we stood mouths aghast as around 25 Boca fans came running from behind, leapt over a small fence and jumped over the turnstiles. Without hope of being able to stop them, the people manning the waist-high turnstiles just had to step back and allow it to happen. Maybe it was the same group of fans we met on the bus three years later?

That was their plan, at least, and we – again, respectfully – declined the invitation, saying that we were meeting people at the pub. I was in two minds, though. It could have been a lot of fun, but how would it have been to hang out with these nutcases as they got more drunk or on to other things?

As it turned out, the game was postponed due to one of those incredible downpours Buenos Aires was subject to, especially in summer months. The postponed game took place the next day. Again, Gregor and I made the trip down and ended up in a different pub with a bigger group of mates. The big screen in La Popular on Avenida Caseros was showing the build-up to the big game and our pints of Quilmes were served in special edition Boca-River tankards. Throughout the game we pestered the waiters to allow us to buy the tankards, but the answer was unequivocally *no*. Despite most people expecting a light and tense match, an entertaining 2-2 draw was played out. Boca Juniors led twice only to be pegged back twice.

When it came to the second leg two weeks later, our plan was the same, although headed in the opposite direction to El Monumental. Yet again, the game would be postponed. We arrived at the ground several hours before kick-off and enjoyed the build-up. The streets were full of people drinking, smoking weed and singing and flares were going off all around. River Plate fans were arm-fanning from the top of street-side kiosks. It was a carnival atmosphere: it was the day of reckoning.

As kick-off approached, we made our way to find a pub where we could watch the game, but few of the restaurants lining the Avenida Libertador were open, and those that *were* open were already full to the rafters. We had to walk several blocks away from the ground in the hope of finding somewhere, but everywhere was full. Once we had found a place to settle and have a beer, the news of an attack on the Boca bus came in.

As Boca's team bus came down the main *avenida*, people began throwing objects, including one-litre bottles of beer. Several glass bottles hit the bus, smashing the windows. Seemingly, at the same time as this was happening, the police were firing tear gas at the crowd. But with the windows smashed, much of the tear gas wafted into the bus. Boca's captain, Pablo Pérez, amongst others, complained of having smashed glass in his eye, and others had their eyes affected by the tear gas. There was chaos in and around the stadium as the news filtered in, inevitably a lot of misinformation initially, but the result would be the same: the game had to be postponed.

The game had been pencilled in for the next day, as was the case with the first leg, which had been rained off. But these were very different circumstances and players would still be injured the next day, Pérez sporting an eye patch from his trip to the hospital. There was no way the game would be on, but the decision to call it off came very late. We had, as had become tradition now, planned to trek over to the ground on the Sunday, but without much faith that there would be a game, we put off leaving. We were just about to leave when the news came in that the game had been called off again.

Boca Juniors claimed that the precedent of the 2015 game and the 3-0 awarded to River then should be applied here. Had that been the case, Boca would have lifted the Copa Libertadores without having to contest the second leg. Many Boca fans said they didn't want this; they wanted to win the title outright. Others felt that River had to be punished. But the circumstances were very different. In 2015 the attack had happened inside La Bombonera. In 2018 it happened on the street outside the ground. Again, conspiracy theories abounded.

Either way, this was a final whose TV rights had been sold the world over. It was the first year that the final was being played on a weekend. CONMEBOL couldn't afford to lose the windfall of this game, a match-up some billed as the biggest match in the history of football. Awarding the championship to Boca Juniors without playing the game was out of the question.

After much deliberation, the game was moved to the Spanish capital 6,000 miles from Buenos Aires as the crow flies. A final between two Argentinian teams not only moved away from Argentina, but away from the continent. They had considered moving the final to Asunción, the Paraguayan capital where CONMEBOL are based. Other South American, Latin American and North American cities were considered.

The Italian city of Genoa offered to host the final, pointing out that Italian immigrants had played a massive role in the establishment not only of the two clubs, but of Buenos Aires and Argentina as a whole. Over 60 per cent of Argentines have some degree of Italian ancestry, with many Italian surnames found in their version of the yellow pages (and on football pitches around the world). In fact, Boca Juniors' nickname is *Xeneizes,* meaning Genoese in the Ligurian language of that region of Italy (also spoken in parts of France). River Plate possibly chose red and white after the region's flag, although this is unsubstantiated. Either way, the link was clear, and the idea could have been marketing genius on the part of the city council of Genoa. As it was, the links with Spain ran deeper and Madrid's Santiago Bernabéu was chosen.

Without away goals implemented over the two legs, a 2-2 draw essentially voided the first leg. Whoever won the second leg would win the 2018 Copa Libertadores. It was the last year that the final would be played over two legs, but the tie now came down to the second leg – it was as if the second leg were the final, just as the 2019 Copa Libertadores would be. The irony of holding the second leg of this unique final wasn't lost on many observers. The tournament, the biggest in South America, was named after the liberators of the continent from Spanish rule. Not to mention the distance. The powers that be knew the stadium would be full as there are many Argentine expats already living in Spain, as well as neighbouring countries with easy access to Madrid. The game had to go ahead, and this is where it would be played out.

I had been to both River Plate's and Boca Juniors' home legs of the semi-finals, which were played on successive nights. I spent Tuesday night in El Monumental and Wednesday night in La Bombonera. The tickets together set me back around £170 but I knew my time in the country was nearing its end. With no guarantee of either leg of the final being played in Buenos Aires, I wanted to get my last fill.

River Plate lost their semi-final first leg 1-0 to Grêmio and it looked like the possibility of a *superclásico* in the Copa Libertadores Final had received a huge dent. But in Porto Alegre a week later, a dubious last-minute penalty saw River win 2-1 and go through on away goals. Boca Juniors won their first leg 2-0 with two Darío Benedetto goals in the last ten minutes, drawing the second leg in São Paulo 2-2. The final everyone had wanted to see had been lined up.

I went back to the same Argentine who had sold me the River Plate semi-final first leg ticket to see if he could get me a ticket for the second leg of the final. I would have loved to have gone to the game at La Bombonera, but being the first leg, I wasn't sure that I wanted – or could even afford – the ticket. If I were going to splash out it would have to be for the second leg.

After a lot of messaging back and forth, my contact told me that he wouldn't sell me the ticket. He had a ticket and we had agreed a price, but the authorities were due to be exceptionally strict on people entering the stadium using other fans' *carnets*, membership cards. He didn't want to take my money knowing I would have only a 50 per cent chance of getting in. I didn't want to pay the money with those odds, either. As it was, that game at El Monumental wouldn't go ahead.

After two legs played over three weekends, with five attempted matchdays, three of which were aborted, the 2018 Copa Libertadores finally had a winner. We had chosen a pub in La Boca to watch the final game. Were Boca Juniors to win, we could expect the streets to be full, and Boca did take the lead in Madrid, but River Plate equalised with a quarter of the game to go. The never-ending saga went into extra time. *Juanfer* Quintero scored in the 109th minute, a left-footed strike from the edge of the box into the top corner, in off the underside of the crossbar. Boca hit the post in the 120th minute and, with the goalkeeper up for the resulting corner, the cleared ball was punted upfield. Pity Martínez punctured the game, running the ball into an empty net. It wasn't surprising that the game ended in a dramatic fashion.

River Plate's historic 3-1 victory at Santiago Bernabéu (5-3 on aggregate) saw their fans from all over Buenos Aires flock to El Obelisco in the centre of town. Our bus back from La Boca took us across Avenida 9 de Julio. We could see the fans, flares and fireworks as our bus slowly chugged down Avenida Santa Fe. We couldn't go home without experiencing this final detail. We hurriedly pressed the stop button to alight and walked the four blocks to where the action was. It was raining but spirits were high, with El Obelisco mobbed by the white-and-red colours of *Los Millonarios*, probably not for the last time.

I was exhausted. The last five weeks had been filled entirely with anticipation for this double-header. However, I would miss all of this. It was the last time for a long time I would see that scene at El Obelisco. With or without me, Argentine football fans would continue to use the town centre as a meeting place to celebrate their club's triumphs. Maybe one day Argentines will fill the streets to celebrate a desperately sought-after national team victory.

I was ready to head home to Europe, but I wasn't quite ready to leave Argentina.

Epilogue

SIX YEARS had passed and my time in South America had taken me to nine of the ten countries on the continent. Whilst I only popped into Ecuador and Paraguay for a matter of hours, naturally I consider them a part of the list. Venezuela was not a viable destination due to the turbulent situation there, although I did briefly contemplate a quick visit from Colombia.

I attended football matches in seven countries, namely Argentina, Uruguay, Brazil, Chile, Bolivia, Perú and Colombia. Each country has its unique relationship with the sport but it was Argentina that gripped me the most. Their football culture with deep roots, legends and anecdotes, romanticism and tragedy was far beyond what I had been expecting to find. Football was extremely important to how I experienced Argentina.

Attending derby matches became a priority and a decent number of clásicos were ticked off: Argentina vs Brazil. Boca vs River and River vs Boca. Racing vs Independiente and Independiente vs Racing. San Lorenzo vs Huracán and Huracán vs San Lorenzo. Newell's Old Boys vs Rosario Central. Belgrano vs Talleres. La U vs Alianza Lima. Medellín vs Atlético Nacional and Atlético Nacional vs

Medellín. Santa Fe vs Millonarios. América de Cali vs Deportivo Cali. Nacional vs Peñarol. A few derbies remain outstanding, on the list for a future visit or sojourn.

Maybe I should never have left Argentina. Buenos Aires had become my home and I had grown extremely fond of porteños and Argentines in general. I felt like a local myself. Having grown up across two different countries, I never really felt 100% at home in either. It wasn't too dissimilar to how Argentines felt a longing for Europe, themselves feeling that they had been displaced. I hadn't been displaced, as such, but found it hard to choose between England and Norway, always missing a detail of the other. Ironically, Buenos Aires was the place I escaped to to avoid the perpetual choice and moving back-and-forth.

It was a form of rebirth. Moving to a new city allows you to start again. Learning a new language is also much like being reborn. Without much knowledge of the language initially, conversations pass you by as if you were a three-year-old child sitting in the company of older family members who are discussing politics. Little by little, you grow and you become more confident and can partake in such conversations. This was very much how I experienced learning Spanish: at times it was uncomfortable, the world was a confusing and scary place. But once I had found my voice, a personality grew and I was able to leave Buenos Aires' gringo bubble. I experienced the continent and her people in a different way.

Argentines were a fatalistic bunch. They were self-reflective, honest with themselves about their strengths and weaknesses as a nation. As Bruce Chatwin wrote in the 1970s: they 'knew the way things ought to be and apologised for the way they were'. A century of military dictatorships, financial crises and unfulfilled potential – not to mention crippling corruption – has led to Argentines partly loathing their own country. Yet, at the same time they are exceptionally proud of what they do well. Whilst without a title since 1993 for the Argentinian national team, football is the one, major thing they do well. And to be able to compete on the international stage – finally being one of the superpowers on a global stage – provides a positive self-image.

South American football – watching, groundhopping, playing – had also given me so much. But my sojourn had to come to an end at some point in time. In 2019 I moved back to Europe. Living so far from home – in a country experiencing another financial crisis and a constantly weak economy – had become a big personal sacrifice. But in the future, maybe I will be willing to sacrifice European creature comforts to enjoy life in the city so dear to my heart, Buenos Aires.

Chronological list of games attended in South America (2009-2019)

Brazil
Estádio do Maracanã, Rio de Janeiro
19/04/2009: Botafogo 0-1 Flamengo (Taça Rio)

Argentina
Estadio El Coloso del Parque (Estadio Marcelo Bielsa), Rosario
03/05/2009: Newell's Old Boys 1-0 River Plate (Primera División)
10/02/2019: Newell's Old Boys 0-0 Rosario Central (Primera División)
El Monumental (Estadio Antonio Vespucio Liberti), Núñez, Buenos Aires
10/05/2009: River Plate 1-1 Lanús (Primera División)
04/06/2014: Argentina 3-0 Trinidad & Tobago (International Friendly)
27/11/2014: River Plate 1-0 Boca Juniors (Copa Sudamericana, Semi-Final, second leg)
13/11/2015: Argentina 1-1 Brazil (World Cup Qualifying)
23/10/2018: River Plate 0-1 Gremio (Copa Libertadores, Semi-Final, first leg)
La Bombonera (Estadio Alberto J. Armando), La Boca, Buenos Aires
17/05/2009: Boca Juniors 2-1 Arsenal de Sarandí (Primera División)
30/03/2014: Boca Juniors 1-2 River Plate (Primera División)
28/09/2014: Boca Juniors 1-0 Quilmes (Primera División)
26/10/2014: Boca Juniors 2-0 Defensa y Justicia (Primera División)
01/03/2015: Boca Juniors 1-0 Atlético de Rafaela (Primera División)

03/05/2015: Boca Juniors 2-0 River Plate (Primera División)

06/09/2015: Boca Juniors 0-1 San Lorenzo de Almagro (Primera División)

01/11/2015: Boca Juniors 1-0 Club Atlético Tigre (Primera División)

24/10/2018: Boca Juniors 2-0 Palmeiras (Copa Libertadores, Semi-Final, first leg)

03/11/2018: Boca Juniors 4-1 Club Atlético Tigre (Primera División)

Estadio José Amalfitani, Liniers, Buenos Aires

10/11/2013: Vélez Sarsfield 0-0 River Plate (Primera División)

Estadio Juan Pasquale, Núñez, Buenos Aires

30/11/2013: Defensores de Belgrano 0-2 Club Deportivo Morón (Primera B Metro)

El Nuevo Gasómetro (Estadio Pedro Bidegain), Flores, Buenos Aires

01/12/2013: San Lorenzo de Almagro 0-0 Estudiantes de la Plata (Primera División)

15/03/2015: San Lorenzo de Almagro 3-1 Huracán (Primera División)

El Cilindro (Estadio Presidente Juan Domingo Perón), Avellaneda

06/12/2013: Racing Club 2-0 Godoy Cruz (Primera División)

24/05/2015: Racing Club 1-0 Independiente (Primera División)

24/04/2016: Racing Club 0-0 Independiente (Primera División)

Estadio Diego Armando Maradona, La Paternal, Buenos Aires

07/12/2013: Argentinos Juniors 1-2 Rosario Central (Primera División)

14/04/2019: Argentinos Juniors 3-2 Independiente (Copa de la Superliga)

Estadio Islas Malvinas, Floresta, Buenos Aires

22/02/2014: All Boys 1-0 Olimpo (Primera División)

Estadio Monumental de Victoria (José Dellagiovanna), Victoria

24/02/2014: Club Atlético Tigre 0-0 Argentinos Juniors (Primera División)

Estadio Don León Kolbowski, Villa Crespo, Buenos Aires

01/03/2014: Atlanta 0-0 Deportivo Merlo (Primera B Metro)

20/04/2019: Atlanta 1-0 Def Unidos (Primera B Metro)

Estadio Arquitecto Ricardo Etcheverri, Caballito, Buenos Aires

31/03/2014: Ferro Carril Oeste 0-1 Unión de Santa Fe (Primera B Nacional)

19/12/2016: Ferro Carril Oeste 3-1 All Boys (Primera B Nacional)

Estadio Julio H. Grondona, Sarandí

14/05/2014: Arsenal de Sarandí 0-0 Club Nacional (Copa Libertadores, Quarter-Final, second leg)

23/04/2016: Arsenal de Sarandí 0-0 Defensa y Justicia (Primera División)

Brazil

Arena Das Dunas, Natal

13/06/2014: Mexico 1-0 Cameroon (FIFA World Cup 2014, Group A)

16/06/2014: Ghana 1-2 USA (FIFA World Cup 2014, Group G)

Arena Fonte Nova, Salvador da Bahia

20/06/2014: France 5-2 Switzerland (FIFA World Cup 2014, Group E)

25/06/2014: Bosnia-Herzegovina 3-1 Iran (FIFA World Cup 2014, Group F)

01/07/2014: USA 1-2 (aet) Belgium (FIFA World Cup 2014, Last 16)

Estádio Nacional de Brasília Mané Garrincha, Brasília

05/07/2014: Argentina 1-0 Belgium (FIFA World Cup 2014, Quarter-Final)

Estádio do Maracanã, Rio de Janeiro

27/07/2014: Botafogo 0-1 Flamengo (Série A)

Argentina

Estadio Tomás Adolfo Ducó, Parque Patricios, Buenos Aires

05/04/2015: Huracán 0-2 Boca Juniors (Primera División)

12/09/2015: Huracán 1-0 San Lorenzo de Almagro (Primera División)

Chile

Estadio Sausalito, Viña del Mar

09/01/2016: Everton 2-3 Unión Española (Pre-season friendly)

Estadio Monumental David Arellano, Santiago de Chile

16/01/2016: Colo-Colo 1-1 Unión Española (Primera División)

Estadio Municipal de La Cisterna, Santiago de Chile

18/01/2016: Palestino 2-1 Audax Italiano (Primera División)

Argentina

Estadio Libertadores de Américas, Avellaneda

21/02/2016: Club Atlético Independiente 1-1 Racing Club (Primera División)

Estadio Mario A. Kempes, Córdoba

23/07/2016: Club Atlético Belgrano 1-1 (4-1 pens) Club Atlético Talleres (Copa BBVA Francés, "friendly")

Estadio Coliseo del Bajo Belgrano, Buenos Aires

28/11/2016: Excursionistas 1-2 Platense (Primera B Metro)

Bolivia

Estadio Víctor Agustín Ugarte, Potosí

11/03/2017: Nacional Potosí 0-0 Jorge Wilstermann (Primera División)

Estadio Hernando Siles, La Paz

28/03/2017: Bolivia 2-0 Argentina (World Cup 2018 qualifying)

Perú

Estadio de la UNSA, Arequipa

10/05/2017: FBC Melgar 2-2 Ayacucho (Primera División)

18/05/2017: FBC Melgar 2-3 River Plate (Copa Libertadores, Group 3)

Estadio Alejandro Villanueva ('Matute'), Lima

31/05/2017: Alianza Lima 0-1 Club Atlético Independiente (Copa Sudamericana, First Round, second leg)

Estadio Monumental de 'La U', Lima

03/06/2017: Universitario de Deportes 1-2 Alianza Lima (Primera División)

Estadio Rosas Pampa, Huaraz

01/07/2017: Sport Rosario 2-1 FBC Melgar (Primera División)

Estadio Max Augustín, Iquitos

25/07/2017: J. Vargas Guerra – Sport Boys (Friendly, cancelled due to floodlight failure)

Colombia

El Campín (Estadio Nemesio Camacho), Bogotá

13/08/2017: Independiente Santa Fe 0-1 Tigres (Primera A)

04/03/2018: Millonarios 3-1 América de Cali (Primera A)

03/05/2018: Independiente Santa Fe 0-1 River Plate (Copa Libertadores, Group 4)

06/05/2018: Independiente Santa Fe 1-0 Millonarios (Primera A)

Estadio Atanasio Girardot, Medellín

27/08/2017: Deportivo Independiente Medellín 1-0 Atlético Nacional (Primera A)

18/11/2017: Atlético Nacional 0-0 Deportivo Independiente Medellín (Primera A)

Estadio Polideportivo Sur, Envigado

24/09/2017: Envigado FC 0-2 Atlético Nacional (Primera A)

Estadio Palogrande, Manizales

25/02/2018: Once Caldas 1-0 Atlético Huila (Primera A)

Estadio Olímpico Pascual Guerrero, Cali

14/04/2018: América de Cali 2-1 Deportivo Cali (Primera A)

Perú

Estadio Nacional de Lima, Lima

11/08/2018: Universitario de Deportes 1-1 Alianza Lima (Primera División)

Uruguay

Estadio Centenario, Montevideo

20/10/2018: Club Nacional de Football 1-1 Peñarol (Primera División)

Argentina

Estadio Nuevo Francisco Urbano, Morón

09/03/2019: Club Deportivo Morón 0-1 Brown Adrogué (Primera B Nacional)

Estadio Ciudad de Vicente Lopez, Buenos Aires

16/03/2019: Platense 3-0 Arsenal de Sarandí (Primera B Nacional)

Estadio Beto Larrosa, Villa Soldati, Buenos Aires

31/03/2019: Sacachispas 3-2 Tristán Suárez (Primera B Metro)

Estadio Afredo Beranger, Temperley, Buenos Aires

07/04/2019: Temperley 1-2 Córdoba (SdE) (Primera B Nacional)

Acknowledgements

Firstly, thanks to YOU for reading this far. I hope you enjoyed this book and the experiences, reflections and stories described within.

Ole Jakob Bugten and Mathijs Steneker acted as proof-readers/crash-test dummies and came with critical but helpful suggestions and advice. If you like the book, it is as much because of their invaluable advice as it is for my experiences. Ole Jakob keeps me on my toes in pub quizzes just as Mathijs used to keep me on my toes on the five-a-side pitches of Buenos Aires. "Play properly," he used to shout. I hope Mathijs liked this football action.

Killian McCabe provided a number of excellent photos for the book, as well as acting as a knowledgeable sounding post on many details regarding Argentinian football, society and culture. Killian was a good friend in Buenos Aires and we played football together on a weekly basis, always enjoying a drink afterwards. It wasn't long before we became groundhopping partners-in-crime.

Bett Moron also provided some wonderful photos. Check out his Instagram for more images direct from Argentinian grounds: instagram.com/elsentimientoinexplicable

I very much appreciated Matías Carro, Juance Saber and William Dalton's assistance on specific chapters and their reflections were incorporated, as I would be daft not to listen to such wise minds.

Helen Coakley, Martín Thompson and Roberto Coll also provided insights to la locura which is Buenos Aires and Argentina. Dan Larter and Leif Uggen – as well as my mum, Wendy, and my brother, Martin, naturally – kept me company throughout my time in South America with regular chats, audio and text messages. Matías Galain is a good friend who also contributed to the way I thought about this project having landed back home.

Also available at all good book stores

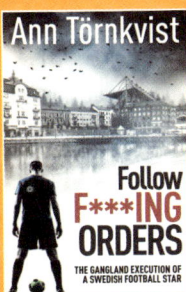

9781785316487

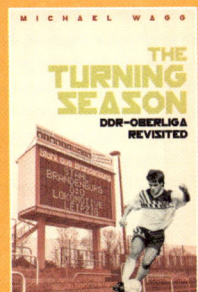

9781785317286

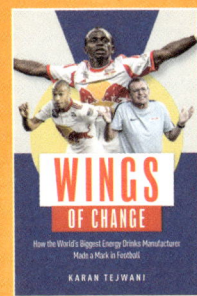

9781785317293

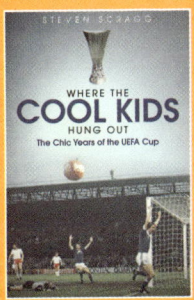

9781785316838

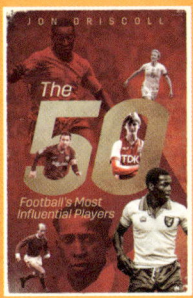

9781785316906

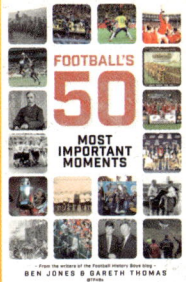

9781785316326

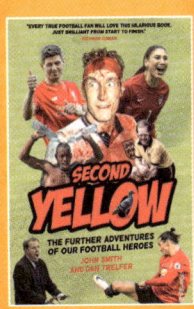

9781785316791

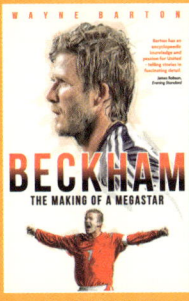

9781785316760

9781785316814